TOTAL SAILING

TOTAL SAILING

TOM HALL

SAN DIEGO • NEW YORK
A. S. BARNES & COMPANY, INC.
IN LONDON:
THE TANTIVY PRESS

The Tantivy Press
Magdalen House
136-148 Tooley Street
London, SE1 2TT, England

First Edition
Manufactured in the United States of America
For information write to A. S. Barnes and Company, Inc.,
P.O. Box 3051, San Diego, CA 92038

Library of Congress Cataloging in Publication Data

Hall, Tom, 1938-
Total sailing.

Includes index.
1. Sailing. I. Title.
GV811.H27 797.1'24 78-75350
ISBN 0-498-02309-5

1 2 3 4 5 6 7 8 9 84 83 82 81 80

to Air and Water

Contents

Preface

This was meant from the first to be a small book of basic feelings of sailing: the very simple, economical sailing book. At the end it still means to be a book of basic feelings, but now it is grown necessarily to medium size to bear the weight of its own substance—still perhaps a basic sailing book, but not as simple as that alone.

As an honest book it would be at least the fundamental how-to-sail book, the bare manual; though if it were just that, it would be enough only as a potent little pamphlet of plain and logical truths: on turning with the tiller and trimming with the sheet, and keeping the balance in the wind. Sailing, most functionally, is simply the practical mechanics of doing these three things; telling how to do them should require hardly a dozen precise pages of plain truth. This book tells such in less than half as many pages, in its very short fourth chapter—which possibly is the measure of its integrity.

That was the safe part, the easy part. It even might have been enough by itself. A book, having fixed upon it and dealt with it, could have effectively stopped without any further involvement. The rest of the pages could have been filled out with harmlessly extraneous materials—a lot of pictures of boats and fittings; diagrams of the sail plans of junks and clipper ships; the inevitable reprint of the entire Beaufort wind scale at the very end; safely incidental facts, somewhat pertinent, altogether cumulative, never venturesome. A book might have been adequate just within these limits; at its very center it probably even could have been an honest book in its way. But *this* book would not be done so easily; it already had larger commitments just to be a book of basic feelings; now it was bound to a basic logic and could not be compromised or indulged. It would go where it must. It had to be a totally unfaltering book of sailing.

Then it must come to the resolution of winds and forces; taking the full, heavy dose of unflinching physics—the basic meanings—while concentrating on the pure sensations—the dynamics. It must pursue this: telling about holding the balance and sailing ahead, going with the wind, then against the wind; being always intent on the feel of forces shifting and changing. The forces are catalytic. The feeling becomes transcendent; it is the experience in air and water. The very essence becomes the understanding of feeling and forces beyond the mechanics of the bare how-to-sail manual. This is the intention of the book.

The book was not done easily. It had to progress in its own singular way to do what it was meant to; very early it took a radical and difficult departure from the ways of all the other sailing books—as it was bound to. It could draw no real insights from the other books, except at complex technical points to refer to advanced texts on sail aerodynamics and subjects more arcane. Two massively competent texts eventually came to deserve virtually all significant bibliographical credit. These were *Sailing Theory and Practice*, by C.A. Marchaj, and *Sail Power*, by Wallace Ross. These two, by their sheer authority, lent this book the secure physical footing it needed. But this book, for its own substance, had to grow by touching directly: having primal encounters with air and water elements—strictly apart from earth and fire elements. It would evolve from the ways the wind would blow, and the waves would roll, and the sail pull, and the boat lean; and from all the rest, beginning with the origins of the phenomenon and coming to the essence itself. With this it would become the book of basic feelings.

Of course the book did not just evolve as I watched passively. I wrote the book and exerted no small effort on it. And I had help; certainly I never could have done it without help. Don Raden, the artist, proved a most resourceful collaborator, producing an impressive volume of cartoon illustrations, working over each picture, adjusting lines, and always imparting his own deft touches of whimsey. Mo Cleland, whom I always will consider one of the most informed and articulate authorities on the subject of sailing, subjected the manuscript to penetrating review. Ken Werrenmeyer, owner of City Sailors, the lakefront sailing school in Chicago, lent his facilities and his full cooperation to the effort of producing this book. My parents probably made the most fundamental contributions. When I was seven or eight and growing up in Michigan, they taught me sailing on our E-scow on Hamlin Lake. Later I attended the University of Wisconsin and taught sailing for the university sailing club on Lake Mendota. Both lakes manifested their influence. Every boat I sailed, every person I taught to sail—all had their effects on this book. I thank them, every one.

But the greatest help of all was that of Lana Cory Hall: researcher, copy editor, critic, advisor, business manager, file clerk—and my wife. She did the book's technical diagrams. She was the one who always was there when somebody had to be. Because she was there, the book is here.

TOTAL SAILING

I hear, and I forget.
I see, and I remember.
I do, and I understand.

—Old Oriental proverb

1
The Boat

Here is the boat. The basic boat.

It is ten or twelve feet long, four or five feet wide, pointed at one end, flat at the other, and round everywhere else. It looks mostly round and not much bigger than a bathtub. It is the boat-shaped boat.

It has one sail. It could have had two, but it would have been presumptuous. One sail is basic, and the rope that controls the sail is the sheet. A rope is a line on a boat, and this line is the sheet. The sail is not the sheet, even though it looks like a sheet. This is the first thing most people learn.

This is, arbitrarily, a good boat: innately better than most—a boat properly designed, well-balanced and proportioned, and so formed into a single, simple shape that is completely equable in water. It goes naturally through water, always in accord with water, never intruding on the ways of the water. It will be light and quick and steady and will ride with equanimity on the flow and swell; it is a presence like the water. This is the way of a good boat.

For this it is a pretty boat, a creation of pure, fundamental curves, all totally functional—curves rounding in and rounding out, coming forward to a soft, clean prow and aft to a tight, tidy transom. All curves together make a spare, compact, uncontrived boat: a whole boat, not a sum of separate parts. The boat has no hard lines, nothing extraneous or aberrant; it is always the basic boat, bare and inviolate, small and artful and never obtrusive. This is the look of a good boat.

It is made of plastic. Let that suffice; nearly all small boats are plastic now. More technically they would be made of glass fibers and polyester resin—of "Fibreglas ©" except the word is a corporate holding of a chemical manufacturer and is not to be infringed upon—so the boat is made of plastic. If it had been made of wood, like old boats, it would be an original art treasure. But now it becomes a rough-crafted plastic copy: sprayed in two layers over a form, popped off the mold, and ground down with coarse-grit sanders. The process is altogether unpleasant, and the boat will smell forever like a chemical plant. But the plastic boat emerges having no certain mortality; so it is to be considered in terms of forever. It is very strong. It doesn't bruise; it breaks only under extreme abuse, and then it is easy to fix. It is synthetically impervious to rot and leakage, and so to the whole complex of biodegredations which ultimately must consume all wood boats. And even if the plastic boat is

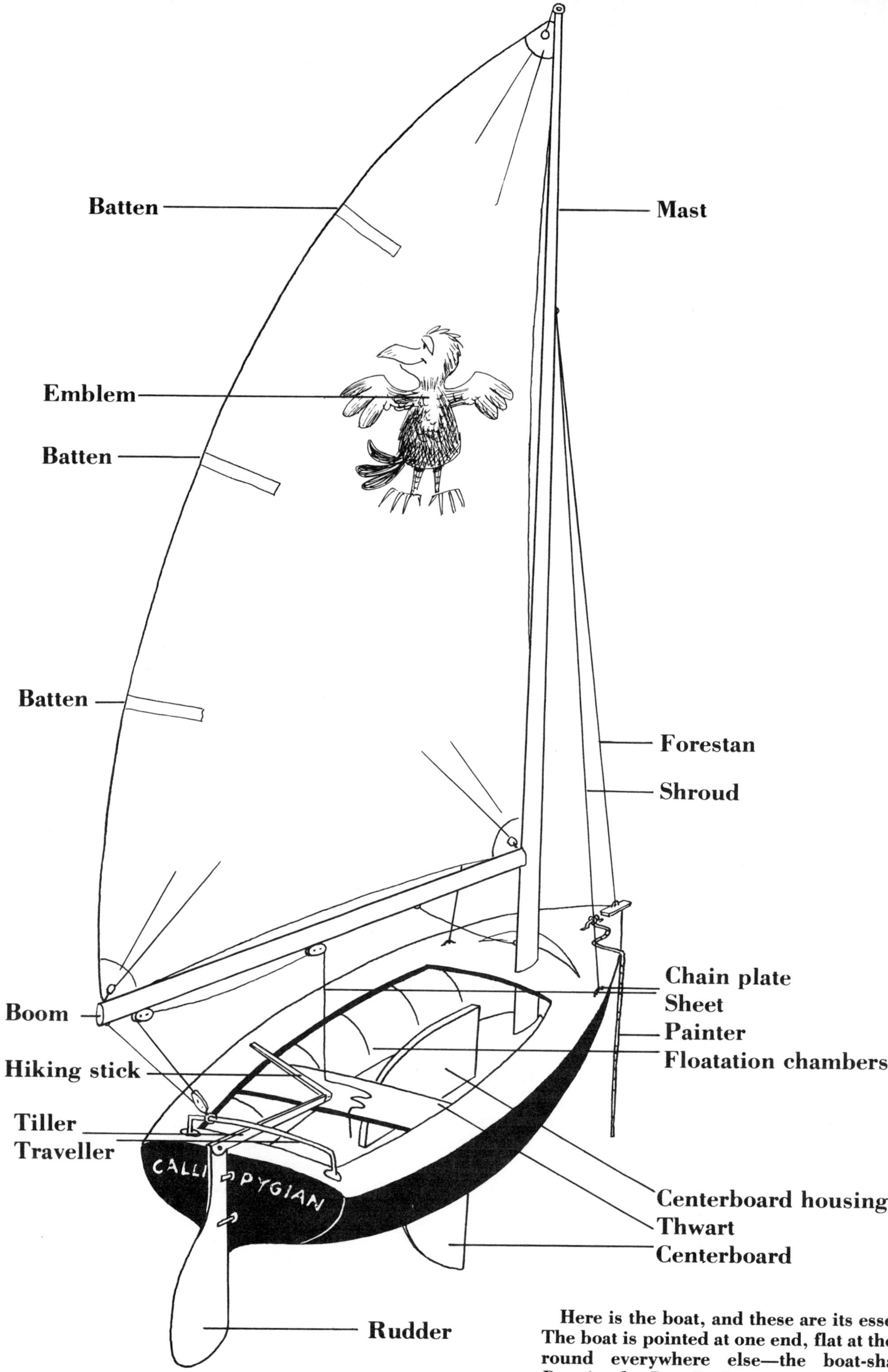

Here is the boat, and these are its essential parts. The boat is pointed at one end, flat at the other, and round everywhere else—the boat-shaped boat. *Drawing by Don Raden*

only derivatively artful, it still is going to be fully as competent as the wood boat: still having the same fundamental curves, the same single, simple shape, completely equable in water. A wood boat may be momentarily perfect; but the plastic boat endures, however crudely it must, as good a boat all the while. Let this be the basic boat.

On the shore, before launching, you walk several times around the bare boat, having a careful look at it. The pointed end would be the front, but you don't call it that. Its name is the bow, so it is the bow, and anything toward the bow is forward. Then the flat end would be the back, but its name is the stern, so it is the stern, and anything toward the stern is aft. Stand at the stern and face the bow—face forward—and the boat's starboard side is on your right, and its port side is on your left. Turn and face aft—or face anywhere—and the same starboard side remains starboard, and the same port side remains port—and so they always will be. These are the first elements of the language sailors speak.

You aren't going to dwell on the language, but it does have to be part of this. It is an old, established language; it comes inevitably in the sequence of events, and for this it is essential communication, however strange it sounds at first. Here is where it begins.

Then on the shore, you put together the boat's machinery. The rigging, the sail, and the rest are elements of machinery. In the most vital sense, all functional parts have to be machinery; and when they all work together, the boat itself will become the machine. It does make an extraordinary machine: prodigious in its way, being both starkly simple and momentously profound—a catalyst in fact, though this is to comprehend later. On the shore now, you attach and assemble and construct the machine. You do the mechanics.

First pick up the mast and set it erect on the ground. The mast is the main spar from which the sail will hang. It stands perhaps fourteen or eighteen feet tall, sometimes over twenty feet; a slender aluminum tube, somewhat resilient, too long to be rigid; not a round tube, its cross section would be more nearly egg-shaped. You can reach around it with the fingers of two hands but not with the fingers of one. Three thin steel wires hang nearly to the ground from about two-thirds of the way up the mast. A narrow groove runs up the mast. A long line, called the halyard, goes up the mast and over a sheave—a pulley wheel—at the very top and hangs down from there, its two ends dangling just above

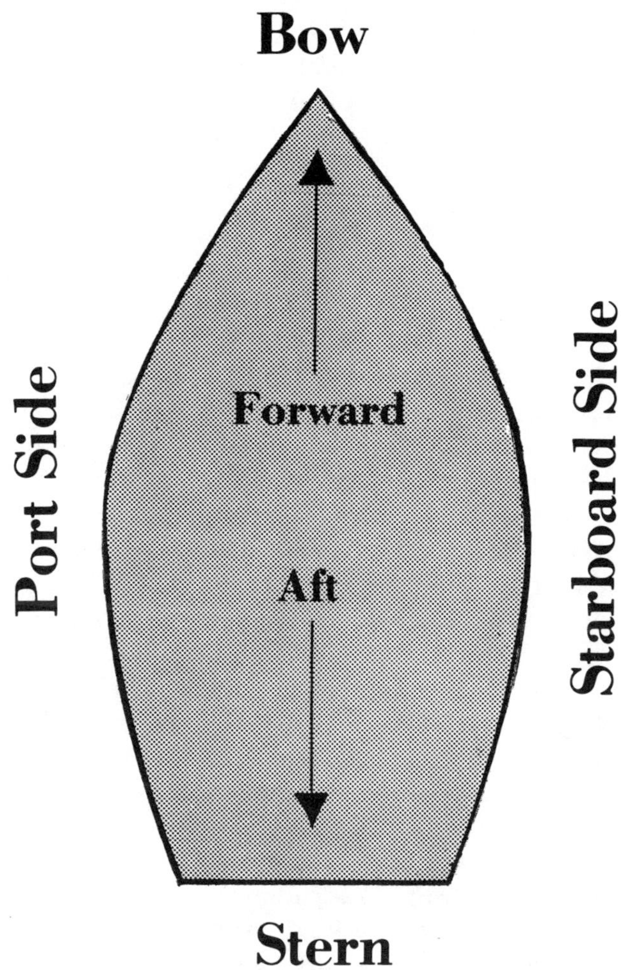

On a boat, the bow is forward; the stern is aft; port is left, and starboard is right. These are the first elements of the language that sailors speak. ***Drawing by Lana Cory Hall***

the ground. With such loose trappings, slightly tangled, the mast stands vaguely like a maypole with ribbons hanging. Let the mast sway just a little; see how the lines and wires swing.

(Masts, like boats, once were wood; their many laminations were shaped by hand and were painstakingly clamped and glued and shaved down. Now masts are aluminum, and factories produce them amid great heat and clatter, turning them out like lengths of pipe—the awesome precision and technology summarily overwhelming all artfulness. But they are all right like this. Masts stand as erect now as ever. If they might seem to stand a little better or a little worse for being wood or aluminum, the difference is more philosophical than practical. You aren't going to worry about it.)

Then lift the mast straight up; it isn't nearly as heavy as it looks. Hold it erect like this, balancing it, and ease it down into its place, forward in the cockpit. The foot of the mast fits very specifically into a shallow cavity called the mast step; or in some boats it may fit onto a stub-like projection, also called the mast step. Set the mast in or on the step, hold it erect, and untangle the three steel wires hanging from above; then attach the wires, by shackles or turnbuckles, to the boat's chain plates. The chain plates are special fittings, so small and unobtrusive that you usually don't notice them; they look like little metal eyelets, one on either side of the boat and one forward where the bow comes to the point. In a good boat the chain plates are very strong and firmly fixed; often they actually are cast into the plastic hull itself. And like this they become anchors for the three steel wires, and the wires become the support cables holding up the mast. With wires secure and tight, you let go and step back. The mast stands erect and alone.

The wire anchored to the forward chain plate is now the forestay. The two wires attached to the two side chain plates are now the shrouds—the port shroud and the starboard shroud—though in some regions, the language takes on variant dialects, and the shrouds are called sidestays. The language, like any language, must have its dialects.

Attach the boom next. The boom is the second spar: another aluminum tube, usually a much shorter and simpler tube than the mast. The boom ostensibly would join the mast at right angles and would hang horizontal over the cockpit—the boat's inner compartment—while the mast stood vertical above it. The boom would extend aft from the mast to a point somewhere over the stern transom—some booms reaching farther, some not as far. But where the mast is the fixed spar, the boom has to be the mobile one. The boom is a pivotal spar, attached to the mast by a uniquely pivotal fitting called the gooseneck; and from the gooseneck, the boom can swing as freely as a conductor's baton—up, down, across, virtually anywhere—and then the linkage of boom and gooseneck can slide up and down the mast together. The boom of course moves because it must; because this is the way the machine is going to work. But you see plainly, testing the boom on the shore, feeling how freely it would move, that even as this boom must have its certain critical flexibility, it still must hold within well-structured restraints—because this too is the way the machine is going to work.

The sheet and traveler will be the restraints. The sheet is the line that is not the sail but rather controls the sail. It does so by restraining the boom; by harnessing the boom to the traveler. The traveler in effect is a short one-track trolley line across the boat. It can be a track or rod or just a length of wire; and a special fitting, a small metal rider, slides along the traveler. The rider is going to be the point of attachment, or point of purchase, being indeed fixed to the boat, even as it remains necessarily mobile and shuttles on the track between the two sides. Then, most simply, the sheet winds several times back and forth between the boom and the traveler, threading its way through the pattern of blocks—pulleys—fastened both to the boom and the metal rider. (The system, or harness, is called block and tackle, an old Navy term originally coined so the tackle rhymed with maple, not with jackal.) The sheet finally emerges from the system and dangles from the boom down into the cockpit; often it goes through one last block fastened to the bottom of the cockpit. Grasp the sheet after it comes out of the last block, wherever that block is; this is where you are going to hold the sheet when you sail the boat.

Stand just behind the boat, aft of the boat, facing forward from the stern transom. Keep holding the sheet with one hand; pick up the end of the boom with the other hand. Hold the boom over the boat, keeping it level—the sheet and blocks hanging below, the whole assemblage linked to the runner on the traveler—then sweep the boom in a long, horizontal arc across the boat. The boom draws the sheet along beneath; the sheet drags the runner

With the boat still on shore, hold the sheet in one hand, the boom in the other, and feel the first elements of control in the machinery of the boat. ***Drawing by Don Raden***

along behind; the rider slides along the traveler; and the entire assemblage comes collectively across the boat. Then the rider halts abruptly at the end of the track; it holds fast there; it establishes itself definitively as the point of purchase. The sheet pulls taut. The boom stops in its arc, suddenly restrained. You have the boom in one hand, the sheet in the other, and you can't sweep the boom farther; you are holding it back with the sheet. The efforts of your two hands come to this deadlock against the machinery of the boat.

You intuitively feel this. You learn the first elements of control from the feel of this. Give an inch with one hand, and you take it with the other; or take it with one hand, and you give it with the other; this is how you are going to run the machinery. So slacken the sheet first. You ease the restraints and swing the boom wider. The blocks draw apart; the arc lengthens. Then just let the sheet run free. You cast loose all restraints and sweep the boom through its full arc; you walk it around and hold it nearly at right angles to the boat; it stops only when you bring it against the shroud. The sheet is fully extended; you hold it at the very end. The boom is out all the way, at the limit of its arc, unrestrained.

Then pull the sheet. You tighten the restraints once again—gaining a powerful advantage in the block and tackle—and you haul the boom into closer straits, back to the boat. The blocks draw together; the arc shortens; you bring the boom to the place over the metal rider at the end of the traveler, the point of purchase. Keep the sheet taut. The boom is close-hauled—fully restrained. This is how it works.

The machinery works the same way when you swing the boom to the other side of the boat. The boom comes across again trailing the assemblage of sheet, blocks, and rider, this time bringing all of it in the other direction. The rider slides the other way along the traveler and stops and holds at the other end of the track. So now, after all this, the traveler is simply the structural conveyance by which the point of purchase makes the essential shift to the other side. Then you slacken the sheet, and the boom swings wider in its arc, finally coming once again to the point where it is nearly at right angles to the boat—now on the other side—and then you pull the sheet, and once again the boom comes back. When the boom swings all ways, through all restraints and non-restraints, then its total arc, the sum of all its arcs, altogether becomes nearly half a circle. This is what you mean to control when you sail the boat.

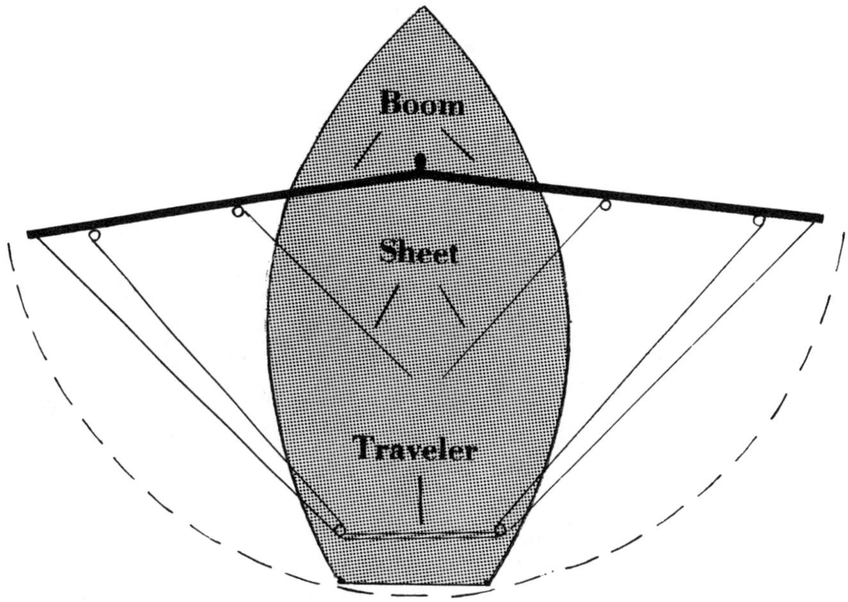

The boom, moving within the restraints of the sheet and traveler, swings in nearly half a circle over the boat. ***Drawing by Lana Cory hall***

The last thing you do on shore is install the centerboard. You mostly learn about the centerboard later, but for now it is a fundamental element of machinery: wide and flat like a plank or blade. It aligns fore-and-aft with the boat; it fits into the boat almost like a knife into a sheath, sliding edgewise into a narrow housing in the center of the cockpit. As functioning machinery the centerboard is going to come partly out of its housing and slide down through a slot in the bottom of the boat: down into the water, once the boat is in the water. And when it is done functioning, it is going to slide back up into its housing: back into the sheath. It can be one kind of centerboard that slides straight up and down like a dagger blade, or another kind that hinges up and down like a jacknife blade. When it is down in the water, it is going to be involved most profoundly with critical balances and forces—and it will keep the boat from slipping sideways; though this is oversimplifying it. Just understand now that the centerboard, functioning or non-functioning, is vital machinery. You will know the rest presently.

As for the mechanics, you install different centerboards different ways in different housings. Some fit in quite easily from above. Others go in with more difficulty from below: going up through the slot in the bottom. Some centerboards are hung on pivot pins, so they hinge up and down. Most have to be connected to systems of cables or lines or levers: to different sorts of apparatus by which you will lower them down into the water and raise them back up—to be, by turns, functioning and non-functioning machinery. So assemble all this. Raise the centerboard up into the housing. Then put the boat into the water.

A small boat is easy to launch. You lower it from a seawall or slide it down a ramp; or you find three friends to help, and together you lift the boat, mast erect, and carry it across a beach and set it into the water. Secure a line to the bow—a very specific line which you call the painter—and hold the end of the painter and let the boat drift there, floating high, like a duck. It looks weightlesss, bobbing on the water, not squatting in it. The boat alone just seems to hang unencumbered over the surface, hardly raising a ripple; just tugging very lightly on the painter. Such are the look and touch of a good boat when it goes into the water.

Tow the boat by the painter, bringing it along the shore to a pier, then out the pier, and away from the shore. For the rest of this you want to be clear of the shore. Tie the end of the painter to the pier, making the boat fast to the pier—this is what the painter is for, towing the boat and making it fast. And the pier is not the dock. The dock is the water next to the pier.

You need to know a good knot when you make the boat fast to the pier—a good knot being

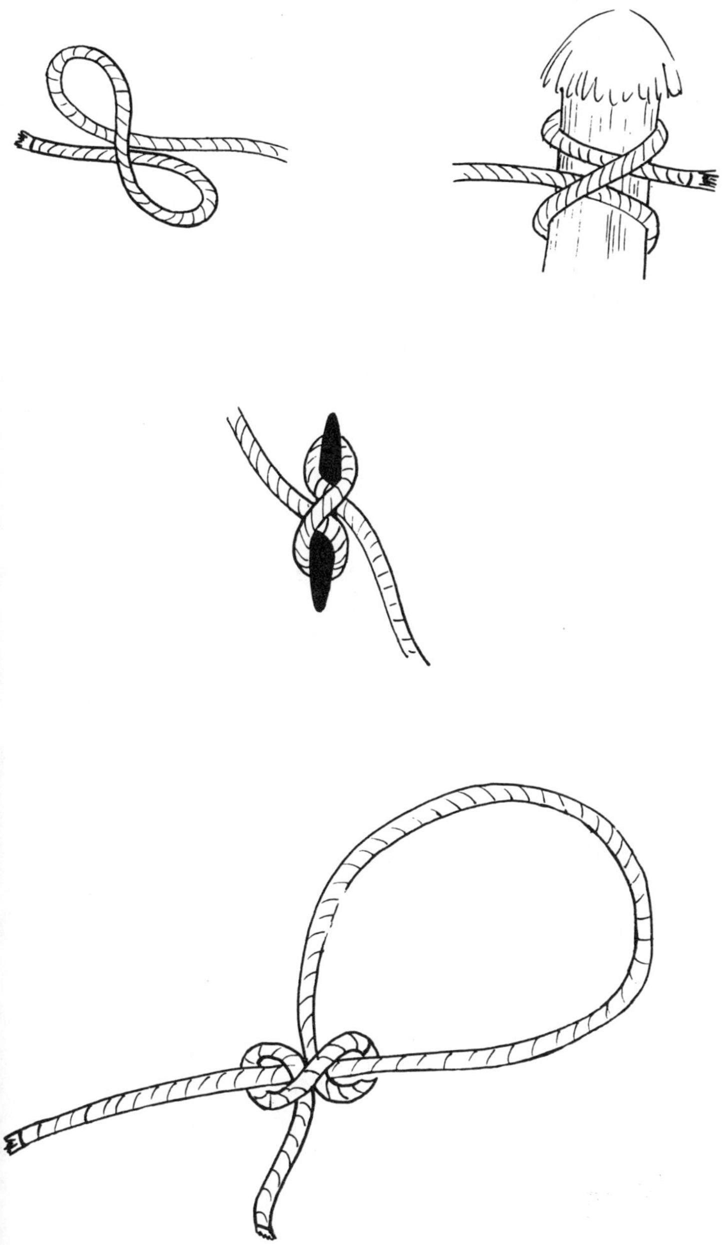

The clove hitch always consists of two loops that become two turns of a line cast on a post, or on a cleat, or—in the Buntline hitch—cast back on the line itself. Regardless of where the turns are cast, the clove hitch is the most useful knot on the boat. ***Drawing by Don Raden***

something rare, a singular bend or turn or clinch of a line, altogether simple and secure, quickly done and easily undone. In all the world there are perhaps only a dozen good knots—the science is so severely limited—and most people, throughout their lives, can tie only a marginally good one in their shoelaces, and they usually don't get it right.

Some day you may know all the good knots, as you should. But now you need two of them for what you are going to be doing—a clove hitch and a bowline—so for now never mind the complex traditions of sailors and knots. Just learn these two and do them right. They are the necessary machinery.

You should learn knots the easy way, from people who know them. But those are uncommon people, even among sailors, so you probably learn knots the hard way, by sitting down and studying them and trying to tie them, and finally getting them right—because, of course, you can't articulate knots; you can only tie them. Tie the clove hitch with two turns around a post, or capstan, or tie a variation with one turn around each of the two prongs of a cleat, or loop the line around a fitting and tie the clove hitch with the two turns going back around the line itself. (You make a very useful sliding loop called the Buntline hitch.) The two turns of the clove hitch actually are so confoundingly easy that there seems almost nothing to learn; the trick is only to arrange the loops so the line tucks under itself and draws tight. The clove hitch becomes your working knot. You tie it more than all other knots; in one way or another it secures nearly all the lines at their critical points, and so it holds the rigging together. It would do almost everything you needed of a knot—except you keep the bowline in reserve.

Learn the bowline by following the old parable of the rabbit emerging from its hole, going around a tree, and going back into the hole. (Bowline tying starts like this and becomes refined into the dynamic exercise in which cults of expert sailors do the knot one-handed, with a single twist of the wrist.) When the bowline is right, it is a fixed, nonslipping loop, and for this it is the unique, ultimate knot and holds as no other knot can. So no matter how many knots you know, you still need the bowline where none other will do. You may need it only rarely, but then you need it very much. You keep it always in reseve.

Then tie a good knot, clove hitch or bowline, and make the boat fast. Then go aboard.

When the boat is small, like this one, you ease aboard most gingerly, especially the first time. Hold the boat alongside the pier; stand on the very edge of the pier and extend one leg slowly and experimentally down into the widest, or beamiest, part of the cockpit, putting your toes in first, as if into cold water. Set your foot down very carefully,

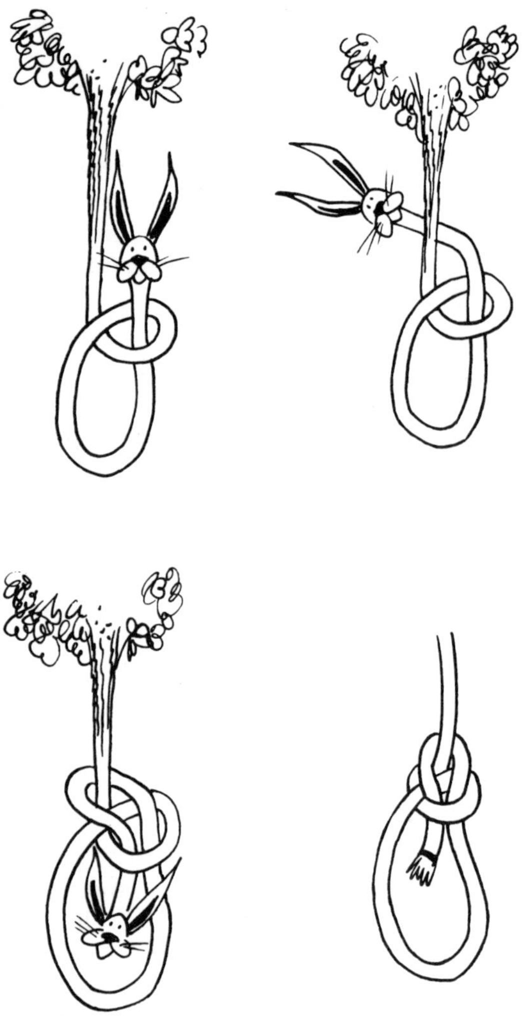

Tie the bowline by following the old parable of the rabbit emerging from its hole, going around a tree, and going back into its hole. The bowline is a fixed, non-slipping loop—the ultimate knot on a boat. *Drawing by Don Raden*

testing the feel and balance. The boat rolls a little, slides, sinks slightly under your weight; in the water it must have this feeling, like nothing on land. It is afloat and moves as you do, or when you do, or because you do; it never can be fixed or rigid or solid under you. You know this just by putting your foot in the cockpit.

Then lower yourself into the boat, the other foot and the rest of you, and still be careful. Crouch low in the cockpit and feel *how* the boat rocks; shift your weight and feel *where* the boat rocks. Once you probably were told never to stand up and walk in any kind of boat, but now you must do it very circumspectly in this kind of boat. You test the boat this way; you begin to learn the feel of it. You need to know the boat just by knowing the feel, because presently you are going to need to know the boat well enough to do things more daring than standing up and walking. So stand up slowly, lean one way, then another. Take a deliberate half step. Hold your balance, try a whole step, then another. Try to

When boarding a small boat, step most gingerly into the widest part of the cockpit—putting toes in first, as if into cold water. *Drawing by Don Raden*

Attaching the helm is always an awkward procedure. Rudder and tiller must be manhandled into improbable places in order to line up fussy little hinge-like fittings. *Drawing by Don Raden*

allow for the way the boat moves. Then try to move with it. You begin to understand about the feel.

You could call this getting your sealegs, but nobody ever uses that term seriously.

In a moment you realize that the boat does have a certain complex stability in the water. It rolls, but it bobs back up. At first it rolls easily; it may seem unsteady. But it rolls harder as it leans farther—or heels farther—and it comes more forcefully back up. It is balanced and ballasted to float upright; as it heels, it becomes counterbalanced and counterballasted against heeling more. You learn this by experimenting. This is a differential sort of stability, but real and of course necessary; it is the basic design of the boat. The boat needs it to sail. You need to know it is there; subjectively you need it to trust.

Assemble the last of the machinery now. The rest of the parts go together with the boat in the water. The rudder is a blade like the centerboard, broad and flat, and it attaches to the stern transom. It can have various profiles, though it is evolved from ancient steering oars and always must look rather like a large paddle. The tiller is a very sturdy stick, usually about four feet long, one end pivotally fixed to the rudder. The tiller and rudder together are the helm, and the helm is the machinery for steering the boat.

You always have an awkward time attaching the helm to the boat. The rudder and tiller together make an unwieldy apparatus that you must manhandle into improbable places. You have to put the rudder over the stern, then lean over after it and fasten it to the transom by an arrangement of fussy little hinge-like fittings. The boat bobs about, and you do intricate contortions, only a scant few inches above the water, sometimes getting your elbows wet, trying to line up small, critical pins and sockets—the pintles and gudgeons—and if you let go, the rudder and tiller together might drop like a stone to the bottom. Each time you do this, you wonder if it is the wrong way, if there should be a right way, some ingeniously quick and competent method of attaching the helm. There should be, but there isn't; so here you are. This is what you have to do when you rig the boat. You just learn to do it and be done with it.

Then when the helm is attached, the rudder hangs on the transom, poised to turn on its pintles and gudgeons. The broad blade of the rudder is down in the water, and the tiller extends forward to the cockpit. Swing the tiller in an arc across the cockpit; the rudder sweeps in an arc through the water, pushing against the weight and volume of the water—and this is how the helm works. This is how you are going to steer the boat.

After everything else you raise the sail. It is made of stiff, heavy, synthetic fabric—of Dacron ©, though the word is another corporate holding—and

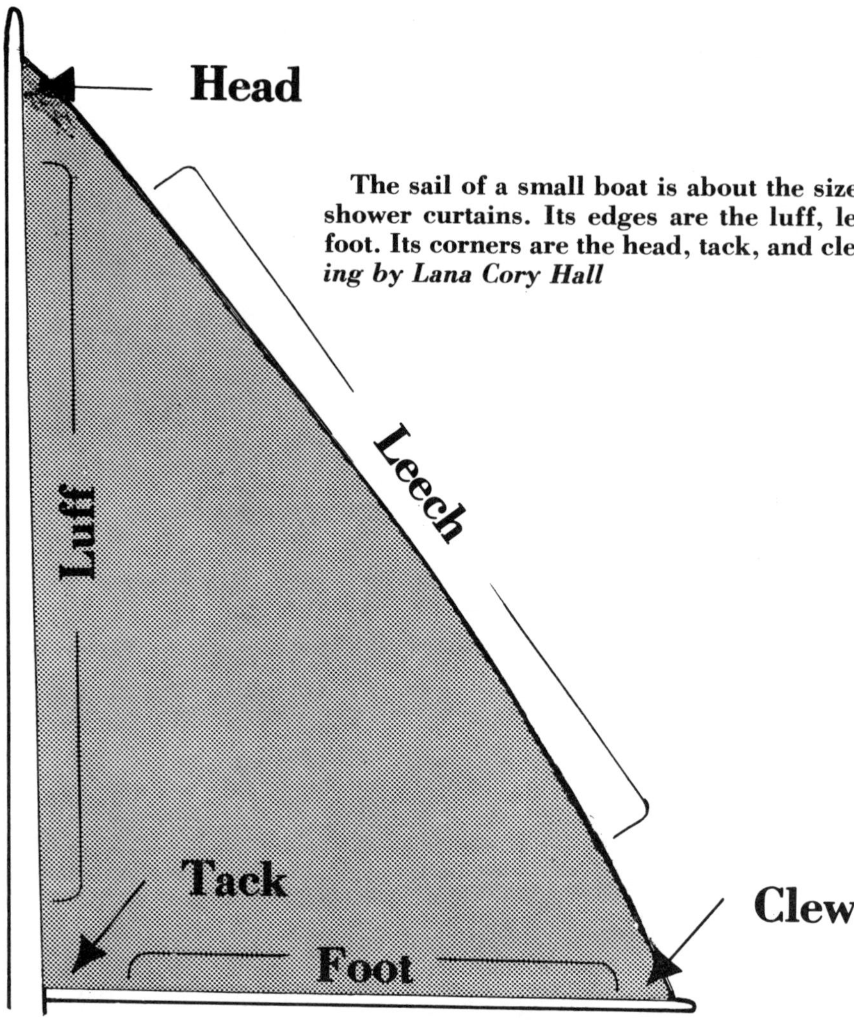

The sail of a small boat is about the size of three shower curtains. Its edges are the luff, leech, and foot. Its corners are the head, tack, and clew. ***Drawing by Lana Cory Hall***

altogether it is about as big as three shower curtains. The three edges of the sail are the luff, leech, and foot; the three corners are the head, tack, and clew. The luff fits exactly into that small groove going up the mast. The head attaches to the halyard: the line that goes up the mast and comes down the mast and hangs over the sheave at the top. The tack attaches to the gooseneck, the fitting that joins mast and boom. The clew attaches to the other end of the boom. The foot of the sail stretches along the boom from tack to clew. The leech is then the remaining edge; it is going to be the sail's trailing edge. You insert three slender hardwood laths—battens—into three special pockets along the leech. The battens keep the leech from flapping; they are a final element of reinforcement.

Then pull the halyard down and hoist the sail up, like raising a flag on a pole. The luff goes straight up the groove in the mast. The sail goes up wide and full and rattling, spreading out like a banner above you. On some boats the sail goes up completely unencumbered; the boom isn't even attached until later. On other boats boom and sail are attached first—sometimes just at the tack, sometimes along the entire foot; this depends on different hardware. The sail goes in any case up the full height of the mast, and you secure the halyard with an impregnable knot in a cleat; wind the line

Pull the halyard down and hoist the sail up, like raising a flag on a pole. ***Drawing by Don Raden***

several times around and across the cleat, then lock it on with a clove hitch. You have to be completely sure about securing the halyard. Some boats even have special hooks for this.

The sail is flapping in the wind and showing the boat's emblem now. Every boat with an emblem carries it high like this.

Make the final adjustments. When you secure the halyard, pull it tight enough to stretch the luff to a certain ideal tension along the mast; the luff should be taut to the point where the horizontal wrinkles disappear but not to the point where the vertical wrinkles would appear; the difference can be only a few ounces. (You would set the luff tension best with a special line called a downhaul; except not every boat has a downhaul.) Then stretch the foot along the boom using the line called the outhaul—but be especially restrained on this. Your impulse is to pull too tight, as if you would draw the sail flat like a drumhead. You have to ease back and deliberately leave the sail sagging, so it will bell out in the wind and form a curve. You will learn presently about the curve.

Notice that the tiller has a hinged extension, another stick, perhaps two or three feet long, pivoting from the end of the tiller itself; this is the hiking stick. Notice also that some boats have wide straps fastened down to the cockpit; these are hiking straps. In a moment you will know what hiking is and what the stick and straps are for. For now just know they are here.

The boat is rigged. The machine is functional.

Drawing by Don Raden

2 The Values

You are going sailing now, allowing that this is neither necessary nor practical. The boat costs too much for what it does. Even if it is clean without internal combustion and works on free energy and doesn't consume petroleum or emit fumes or make noise, it still can never be materially productive; it is always too much machinery for something that just moves through water. Its value is only that it does what it does because it is what it is, and in this it provides a unique and fundamental experience. In this it is rare.

You go sailing only when you know you will encounter no serious danger; sailing isn't worth that. So you sail only if you can swim first. You can swim only if you *know* you can swim; if you don't know, you can't. And if you can't, you already are in grave danger just being in this boat tied to the pier. Try this: tap your toe on the floor of the cockpit. There is 1/8 inch of plastic under you, and then there is the water. The water is the final reckoning. If you aren't ready for it, then get out of the boat while you still can. And don't try to think that a life preserver would save you. Don't ever trust your life to a life preserver if you can't swim. It is a false security, an absurd contrivance for a serious failing. It might make you safer if you can swim, but it never will make you safe if you can't. So keep a life preserver as a presence in the boat, but don't depend on it. Believe in it only when you don't need to.

Notice about the boat: in its essential structure are large compartments, shut off, sealed tight and filled with air and urethane foam. These compartments always crowd the cockpit. Sometimes they bulge so large that they reduce cockpit space down to a narrow trench in the center of the boat. Sometimes the entire boat is a single sealed compartment, and the cockpit might be just a depression no larger than a bucket, in which you might put your feet. And if the boat is awash, or if it capsizes, then it is buoyed up by the air sealed in the compartments, and it stays afloat regardless. All the compartments together comprise the boat's flotation. This is what keeps it from sinking.

The boat is regulated by law; it may not sail until it will not sink. You are not regulated. You stay afloat by minding values.

Then attend to necessary details. Empty your pockets of keys, money, wallet—all your worldly possessions—because nothing ever stays in pockets when you sail a boat. You will understand this soon enough; at moments you will sail while seeming to hang nearly upside-down. Stow your things in a locker that latches very securely, or if the boat doesn't have a locker, tie everything in a sailbag and lash the bag to the mast. Keep only your wristwatch, because you usually need to know time, but make it a waterproof watch and expect it to get wet. Expect everything to get wet; you especially must allow for getting wet, even though you make every effort not to. This is most fundamental of all.

Finally, when you first set out, bring someone to guide you: someone who can sail. In theory you could go out alone, and probably you would come back all right; people have done this and have told improbable stories afterward. But you would have bad times. You would want help and wouldn't have it. You would be chronically embarassed at least, gravely endangered at most, and never mind which is worse; either way you would risk more than any of this is worth. Bring a guide, and you temper the adventure. You learn to sail, and the guide is just there keeping the values. The guide will be invisible hereafter, so you don't doubt yourself—but still will be here so you don't destroy yourself, or just make a fool of yourself.

With this you ease the centerboard out of its housing and down to its setting in the water. You cast off the painter—you untie it—and set the boat loose, and sail it.

You don't know how to bring the boat away from the pier yet; so just push off this time: give the boat a strong, simple shove toward open water. Then let it drift. Let it be detached. Hold the slack sheet very lightly in one hand. Hold the tiller in the other. Watch the sail hang and flap. And wait like this. Be calm; and just for a moment, trust the machine.

The machine is working. It never actually begins working; it just collectively is working because everything is simply if variously *there* when all the parts are together. The boat becomes tense. The sail quiets, stiffens, tightens, curves out. The boom swings over. The lines draw taut. The small metal rider slides along the traveler and stops with a sharp, hard impact at the end of the track. The sheet pulls in your hand. The tiller stirs. Wind blows. Forces rise. The machine is underway—the entire machine, moving ahead now, going incredibly, logically forward.

It is easy. The boat sails like this, just because of what it is, and where it is, because it is in both wind and water, and you hold both sheet and tiller. You plainly feel this: the wind comes; the machine works; the boat goes. The boat bobs, rocks, splashes, slides; bounding over smaller waves, bouncing through larger ones; making sloshing and gurgling noises underneath, leaving a modest trail of bubbles behind. It goes a little roughly; it does ride rougher than it appears to; but it goes bountifully, on gathering forces—pushed, pulled, pressed, and always driven ahead. You sail now, and it feels good. At this point you don't even need to understand. You hold the sheet and tiller, and the boat sails away to open water; going bountifully out to sea.

(It has to go to open water. It needs at least a clear mile of open water. It would have no value in those shameless little suburban sinkholes measuring barely a few hundred yards across but marketed so ruthlessly as open water.)

You learn two things on the way to open water. These are always the first two things you actually learn about sailing:

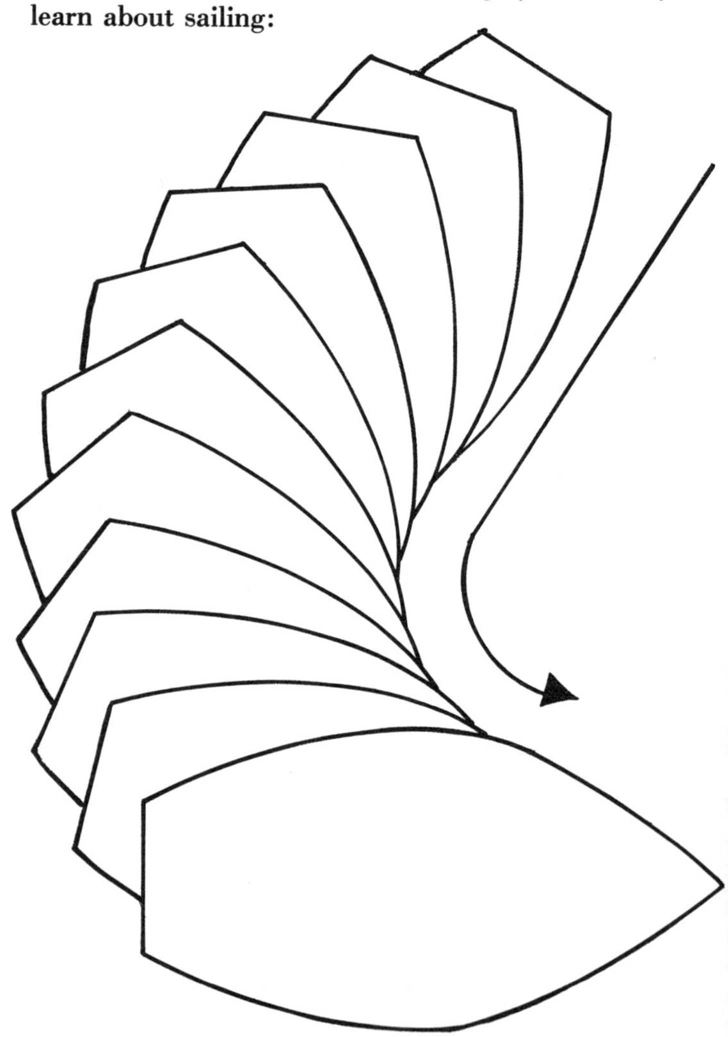

The boat doesn't turn. It swerves. The stern swings one way, so the bow points the other. ***Drawing by Lana Cory Hall***

When you point the tiller one way, you turn the boat the other. Point starboard; you turn port; point port; you turn starboard. And this is how you steer. This is because the boat is on water, not on tracks; and it doesn't really turn; it swerves. Point the tiller, and you set the blade of the rudder obliquely against the water; and the mass of the water obliquely deflects aside the momentum of the boat driving ahead. Then the stern swings sideways, as it must, while the boat is going forward; and sliding both sideways and forward, the boat swerves around. So in fact you turn the boat by swinging the stern where you point the tiller, and this is really how you steer. This is the first thing you learn.

The other thing is that the boat heels. This is part of the way it works: it leans to the side as it sails ahead; leaning variously with the weight of the wind blowing into the sail. Right now it might lean only slightly: one side rising higher, the other sinking lower. In stronger wind it might lean all the way to its limit and sail tenuously on its edge, just hanging there on the verge of capsizing. Capsizing is overturning—the abrupt and unwarranted end—and however the boat heels, it always must lean toward potential capsizing. If you didn't know that before, you know it now, by your raw instinct for self-preservation. Because now, indeed, the boat is heeling.

You go instinctively to the boat's weather side, or windward side—the side that rises higher. The sail, with the weight of the wind, is over the lee side, or leeward side—the side that sinks lower. (Lee rhymes with tree, leeward with steward.) And as the boat leans to leeward, you lean to windward, applying your own weight as a counterbalance to the wind's. You hike like this. You hook your toes under the hiking straps; you steer from the end of the hiking stick; and you extend yourself past the edge of the boat and exert your own leverage against the heeling. You hike, and the weather side comes back down. The lee side comes back up. You hold the boat down flat on the water, not heeling, and sail it forward.

This is right. The boat should be flat. It is true and balanced when flat. When it heels, it is unbalanced and misaligned and sails badly—though it has reasons for heeling, and does heel, and often must heel; and you will come to understand this. The boat could heel with a splendid arrogance and hang up on its edge, its radical limit; though it would be all wrong and hardly would sail at all; and you will understand this too. So just learn now that the boat heels when it needs to heel, but you sail it best when you hold it flat. The boat is meant to sail flat; it is conceived and designed to sail flat. This is fundamental.

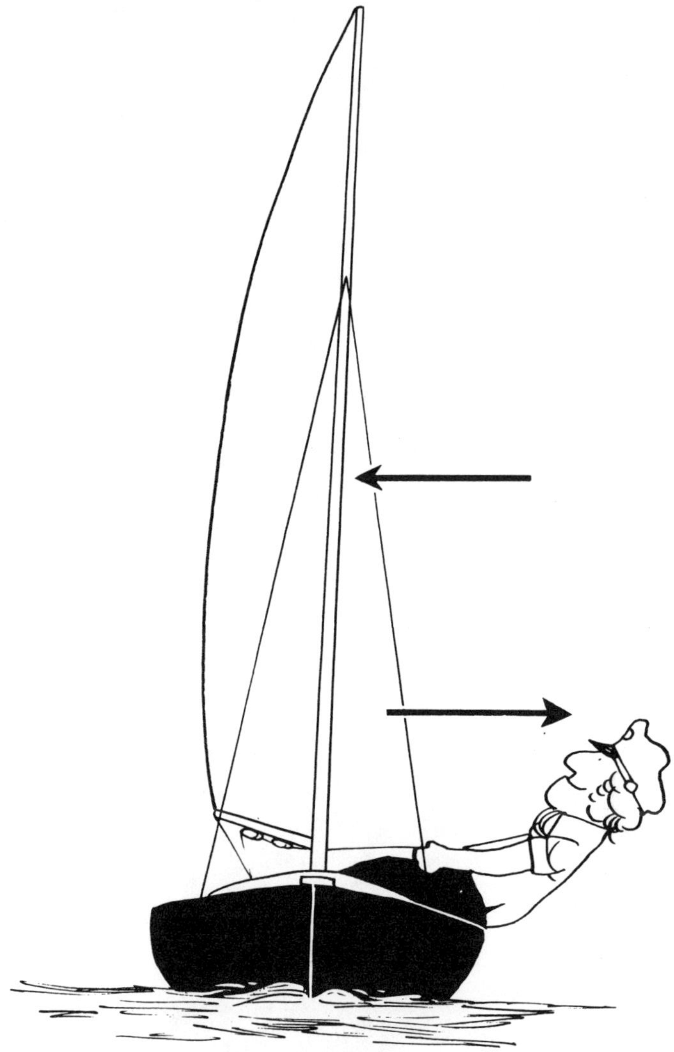

Sailing the boat flat, the skipper hikes out—leans over one side—to counterbalance wind and sail forces that would heel the boat toward the other side. *Drawing by Don Raden*

In open water now, sailing flat, you first find the essence. You begin to feel the ways the boat moves with the elements—driving with the wind, riding with the waves; going as air and water do. It belongs to air and water now; it has become a phenomenon of air and water; a resolution of air and water. It has the forces and rhythms of both; it goes where it will, being always in accord with both. Now you can feel it like this—working because it is what it is, and where it is; and because you hold the sheet and tiller. You have to come this far to feel this: out into open water.

This is why you sail the boat. The experience is part of the essence; you are part of the phenomenon. When the boat sails, you belong to the elements. Now you are with the elements. This is where you begin to learn.

Start learning the wind. The wind is always first.

3
The Wind

You have a fair wind. It is clean and steady, without turbulence, and it blows in moderation, so the waves are small, without white caps. Ideally, this wind blows at an angle toward the shore, and you can stand there and lick your finger and feel for it, which is a little silly. Or you turn around and feel it in the backs of both ears, which is a better way. Or you watch smoke drifting, or waves rolling, or dark spots sliding on water. You don't see a fair wind, but the signs define it, and you can be detached about it; it is very simple from shore. You don't care about it because it doesn't affect you much. And you know where it blows because you touch the ground and know where you are.

But now in a little boat you sail away from the shore, not realizing what is different. Now you do care about wind because it does affect you; but now you don't know where it blows because you don't touch the ground and don't know where you are—and you don't understand any of this yet. You just go happily out to sea, sailing by a charm. You have the sheet and tiller and the good sensation of the boat sailing because of something you are doing. And whatever you are doing, it is not difficult. You might wonder vaguely if you ought to be preoccupied with wind, but you aren't because you haven't yet learned to be, and for just this moment you don't want to be. You are content to let it blow and not ask where, then it won't interfere with the way you sail the boat. And you know even as an innocent that this is absurd, and you are in a fool's paradise, but you keep going as far as you can like this, and the boat sails as long as the charm holds. Then you encounter the wind.

It happens quickly. You don't have time to think. The wind indulges you; it lets you sail out to sea; it waits. Then abruptly it turns on you. You make a wrong move or don't make a right one—the difference is slight—and in that awkward instant, when you are off-balance, the wind is upon you. It seizes you from behind, wrenches the boat one way, flings the sail another; it spins you around, heels you precipitously, stops you with a lurch; it leaves you flapping and floundering in the swells, sets you adrift like flotsam: all this without actually becoming violent. You float away strangely unshaken but profoundly impressed and only half curious about what you didn't do right. Now you have felt wind, and you are enlightened most forcefully. After this you live with a basic and abiding awareness of wind. It is elemental like water.

You begin to understand what is happening.

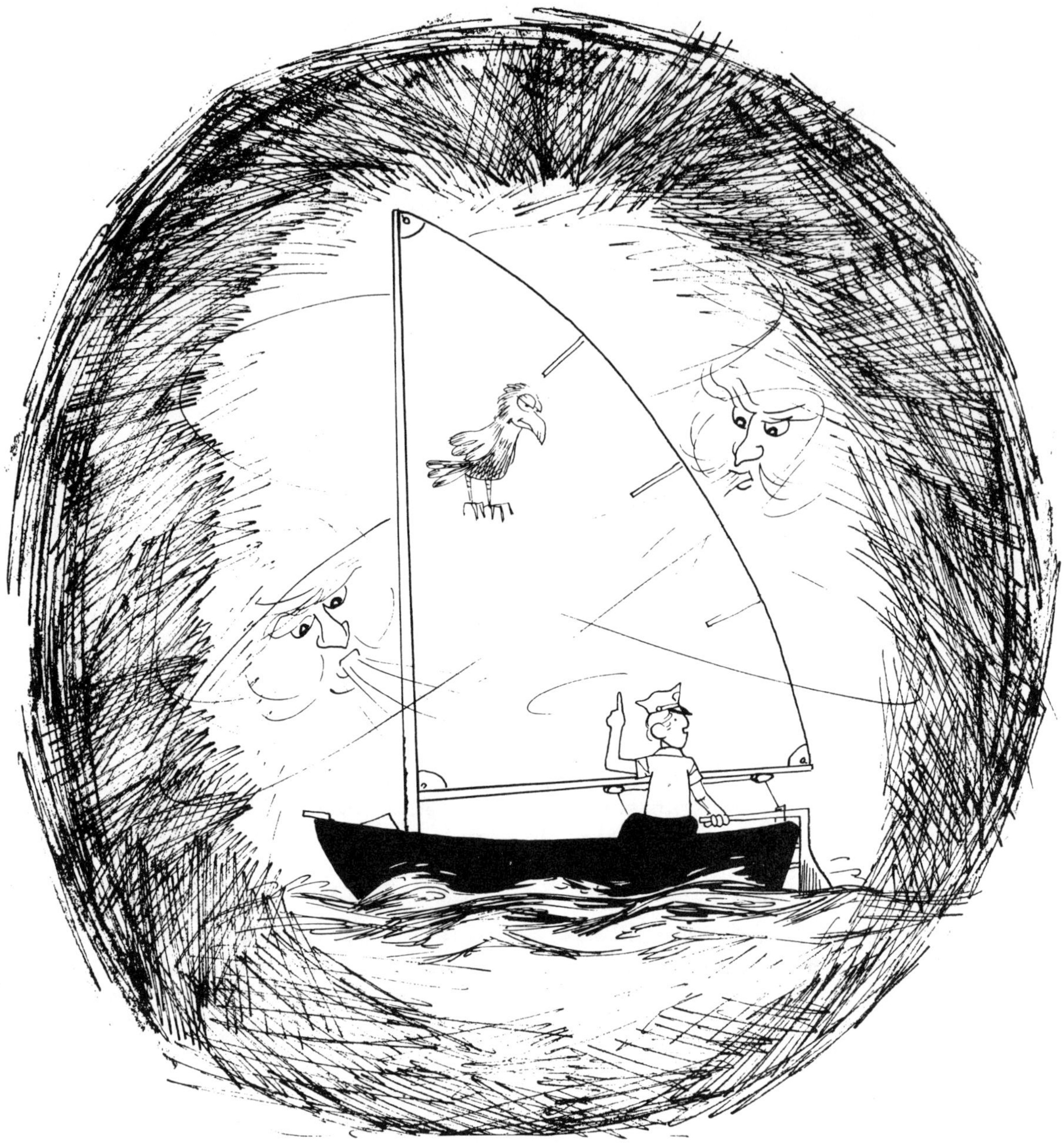

Lost in the wind. ***Drawing by Don Raden***

Now you do know wind. It doesn't blow away, like on shore; it is omnipresent here, the primal force. It blows and everything moves. Masses stir. Waves roll. You go too; you are part of this. You have come here and become one of the things in the wind. You didn't mean to commit yourself this way; you didn't know, but here you are. Now you have found the wind.

The discovery is only partly illuminating and—in fact—not really reassuring; altogether it might reveal just enough so that now you know wind but don't know what to do about it. And this might not trouble you, except now you are sufficiently aware of what you do know, and you feel obligated for what you don't. And the moment you first grasp at this or try in some way to reason it out, sailing itself suddenly confounds you. Out in the wind you begin to think with your sheet and tiller in your two hands; you are about to have the first sensations of the logic in what you are doing. Then abruptly you are lost, and you don't know how or why. It happens so strangely. You are disoriented, directionless; the logic is in the wind somehow: intangible. Nothing is fixed or firm. Everything is heaving or tossing or rising or sinking, shifting you this way or sliding you that. You search for some line or point; you want very much to align yourself with something. But your bearings are vague, and you find only air and water. Then you remember how easily you sailed here, completely oblivious of all direction, and you wonder. You fantasize about boat, waves, and wind, all in suspension. You would freeze them where they are and walk out on the water and view them from the detached perspective—like on land—and then everything would be resolved. But you are not so gifted. There is no perspective and no resolution. You see where you are; yet, you are blithely lost, and you just keep sailing the boat, trying to understand.

All this is necessary. This is how you progress. You sail out of a fool's paradise and into a cheerful chaos, and you can only hold on to your sheet and tiller and keep going. Try not to struggle; just hold on and ride the boat, and mostly it sails for you, even if it sometimes balks and plunges, and the sail thrashes. You need to concentrate on wind now. You are blowing with it, groping through it; you have become immersed in it. And still you don't know what to do about it. You try to look for signs. You hang out strands of yarn to see where they flutter; you watch again where the waves go. But this

The great enlightenment comes with the discovery of the center of effort, the focal point of all forces in the sail. ***Drawing by Don Raden***

doesn't help. You are now so close to the wind and so involved with it that signs by themselves no longer are enough. You simply keep going, and gradually you realize that you can't just know wind. You have to be intuitive about it. You need a very basic feeling for it. And you don't have the feeling yet, and so this is how and why you are lost. It helps a little, understanding just this much.

But for a while you must go on sailing while lost in the wind. There is no avoiding this; it is the hardest and most critical part of the learning process. How long you must be lost depends on who you are. Some people require only a moment. (Airplane pilots are traditionally quick because they already have insights on wind.) But you, like most people, probably need half an hour or less—or perhaps an hour or more. A few people need two or three hours. Such differences aren't important. No matter who you are, you don't get hopelessly lost in wind. You never think of despairing. All this while, in fact, you actually are very near to what you are after. You just need to keep going.

And then you do have it. The feeling. The wind. It was there all the time. It is so uncommonly simple. There comes a moment which is no different from any other, but it is like the moment you learn to ride a bicycle; suddenly you can do this. You aren't lost any more. You know purely by reflex that you are here, going this way, and the wind is there, going that way; and as neatly as that, you have the whole logic. You feel it intuitively. You are sailing the boat with it, steering so very deftly through the wind. You know where the wind blows. It is so *uncommonly* simple.

From now on you are all right. You become very certain about wind. You can watch the signs once again and see how wind comes and where it goes and what it does; and for a while you are satisfied simply to have the feeling for it and to hold it in your sail when you need it and to spill it out when you don't. But soon you do better. You begin to refine the feeling. You learn almost instinctively to think of wind scaled down just to the specific forces that are in the sail and driving the boat—and then, more hypothetically, to think of those forces resolved still further, down finally to a plane geometry, with a single, sinuous line bearing on a single, definitive, focal point. The point is the center of effort, and, plotted mathematically, it is always low and forward on the sail, two or three feet aft of the mast and two or three feet above the boom. The line is the wind axis, and it begins where the wind does and extends across half a continent to the point in the sail, and now you can sense its last half-dozen yards. You resolve the omnipresent wind down to this, and you are never lost again.

After this you finish learning to sail the boat. Everything else is mechanics and maneuvers, and there are many more lines. But these few yards of the wind axis make the basic line. All other lines are measured from this one; they could not exist without it. The wind axis is where the wind blows. It is more important than anything.

4
Turn, Trim, and Balance

So now have a look at the sail spread across the wind. The sail forms the essential curve; a lovely, mathematical curve, bare and functional and altogether vital like logic itself. It is smooth and near-rigid with tension—the pure, basic shape, cut and stitched to bend and hold just this way. Touch it; you can drum your fingers on it. Prod harder against it; you feel the forces gathered in it. This is not the ethereal thing it seems. This is something very important.

You see plainly that the boat sails forward because the wind fills the sail, and the sail curves this way; you sense this even more when you take the sheet and tiller and become part of the phenomenon. And you realize, as you sail along, that with these two controls in your hands, you actually are holding the curve there in the sail, but you aren't quite certain what you should be doing with it. You just feel responsible for it because you are connected to it. So you start experimenting—setting the boat firmly on a straight course across the wind and beginning to test your controls. You mean simply to learn what you can do. Here, in fact, is where you really begin to sail.

Slacken the sheet now. Let it slide very slowly through your hand; let the tension ease. And watch what happens. The sail swings by degrees out over the water. The wind begins to spill out. The curve softens; imperceptibly at first. It seems to sag just a little, though you can't be sure. Then you see it quivering at one point near the mast, and as you watch it here, it begins to collapse. You keep playing out the sheet, an inch at a time, and you see the entire curve gradually deflating like a balloon. For just one moment, when half-deflated, it becomes a feeble sort of S-curve; but it keeps sinking until eventually it is gone altogether, the last of it sliding off the sail's trailing edge. Then the sheet lies limp in your hand. The sail hangs empty, flapping like a rag in the wind—"luffing" in nautical language. The boat falters and stops and lies adrift, rocking loosely, not sailing any more.

Float here for a minute. The boat drifts, relatively secure with the wind gone from the sail, and you are not even surprised at the way this has happened. It all felt so logical. You just let go and everything stopped.

Now pull the sheet back in: slowly, like you let it

out. (You pull with both hands, as one of them simultaneously holds the tiller, which isn't as difficult as it sounds.) The sail comes back gathering wind once again, catching the first elements in its trailing edge. It stops flapping, begins to stiffen, then to fill. The boat heels a little and seems to nudge forward. You feel lines going taut. You keep pulling, and you see the curve forming; it is just a vestige at first, then the feeble S-curve, and then the whole curve, sliding across the sail, filling it out. You pull in the sheet until the curve fills everywhere except at a single point still quivering near the mast. You pull in another inch, and the quivering stops. And then you pull in just a little more—a quantity you don't measure yet—applying tension down to the critical ounce that turns the curve hard and rigid again. Now hold the sheet right here. The sail is trim; it is set exactly right. The boat sails without effort, just riding with the waves. It is light and free. It feels good.

But you want to pull still harder, and so you do, just to test the power in the sail. You feel the first surge with one slight tug; the boat leans and strains and pushes harder through the water and leaves a wide wake behind. Pull more strongly, and the boat heels up on its side and pounds mightily against the waves and sets the spray flying; and you ride out on the high edge, exulting in the force and spectacle of this. Then you have to pull still more, just because the urge is irresistible. You never want to let go again. For a while you can't help but sail this way: simply powering the boat, pulling compulsively on the sheet—until finally you are just clinging there, clutching raw power, stretching every line to the limit in a crashing crescendo of power. And then you realize with sudden insight that the boat is scarcely moving forward.

This is very odd. The boat indeed is seized with near-paralysis. You can feel the great forces it has gathered, but somehow those same forces also have gathered against it. And now it is bound up in forces. It is cramped with power, laboring prodigiously but moving only painfully, or sometimes not moving at all. And you made it do this. You pulled the sheet in too tightly. You overtrimmed, and you didn't see what was happening, and now you must let go. Let the sheet run out. Let the power slide away. You still don't want to do it, even now. You have to force yourself, and it almost hurts.

But you do the right thing. The sheet plays out slowly. The boat eases and settles and then goes forward again, rather tenuously at first but then more certainly. You need to watch closely to see just how

With the sail pulled in too tight, the boat heels up on its side—and scarcely moves. It is cramped with power: bound up in the forces that are supposed to drive it. ***Drawing by Don Raden***

it moves because you don't have the feeling for this yet—the feeling being complicated for you because until now the boat went better only when forces gathered, but now it goes better as forces slacken. It sails now with diminishing effort, which you do feel, and with increasing speed, which you try to see and learn later to feel. You keep letting the sheet out, however reluctantly, sailing for the moment by faith alone, holding to a conviction that the boat really is going better.

Then you finally stop the sheet when the sail is trim again—just as the curve is about to soften into the first imperceptible sag before it begins to quiver next to the mast. Except now, when you slacken a sail trimmed too tight, you can't actually know when the curve is about to soften, because it holds rigid to the last instant, never showing you a sign; so in fact you must keep slackening deliberately, until the curve really does soften and sag and perhaps even quiver slightly; then you pull back just enough so it hardens again. And then the sail is trimmed. The boat is light and free and moving well, not laboring any more, and you understand this without difficulty. Once again, it feels good.

From now on, you trim the sail constantly. You keep working the sheet, easing it by inches, tightening by halves, then easing still more against the urge to pull still tighter. (You retain the urge even now, when you know better: chant silently to yourself, "When in doubt, let it out.") You get so you trim the sail as a basic skill and as an exercise in subtleties and disciplines; you make the very small adjustments and very temperate judgments which are very good for the way you sail the boat. One day you might do this well enough so that you trim by feel alone, but don't expect that so soon; you do it later, when you are expert. Now you simply know about the sheet, which isn't so hard but still is satisfying. It is something most essential.

Then you begin to test the other control: the tiller. Steer the boat to windward with it. You know where the wind comes from: now turn that way, experimentally, easing the tiller the other way. Hold the sheet tightly; don't pull it in or let it out from now on; just keep it in place. And watch the sail. It softens, sags, and quivers; the curve slowly collapses. And once this begins, it doesn't surprise you. It happened before when you let the sheet run out; now it happens again. The boat turns upwind. The wind spills out. The sail flaps. You know all about this.

Now steer back to leeward; slowly, keeping your hold on the sheet. And the sail begins to fill again; the curve takes shape and of course you expected this. You keep the boat bearing steadily downwind—bearing off—until you have it on a heading where the whole curve forms except for the quivering next to the mast. Then bear down one degree more, and the quivering is gone, the curve is hard, and the sail is trim. You trim it with the tiller this time, where before you trimmed it with the sheet, but it is indeed trim, and the boat is sailing. The feeling is the same. It feels good.

Experiment further. Steer even more to leeward. Hold the sheet and turn the boat; deliberately force the boat away from the wind. It leans again; it heels up on its edge and teeters precariously and makes the wide wake astern. It still moves forward, but it is sluggish now, not driving any longer; it just wallows through the water, pushed ahead only by the weight of the wind behind. And now it is hard to steer. It fights you; it pulls the tiller against you; it keeps trying to head itself back into the wind. Make it go like this for a while, even though this is wrong. Keep holding the sheet and keep forcing the boat until you are sure of how it feels when it is wrong this way. You need to know the feel.

Then steer back to windward. The boat settles slowly; coming down from its heel, beginning to sail flat again. It balances under you, gathers forces, and starts to drive ahead. You can steer it easily now, even precisely, just nudging the tiller. Bring the boat steadily upwind until the sail quivers, then turn back one degree, and the quivering stops, and the sail is trimmed. You can feel the boat sailing very nicely. It is right again.

Now keep the sail trim just by working the tiller. Steer along a fine edge, testing constantly; push the boat tenuously upwind, then downwind, and keep bringing it back, trying to hold it always on the critical heading where the curve in the sail is about to soften. Work the tiller now like you worked the sheet before, making very small adjustments and very temperate judgments. Sail like this until you are sure you do as well with the tiller as with the sheet at keeping the sail trim—that you know both.

Then finish the experiment. Take full control and sail the boat by the sheet and tiller together. Ease the sheet once more—almost ritually now, completing the formalities—and the sail quivers once more. And where, before, you pulled in the sheet, now steer to leeward instead, and the quivering stops. Then pull in the sheet, and the boat leans and labors, but steer to windward, and the leaning and laboring stop. Then hold the sheet and force the boat still farther to leeward, and the boat heels and wallows, but then ease the sheet, and the heeling and wallowing stop. The boat settles and drives. Whenever it is wrong, however it is wrong, you make it right with the sheet and tiller.

From now on you work the sheet and tiller simultaneously, pulling in while heading upwind, easing out while heading downwind, and continually, incessantly testing and fixing and feeling for the trim of the sail.

From now on, this is how you sail the boat.

5
Unflinching Physics

You come now to the point where you take the physics lesson, as eventually you must, because sailing itself, being ultimately a resolution of forces, is in fact plain physics. Inevitably you become caught up in physics. You have a part in it; you become a part of it. And now you must face up to it forthrightly. You are going to like this kind of physics.

Begin again with the wind. It is basic, constant wind—you presume it constant—the true wind. You know where it blows, and you sail the boat, and until now you do well enough. But wind from now on will not be this easy. There is another wind which you don't feel directly: an odd, passive headwind that doesn't really blow but is generated just by the boat moving forward. Joseph Conrad called this wind a "draught of air fanned from ahead by the speed of the ship." He did feel it directly on the deck of a freighter steaming through a flat calm. Call this the false wind, or call it just air resistance; by any name it is an obstacle permanently before the boat. It comes always from ahead; you must sail always dead against it. The true wind comes from its own source across a continent, and you sail different ways along it or across it or even obliquely against it. But to make the boat move forward, you must sail in both winds regardless. You cannot have either wind without the other.

Then the true and false winds meet as they must in the curve of the sail. They converge there. Scaled down to the geometry of their two bare axes, they come from their two separate sources to the center of effort, the single point. And there, together, with forces resolved, true and false winds merge into a single composite wind coming in on a vector—bearing in on its own axis exactly balanced between the other two. The composite is the apparent wind: two winds in one, both true and false.

Apparent wind sounds at first like a hypothesis or an illusion or something intangible. But this is real wind. This is what you feel in your face; it is what fills the sail and makes the curve; it is the wind that does the actual work of sailing the boat. It is wind blowing exactly where the wind *appears* to blow. You probably could sail a long time happily innocent of apparent wind, but you would be sailing with distorted notions about wind. You want to know apparent wind. You need this.

Apparent wind is not complex, but it does have a

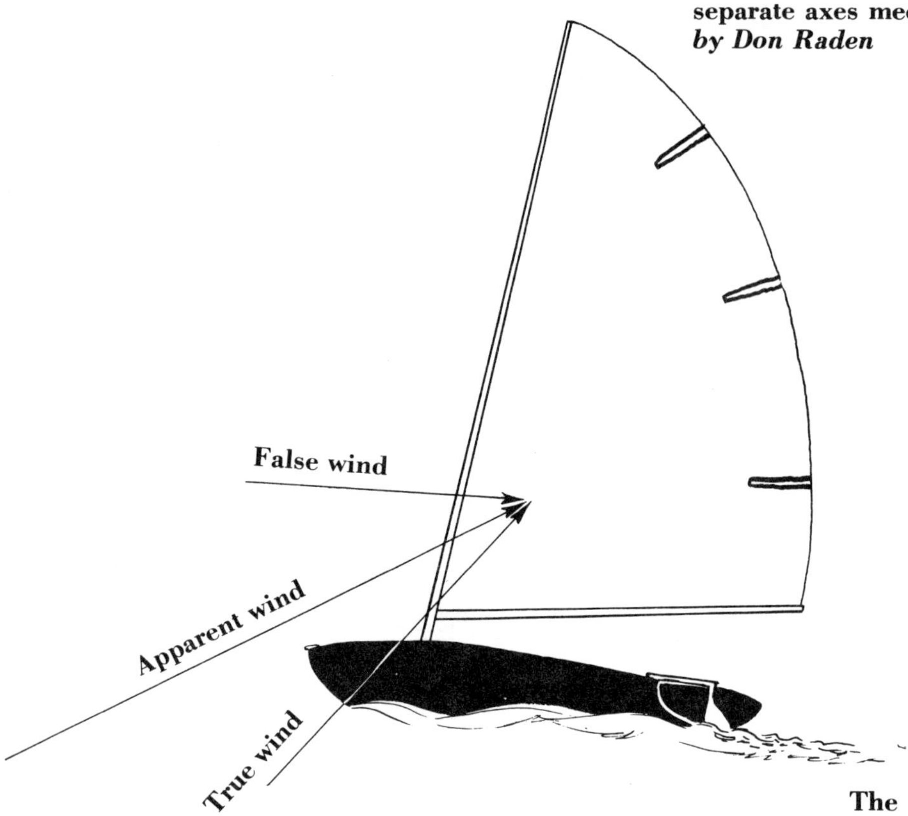

The true wind, the false wind, and the apparent wind converge in the curve of the sail. The three separate axes meet at the center of effort. *Drawing by Don Raden*

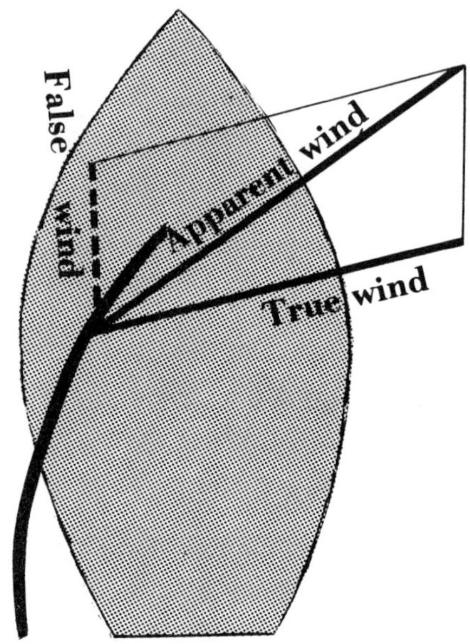

The apparent wind becomes resolved in the merger of true and false winds. Its axis is charted as the diagonal of a parallelogram made of true and false winds. *Drawing by Lana Cory Hall*

certain unique mobility, being partly self-determined and subject to a quick and busy logic. As a physicist (for a moment) you chart its axis as the diagonal of a parallelogram made of true and false winds, and you see the parallelogram changing configurations—slanting over, stretching out, shrinking in, squaring up—as the boat turns upwind and down, sailing faster and slower. The diagonal lengthens in some configurations, shortens in others; it makes wider and narrower angles with the axis of true wind. The overall pattern emerges in a progression of parallelograms. The true wind holds constant—presumed constant—and the apparent wind shifts and changes incessantly, often radically; it does this just by the rules governing forces moving and merging. The apparent wind blows variously weaker and stronger than the true wind, shifting nearer to the true wind and veering farther from it. Sometimes it is a better wind; other times it isn't. But it never is the same wind, so long as the boat keeps sailing. True and apparent winds are the same only when the boat lies at anchor.

Those bits of yarn you hang from the shrouds—the telltales—mean to show you where the apparent wind blows. They don't do that exactly, because they are deflected by extraneous currents, but they do give you a fair enough idea. The strands of yarn flutter distinctly apart from the direction the waves roll, and the waves roll with the true wind. You can see in this, imperfectly but adequately, the margin by which the apparent wind is not the true wind.

The apparent wind is to sail by. The true wind is to measure from. You trim and balance in the apparent wind. You draw perspectives from the true wind. You need both winds; each must be there for the boat to function in the other. Just remember how they are different from each other. And remember how different they are from each other.

Now put wind and sail together in the pure state of trimness. Reduce everything down to the bare, basic lines: just the curve of the sail and the axis of the wind. You may have wanted the lines to show a sail set squarely across the wind—spreading broad and full, billowing out like a parachute—but this

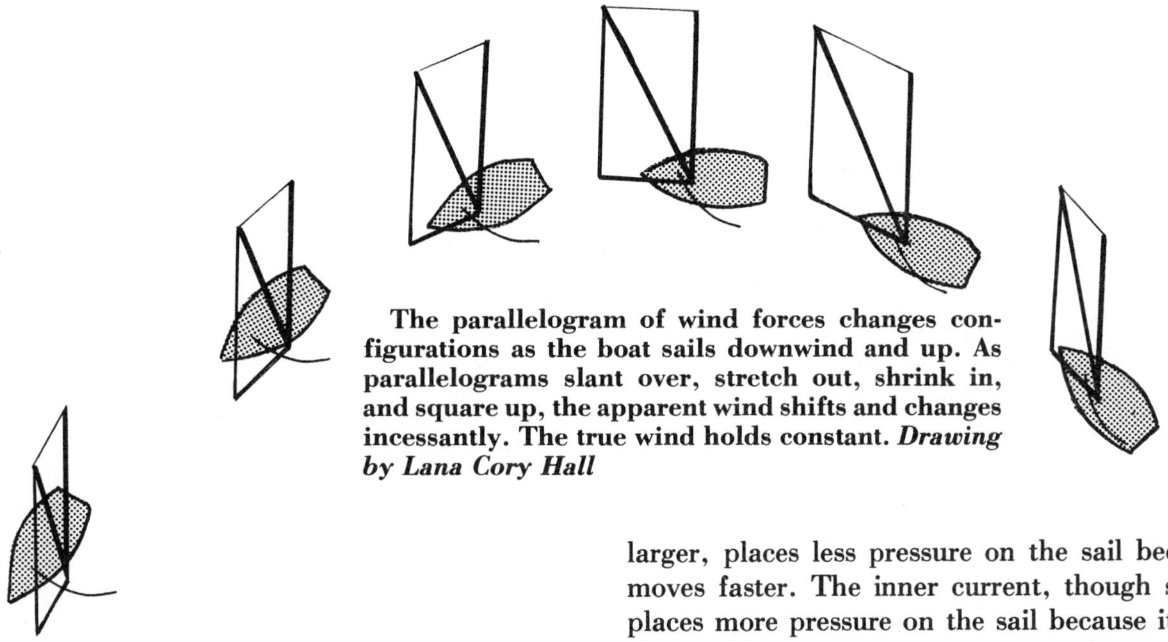

The parallelogram of wind forces changes configurations as the boat sails downwind and up. As parallelograms slant over, stretch out, shrink in, and square up, the apparent wind shifts and changes incessantly. The true wind holds constant. *Drawing by Lana Cory Hall*

sail won't be like that. This sail is sharp and slender, like a blade. It slides edgewise into the wind; it figuratively *slices* into the wind. It curves inward to stop on the point where it is exactly tangent to the apparent wind. And you hold it here. This is where the last quiver stiffens and the curve hardens; you keep trimming the sail so it is constantly in this one position in the apparent wind—even as the apparent wind keeps shifting and the boat keeps turning. Now you can feel forces building in the sail; they are more than just the wind blowing. The sail is under power. It takes flight.

The sail is a foil. The curve is a catalyst. It is the curve of a bird's wing and a farmer's plow; and the boat sails like the bird flies, because the sail divides and turns the wind like the plow divides and turns the earth. It is all incredibly smooth and neat. The sail is held trim, and the curve adds no energy; the curve isn't even in the wind's way, not really. It is simply there and is the right shape—the catalyst—and the wind slides onto it and separates into two currents; the two currents of wind come out of the free air stream and slide around the two sides of the sail. Both currents turn on the curve, bending aerodynamically on the curve. One current turns outside the curve and grows larger but moves faster and stretches thinner. The other current turns inside the curve and grows smaller but swells wider and moves slower. The outer current, though larger, places less pressure on the sail because it moves faster. The inner current, though smaller, places more pressure on the sail because it moves slower. The two pressures press together on the sail and against each other, and the greater pressure pushes harder, and the margin by which it pushes harder is the power of the sail. This will drive the boat.

And this is the catalytic effect: the difference between the two pressures generates a greater force than that of the wind blowing past.

The aerodynamics in this are both marvelous and complex. The outer current is actually siphoned around the sail's convex surface; it is a stream of air going through a powerful nozzle effect outside the curve—air driving into narrowing straits, rapidly accelerating, stretching thin, then scudding away through widening straits—and while it is the larger current, it still represents more velocity over the sail than weight upon it. The inner current, by contrast, seems neither drawn nor driven; it is a remnant of wind gravitating into the sail's concave surface—slowing, spreading, accumulating mass and volume—and while it is the smaller current, it still is more weight on the sail than velocity over it.

The whole phenomenon in fact is a pure application of Bernoulli's law, which was defined in 1738 and which says irrefutably that air moving faster does indeed exert less pressure on the surface it moves over, and air moving slower does indeed exert more pressure. And this all has to work, so long as birds fly.

Sailors have a separate understanding: their own kind of physics, less accurate but more practical. Sailors know two forces that power the boat. They

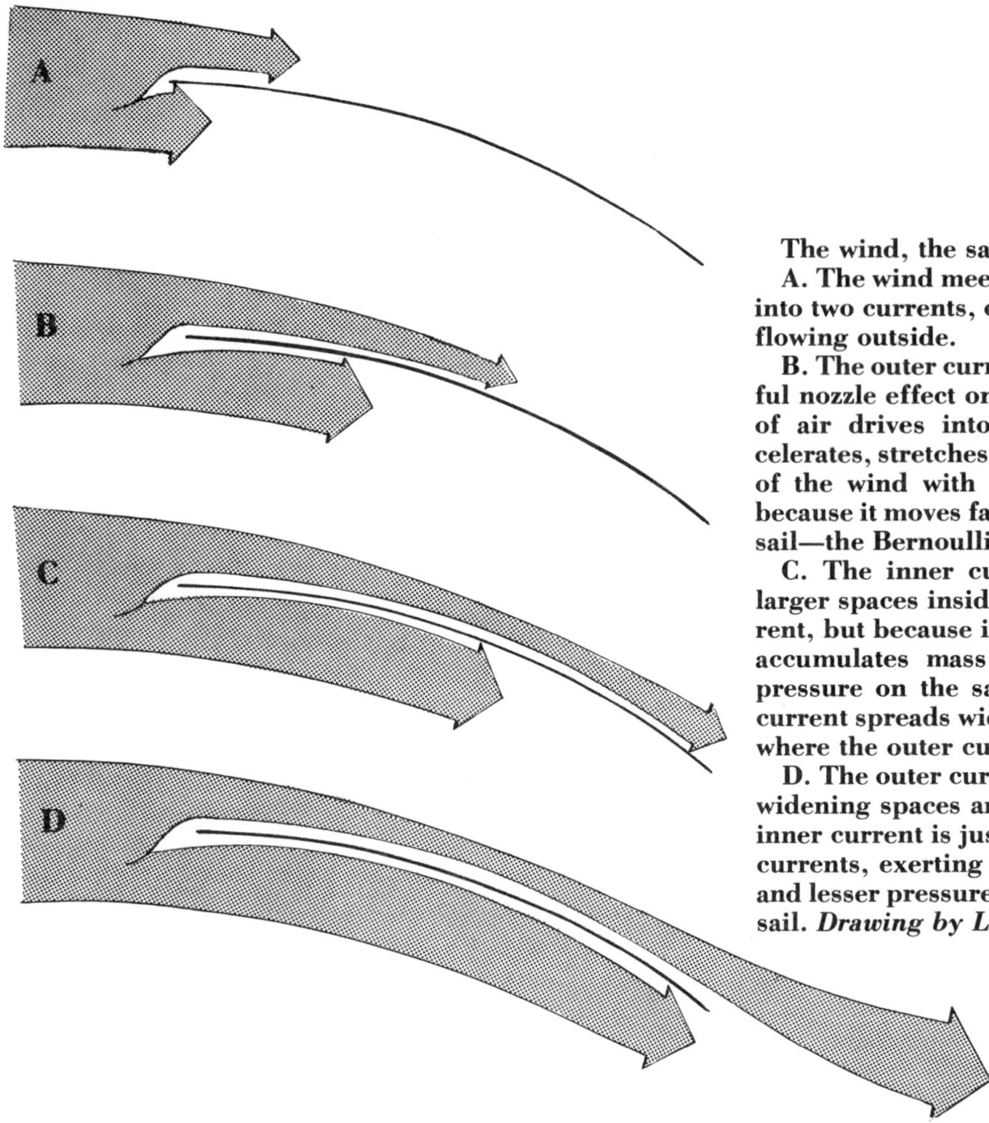

The wind, the sail, and the Bernoulli effect—

A. The wind meets the edge of the sail and divides into two currents, one flowing inside the curve, one flowing outside.

B. The outer current is siphoned through a powerful nozzle effect on the convex surface. The stream of air drives into narrowing straits, rapidly accelerates, stretches thinner, and pulls the larger part of the wind with it. It is the larger current, but because it moves faster, it exerts less pressure on the sail—the Bernoulli effect.

C. The inner current slows and gravitates into larger spaces inside the curve. It is the smaller current, but because it moves slower, it spreads wider, accumulates mass and volume, and exerts more pressure on the sail's concave surface. The inner current spreads widest at the deep part of the curve, where the outer current stretches thinnest.

D. The outer current goes scudding away through widening spaces and is off the sail and gone as the inner current is just reaching the trailing edge. The currents, exerting greater pressure outside the sail and lesser pressure inside, generate the power of the sail. *Drawing by Lana Cory Hall*

know the greater, inner pressure as a force that pushes the sail. And they know the lesser, outer pressure as a force that pulls the sail—or sucks it, or draws it, or lifts it; they tend to grope after verbs, never finding quite the right one. They know this even realizing they are technically wrong: the lesser pressure does not really pull and is not really a force; it is a relative void that the greater pressure pushes into, a non-force. But sailors do not reckon with non-forces; they believe only in forces, and they feel this force pulling, even if it is a non-force. They sail much better just knowing it as a force. Its effect is the same. Its value is the same. For all functional purposes, the force pulls the sail.

Sailors (and physicists) also know that the pulling force (or non-force) is twice as strong: it pulls twice as hard on the sail's outer surface as the pushing force pushes on the sail's inner surface, (because the outer wind current gains twice as much velocity outside as the inner wind current loses inside, and the outer pressure drops by twice as much as the inner pressure rises). But the pulling force also is most precarious; it is quickly disrupted and drastically weakened just by small misalignments and imperfections, (because the outer wind current is impelled to such high speeds that it can hold only tenuously intact around the outer surface; the current breaks and deflects against minor obstacles; if a sail is set too tight, the outer current actually peels off like the skin coming off a banana). Sailors know that the pulling force, by its own dynamic instability, is the critical element in sail power. When the pulling force is right, the boat is driven at high power. When the pulling force is wrong, the boat is pushed at low power. There will be more on this.

Here is where the boat itself becomes a factor.

The boat is reality. The boat is machinery. It is less than a perfect state; it is more than bare lines. It must complicate simple function; it must corrupt pure theory. The boat is a structural presence in the wind; it must manifest a certain bulk before the wind. Every structural member, every deck cleat and guy wire, must become a foreign object in the aerodynamics of the wind and the curve. In real life you have to reckon with this: when the boat sails, the presence must compromise the phenomenon.

The mast is the real spoiler. It is in the worst possible place before the curve of the sail, like a slug of pig iron before the blade of a plow. The mast blunts the sail's sharp edge—the very crucial forward cutting edge that should slice into the wind like the plow would slice into the earth. The edge is swallowed in the mast's monolithic structural machinery, and that mass of machinery must bull and muddle as it can into the wind, trying very crudely to push the wind into the two currents that are supposed to make the critical turn upon the curve—like plowing with pig iron.

The currents get messy now. The mast, however streamlined, still is a mass in the wind: structurally necessary, even as it causes things to verge toward aerodynamic catastrophe. (There have been some interesting experiments at rigging boats without masts and at building masts without mass, and some occasionally brilliant contrivances have evolved; but so far the ones that have worked haven't been practical enough, and the ones that have been practical haven't worked well enough.) The mast must remain always a serious obstacle that the wind encounters on the way to the sail. And the encounter is traumatic. The wind figuratively shatters on the mast. It veers into awful contortions which you do better not to brood over. Those currents—which in theory would have been charted in flowing, rythmic lines—now scramble like eggs. They are diverted into sudden frenzies; they become warped and cramped and terribly misdirected. You would need to study them in wind tunnels, and even there you would find them only dimly rational. The shock on them has been this severe.

Still, these currents do get past the mast, even if they are not the currents that might have been. Something in them retains an innate momentum of sorts—an obscure but somehow consistent element that does keep moving, however damaged and fragmented and hampered by complexities. A

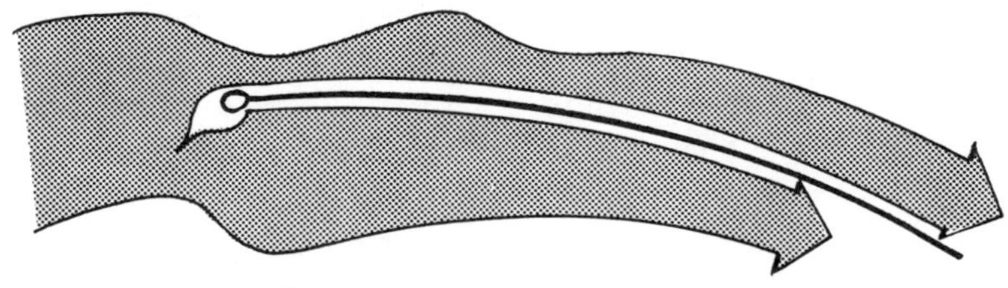

On an actual sail, the wind figuratively shatters in getting past the mast. The wind currents veer into awful contortions (here greatly simplified) and generate only a distorted fragment of sail power. ***Drawing by Lana Cory Hall***

larger, faster current, though broken and tangled, does continue outside the curve, moving uncertainly and indirectly but still gaining a haphazard kind of velocity. A slower, smaller current, less affected—somewhat misshapen but still largely intact—goes more surely inside the curve, still gravitating doggedly across the sail. The two currents turn on the curve. The outer current, going faster, exerts less pressure outside; the inner current, going slower, exerts more pressure inside. The outer current pulls; the inner current pushes. The pull and push, the differences between greater and lesser pressures, make the power in the sail. It all still works.

But at best this is only a distorted fragment of the power that theoretically would have been. The forces of course are badly weakened. The most ponderable of them are shifted forward in the sail and crowded there, unevenly, uncomfortably, untidily. The forces aft dwindle down to mere balancing elements, having only marginal push or pull at the sail's trailing edge. Currents generate their best driving forces as they go down into the deep part of the curve; they are too diffuse and distorted to generate much significant driving force as they come out. Past the deep point, the two currents become more nearly the same current: flowing more passively across the sail, having little difference in weight or pressure; and finally they slide off the edge. The overall patterns of currents and forces are complicated, often unsure and quite hypothetical—but never mind. That would be more than you need.

Just understand, of the forces—however they still pull and push—the heavy parts are forward; the remnants are aft. The state of trimness is not pure; it is hereafter an imperfect state. You settle for this distorted fragment of sail power to drive the boat.

Except you wrest one extra element of force from

the sail; though it is an ill-favored element, contrived out of the overall damage itself. Pull the sail out of the state of trimness: pull it 5 degrees tighter than trim. You cramp the curve just this much across the wind. You bring the inner surface this far into the smaller, slower current; you bring the outer surface this far out of the larger, faster current. And you feel a very palpable surge of new power in the sail.

This is something that happens between the fitfulness of the outer current and the doggedness of the inner. The outer current can't hold to the curve of the sail pulled tighter than trim; the bend is too cramped, the contortion too severe. The current begins to veer off, as if by centrifugal force, first at the trailing edge, then forward—like the skin peeling off the banana. When the sail is 5 degrees tighter than trim, the current veers off the aft two thirds of the convex surface; it holds only to the forward third. This is separation. More scientifically, it is the loss of laminar flow.

Where the current separates it leaves a bad thing called the stall zone: a cavity of wind eddies churning next to the lee side of the sail. Think of the stall zone as a large flaw in the wind and expect no good of it. The eddies are insidious. They disrupt currents and pressures; they manifest uncertain forces; they effectively sap power wherever they touch. But now the eddies touch only the aft two thirds of the sail, where most of the power that would have mattered is already lost. The eddies can churn here as they will; very little of any significance is left for them to sap away.

But the outer current does hold to the forward third of the sail. It still turns, but now on a shorter arc; it does the same contortion around a third of the sail that it did before around the full sail. It flows faster around the shorter arc; it pulls harder on the lesser sector; it concentrates forward forces

With the sail pulled 5 degrees tighter than trim, the outer wind current peels off two-thirds of the convex surface—like the skin off a banana—and leaves a bad thing called the stall zone: a cavity of eddies churning next to the sail. ***Drawing by Lana Cory Hall***

that would have been dissipated aft. All this is somewhat hypothetical, but you feel these concentrated forces—abruptly heaving forward, exerting this last extra lurch, graceless but significantly potent. The lurch is genuine power, however bent and misbegotten, the final element of sail power. Feel it just once, and you settle for it without a qualm.

(Inside the curve, the slower, smaller current still moves resolutely, the more certain, more contained current. It turns harder on the curve cramped 5 degrees tighter, but it masses against the concave surface and keeps its weight on the sail. Whatever its damage, it never stops pushing.)

Then at this setting, 5 degrees tighter than trim, the forces strengthen with the lurch outside; they don't weaken inside. And all the forces together become the total force, which finally measures out at about half the theoretical force of the perfect sail in the pure state of trimness—which of course could never be. The state of trimness now becomes only an aesthetic condition, quickly sacrificed for extra power.

But the total sail force, though damaged and corrupted and restricted to narrower confines, still is a force surviving impressively: still the manifestaton of Bernoulli's law. It still pulls twice as hard outside as it pushes inside. It retains its catalytic effect; as raw sail power, it is altogether a greater force than the wind that gets past the mast. And though it evolves out of elements of aerodynamic chaos, it still proves to be a singularly stable, straightforward, persevering force: the strongest possible force that actually can drive the boat. A very good force, regardless.

As you come to know the total force, you begin to resolve it, like the wind. You know it first as all forces in the sail, the greater ones forward, the lesser ones aft. Then you see it as greater and lesser-forces balancing and counterbalancing in the sail—patterns of forces being sized and scaled, defined, aligned, combined: pulling and pushing forces finally, effectively becoming resolved down tothe single line of force, the bare axis of total force. The force axis is one line going out from the sail just as the wind axis is one line coming into the sail. Two straight lines: this is how sailors come to know the forces that drive the boat.

Chart the geometry of this. There is the curve of the sail, the axis of apparent wind coming in, and the axis of total force going out. The curve is contrived. The apparent wind axis is determined. And

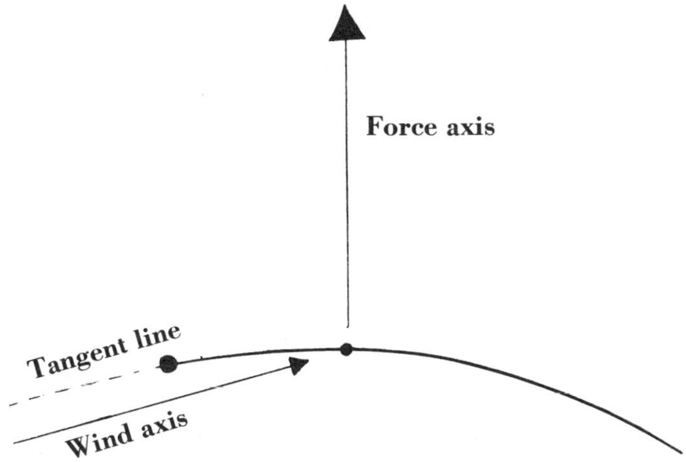

In the bare geometry, there is the curve of the sail set 5 degrees tighter than trim in the apparent wind. The wind axis comes in parallel to the tangent line. The force axis goes out on a radius line. The two axes meet at the center of effort. *Drawing by Lana Cory Hall*

now the total force axis is derived: the final factor. The wind axis comes in beside the tangent line—once removed from it but parallel to it—and the force axis goes out on the radius line, or canted slightly ahead. The two axes meet at the sail's center of effort, that aerodynamic focal point. It is one third of the way aft on the curve. Chart it there.

(The actual center of effort is not a fixed point. It hovers fitfully, fidgeting about because of forces and pressures. It fidgets mostly within an area about the size of a tea saucer; though it does shift farther aft in heavy wind with the boat heeling, which is a special condition. For your purposes the point needs to be fixed hypothetically in its one place, one third of the way aft on the curve: there to be the definitive center of effort. You establish it—definitively—in this one place, as if you would stop the point in mid-hover and hold it—hypothetically—upon the very center of the tea saucer. From now on you presume it fixed here. You are allowed this; you must have this: the one place where wind axis and force axis meet.)

Then so long as the sail stays 5 degrees tighter than trim, the axis lines hold as if welded. The wind axis comes in to the center of effort, the force axis goes out from it; and with all forces resolved, the two axes meet at a very specific angle of 105 degrees—the dogleg angle hereafter because it is rather like the anatomical bend of a dog's hind leg. The angle is the very geometric principle by which the boat sails. It is the critical change of direction in the fundamental lines of force; it is the manifestation of the total sail force materializing out of the apparent wind and bearing 75 degrees back against it—these 75 degrees actually being the other perspective on the same 105 degrees—and this is the whole difference between the boat sailing and flotsam drifting. Flotsam goes where the wind blows: the boat is pulled 75 degrees away from where the wind blows. Everything works from now on just because of this. Because the wind comes in one way and the force goes out another.

But this whole state, 5 degrees tighter than trim, still is as fragile as it is functional. The sail and the wind must stay together in this single, most critical setting; in the delicate art of trimming you work fix-

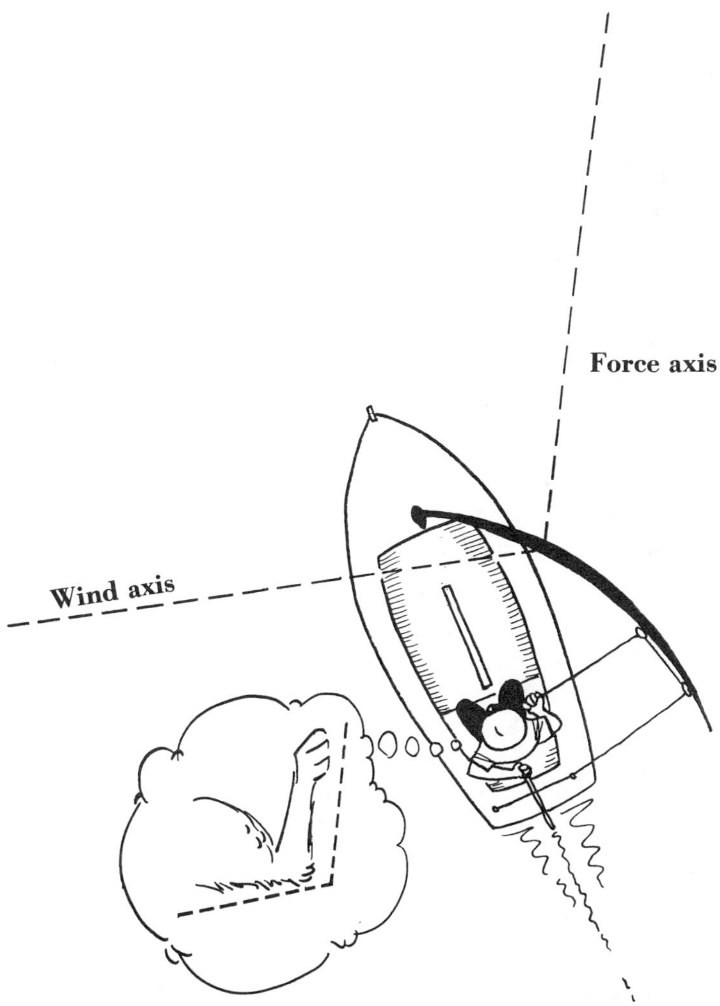

Wind axis and force axis meet at a very specific angle of 105 degrees—the dogleg angle, because it is rather like the anatomical bend of a dog's hind leg. *Drawing by Don Raden*

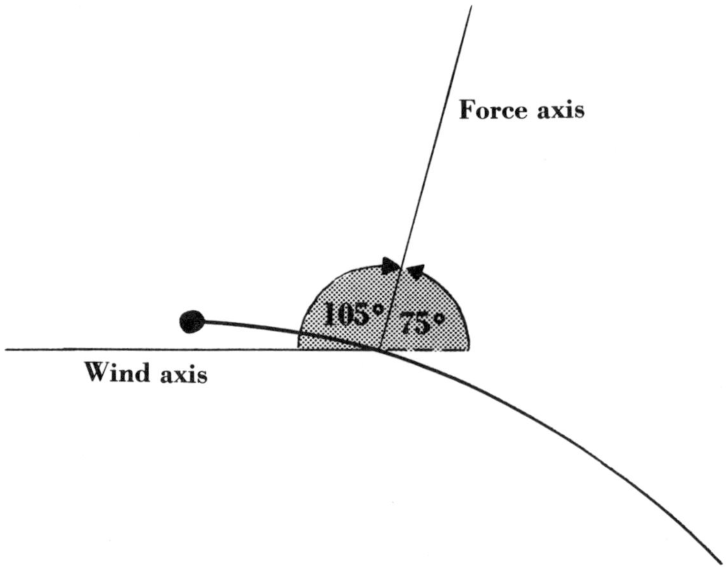

The dogleg angle from the other side: total force pulls 75 degrees back against apparent wind—these 75 degrees being the other perspective on the same 105 degrees. ***Drawing by Lana Cory Hall***

edly at keeping them precisely so, even as the wind blows and the waves roll. You pull in the sheet, let it out, keep the balance, mind the telltales; you constantly test and feel and make fine adjustments. You mean most expressly to keep all lines of force exactly in place, however the boat turns and the wind shifts and changes. Then the curve is right, the currents turn, the pressures press, and the forces pull and push their hardest. It all works, but the tolerances are stringent. If the sail is 3 or 7 degrees tighter than trim—not 5—it already begins to lose power. The curve is wrong, the currents veer out or bend in, the pressures diffuse, the forces dissipate. If the sail is mis-set just 5 degrees—either way, too loose or too tight—it must sacrifice as much as a quarter of its total force. You will learn more on this.

The finest skill in sailing is to maintain the adjustment of the sail. Concentrate always on the ideal state—to keep the adjustment always constant within one degree of 5 degrees tighter than trim—and presume this now, for the physics. Though figure in real life that you will do quite well just to keep the adjustment within less than 5 degrees, plus or minus; nobody actually does better than to hold within 3 degrees anyway. In real life the conditions are so imponderable.

The boat is reaching when it sails 5 degrees tigher than trim. Reaching is the best kind of sailing and the largest part of sailing. Beyond reaching, the boat must sail other ways, that aren't as good; you will learn about this. In reaching now you measure the best of the sail power. The sail is small, perhaps 70 square feet, and most of the power is in the forward third: a sector smaller than a shower curtain. In 10 knots of apparent wind the sail generates about 400 pounds of total force. (The force is always somehow proportional to the square of the apparent wind speed: here, so things are simple, the force in pounds is four times the square of the apparent wind speed in knots—which actually is about right.) The 400-pound total force very nearly equals the combined weight of a small boat and a medium-sized crew; it pulls both together briskly enough, giving the boat a speed of about 5 knots, 75 degrees toward the 10-knot wind. If the wind speed would double, from 10 knots to 20, then on this same sail, the total force would redouble by the square, from 400 pounds to 1600—four times the weight of boat and crew. This is the kind of power you have in the sail. You acquire a deep respect for it.

This same 400-pound total force, spread across the sail's 70 square feet, averages out to just 5/8ths of an ounce pulling and pushing on each square inch—establishing in a simple though fussy calculation that the difference between inner and outer pressures is now only 1/370th of the standard atmospheric pressure of 14.7 pounds per square inch. That minute fraction is the measure of sail power.

What remains is to sail all the courses other than 75 degrees toward the wind—to turn upwind of this one heading where the force pulls straight ahead, and to sail the other ways, where it doesn't. The other ways are where boat and force go awry to each other: The boat still must sail forward while the force now pulls at an angle, still forward but now also sideways; both at once, both obliquely. The boat will, and it does.

The boat has its capacity for this. It is a machine functioning selectively on elements of forces—on component forces; it moves most fundamentally by component forces. It goes forward on the cumulative impetus of all forward components: the driving force, all the elements of the total force exerted forward, however obliquely. But the boat braces rigidly against the collective weight of all sideways components: the pressing force, all the elements of the total force exerted sideways

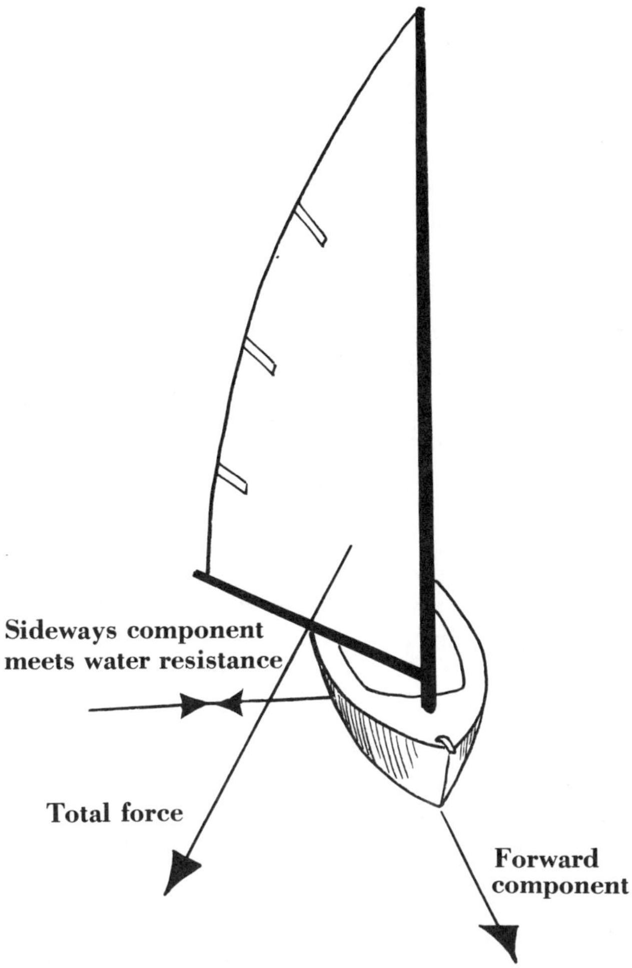

The boat is braced sideways and driven forward. The total force pulls obliquely, partly sideways, partly forward. The sideways component meets the resistance of the water. The forward component drives the boat ahead. *Drawing by Don Raden*

—however obliquely. The boat has this structural resistance to any force exerted in any direction except dead ahead. This is basic.

The resistance is integral, like the force itself. Resistance is water on the centerboard, like force is wind on the sail. The centerboard is the broad blade under the boat, like a fin on a fish. From ahead it is only a sharp edge slicing through the water, effortless in effect. But from aside it is a great, flat plank set squarely against volumes —tons—of water; and if it is pressed sideways, however obliquely, by whatever components of the total force, then the water is there in comparable weight, massing back. The water is the equal of any force pressed against it; it is as ponderous as any force is powerful. The water is the source of all resistance.

(In the physics, the components would be charted as another parallelogram—a rectangle, in fact—with the total force as the diagonal. The components keep a balance about the total force, diverging from it but always equivalent to it, exerted cumulatively as it would be exerted singly. The components are the total force resolved once more.)

The boat sails, powered by wind, braced against water, pressed and driven by components of force. In the final resolution the boat is propelled forward between force and resistance like a slippery seed you squeeze between your fingers. It comes to this.

Then:

Steer the boat upwind. It goes harder against the

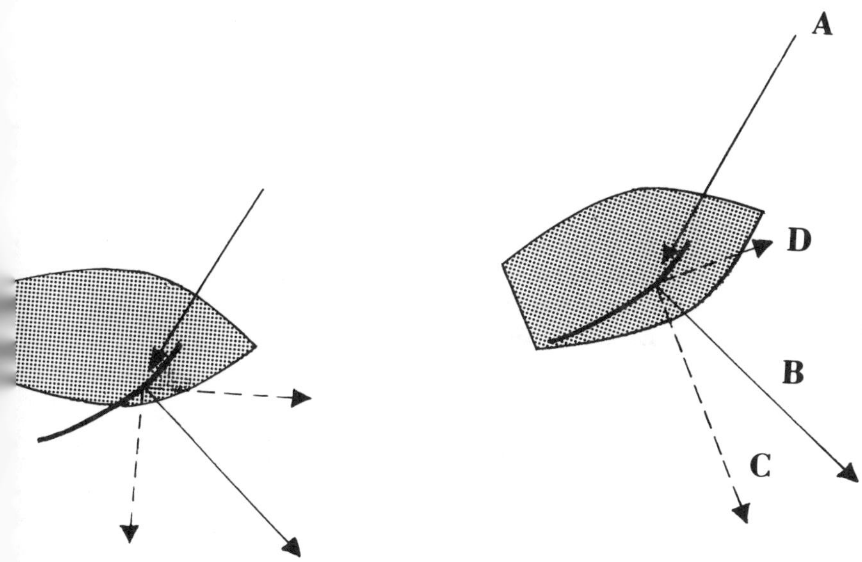

The boat turns upwind: Then:

A. Apparent wind blows harder as boat sails harder against it.

B. Total sail force pulls harder as wind blows stronger but pulls more sideways and less forward as boat and force turn more askew to each-other—and come farther out of alignment with each-other.

C. Sideways component/pressing force presses harder as total force pulls harder—and presses harder still as boat and force turn more askew to each other; total force strengthens and pulls boat more sideways, less forward.

D. Forward component/driving force drives harder as total force pulls harder—but drives less hard as boat and force come farther out of alignment with each other; total force strengthens but pulls boat less forward, more sideways. *Drawing by Lana Cory Hall*

apparent wind it sails by. It makes the apparent wind blow stronger, by the rules that govern forces moving and merging; it makes the total force pull harder because the apparent wind blows stronger. But it turns more askew to the total force pulling harder. It makes the force pull more sideways to make the boat go forward. It makes the total force a greater force worse directed.

The driving force: the component force—the elements of the total force exerted forward—strengthens as the total force pulls harder but then also weakens as the total force pulls more aside and not as much ahead. It drives the boat variously, more and also less.

The pressing force: the component force—the elements of the total force exerted sideways—strengthens as the total force pulls harder and then strengthens still more as the total force pulls more aside and not as much ahead. It presses the boat doggedly, more and still more.

Then:

Steer the boat downwind. It goes easier with the apparent wind it sails by. It causes the apparent

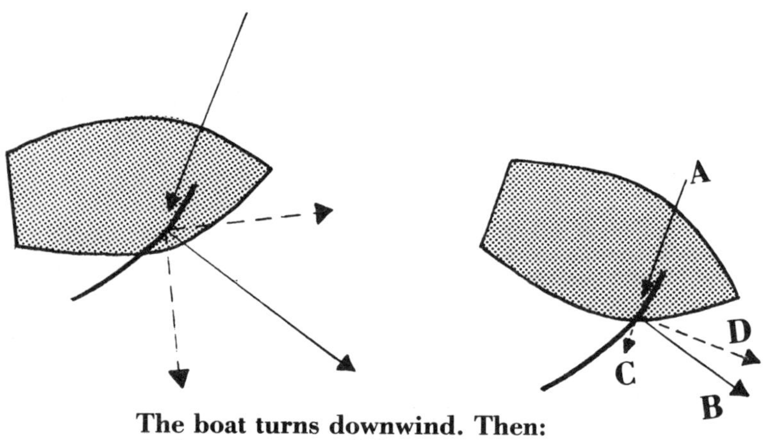

The boat turns downwind. Then:

A. Apparent wind blows lighter as boat sails easier with it.

B. Total force pulls less hard as apparent wind blows lighter but pulls more forward and less sideways as boat and force turn less askew to each-other—and come nearer to alignment with each-other.

C. Sideways component/pressing force presses less as total force pulls less—and presses still less as boat and force turn less askew to each other; total force weakens and pulls boat less sideways, more forward.

D. Forward component/driving force drives less as total force pulls less—but drives harder as boat and force come nearer to alignment with each-other; total force weakens but pulls boat more forward, less sideways. ***Drawing by Lana Cory Hall***

wind to blow weaker by the rules that govern forces moving and merging; it causes the total force to pull less hard because the apparent wind blows weaker. But it turns less askew to the total force pulling less hard. It allows the force to pull more forward to make the boat go forward. It makes the total force a lesser force better directed.

Now the driving force weakens as the total force pulls less hard, but it also strengthens as the total force pulls more ahead and not as much aside. The driving force drives the boat less, and also more.

The pressing force weakens as the total force pulls less hard, and it weakens even more as the total force pulls more ahead and not as much aside. The pressing force presses the boat less, and still less.

You come to understand this. You steer the boat among the permutations and combinations of greater and lesser forces better and worse directed. You drive it with the lesser parts of greater forces or the greater parts of lesser forces. It sails like this, even past the limits where it no longer reaches.

There is the windward limit. You steer upwind to it, trimming in the sail; you are there when the sail is all the way in. And there is the leeward limit. You steer downwind to it, trimming out the sail; you are there when the sail is all the way out. You can sail the boat past both limits, but not like you sailed it to them, not with the sail 5 degrees tighter than trim. Beyond the limits, the sailing isn't as good.

You come to the edge of the leeward limit on the heading 75 degrees toward the wind, where the total force pulls dead ahead. Steer down to here, trimming out the sail until it is nearly at right angles to the boat. You can't let it out farther than this, or you wouldn't if you could. (You learn these mechanics later.) So just steer past the limit, 5 degrees farther to leeward, 6 to be certain—just turning the boat and keeping the sail at right angles. Turn the boat this far, and you bend the sail this much across the wind. You cramp the curve 6 degrees.

Then the bend is too tight, and the larger, faster outer wind current can't hold any longer to the curve and can't make its critical turn: not even around just the forward third. The current separates, veering completely off the sail, peeling away like the banana skin, and then it isn't even the current any more. It is only the wind crashing into the mast, spilling around it, and reeling away. It leaves a vastly expanded stall zone behind the

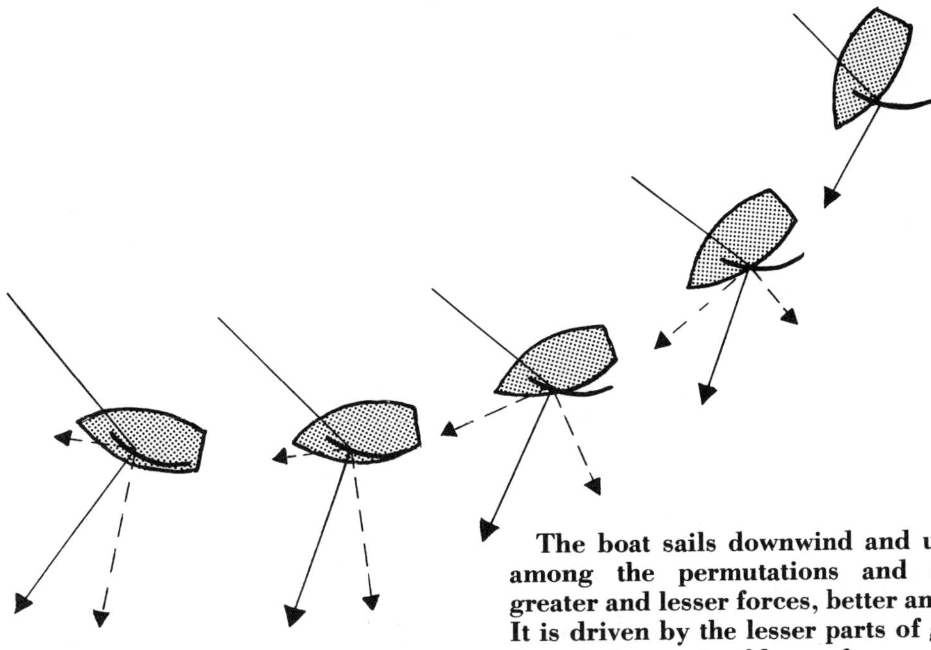

The boat sails downwind and up, being steered among the permutations and combinations of greater and lesser forces, better and worse directed. It is driven by the lesser parts of greater forces, or the greater parts of lesser forces. *Drawing by Lana Cory Hall.*

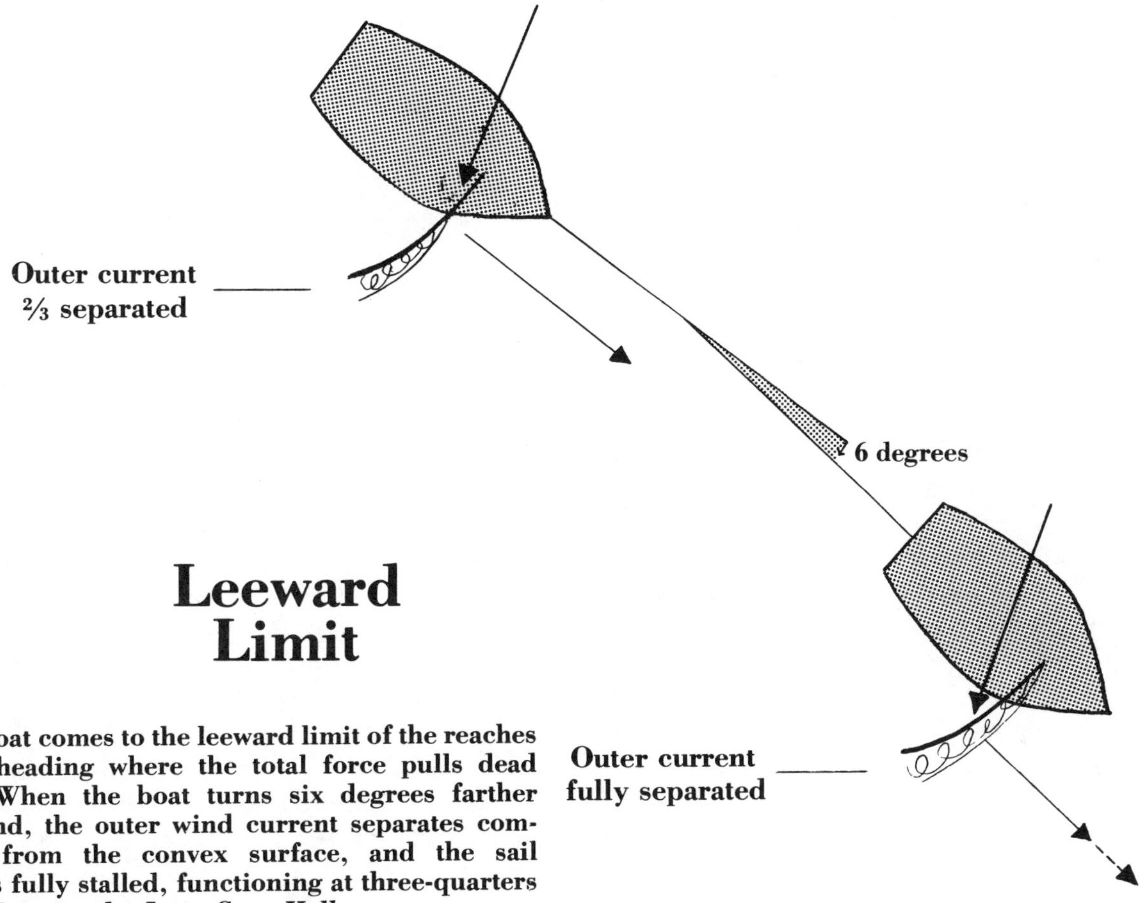

Leeward Limit

The boat comes to the leeward limit of the reaches on the heading where the total force pulls dead ahead. When the boat turns six degrees farther downwind, the outer wind current separates completely from the convex surface, and the sail becomes fully stalled, functioning at three-quarters power. *Drawing by Lana Cory Hall* sail—an appalling aerodynamic chasm of whirlwinds and turmoil and forces in foment. It summarily siphons out the best of the pulling force, the dynamic part of the total force. There is no catalytic effect in this. There is no laminar flow. Bernoulli's law no longer applies. The sail simply is left in the way of the wind.

In this state the sail is said to be fully stalled; though the term is a bad one; it sounds as if the sail doesn't work. In fact it still does work, simply because the slower, smaller inner current still pushes inside the curve. The current must bend harder in the curve; it may become jammed or blocked now, and it may begin spilling around the sail's trailing edge. But it still keeps pushing inside against the turmoil raging outside. The pushing weighs heavier by sheer perseverance than the raging weighs by happenstance, and the difference is a rudimentary sort of sail power—plain pushing force, less force than before but still very real.

Keep steering downwind after this: turning the boat and holding the sail at right angles, fully stalled. You are bending the sail still harder across the wind, cramping the curve even tighter. The wind simply pushes. It blows into the sail and spills around the edges and goes reeling off. It pushes with only about three quarters of the former total force, varying somewhat but still averaging out to this. But now the three-quarter total force is exerted always dead ahead; the force becomes a fixture of the boat—resolved upon a new axis that is aligned with the boat and set upon a new center of effort, this time at the geometric center of the sail. The force is all driving force; it becomes its own forward component. There is no more pressing force; there is no sideways component.

The force axis and the wind axis now verge slowly together as the boat turns downwind. The axes are no longer at the dogleg angle. There is no more dogleg angle.

You become circumspect about the three-quarter total force of a stalled sail. It is crude, not a good force; you generally abhor it, except you need it just to drive the boat downwind past the reaching limits, where there are no good forces. You do abhor it, most specificially, when you don't need it—when reaching across the wind, within the limits, and there *are* good forces. Then if you pulled the sail too tight (as you once did, experimentally) you would wrench it unbefittingly into the full stall and lose the good forces. The three-quarter, not-good force would push almost entirely sideways: nearly all pressing force this time, only scant driving force. And the boat would come to the state of near paralysis. It is all a horrible mistake; this is why you trim the sail so carefully.

Then go to the windward limit. Steer upwind, pulling in the sail, keeping it 5 degrees tighter than trim. Reach across the wind, then into the wind, turning toward the axis itself. When you can't pull the sail in any more, you are at the limit: the last

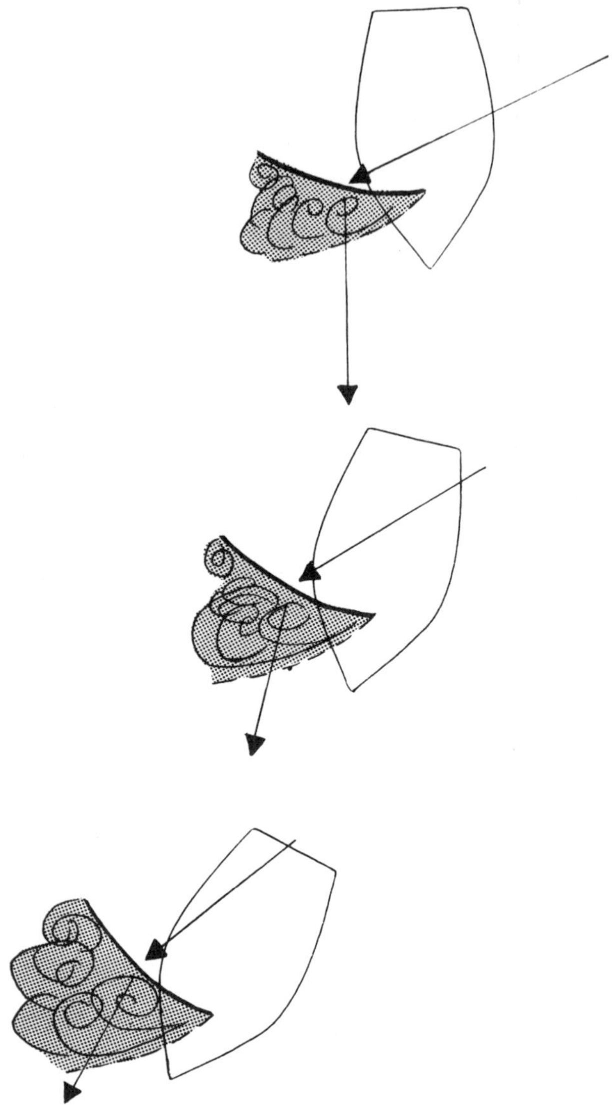

Beyond the limit, the boat keeps turning to leeward. The sail is bent harder across the wind, the curve cramped tighter. The stall zone widens behind the sail. The wind only pushes. The sail remains at three-quarters power; through the three-quarter total force continues to push dead ahead. *Drawing by Lana Cory Hall*

When the sail is pulled too tight—overtrimmed—it is wrenched unbefittingly into the full stall, and the three-quarter total force pushes almost entirely sideways. The boat hardly moves, being bound up in forces. *Drawing by Lana Cory Hall*

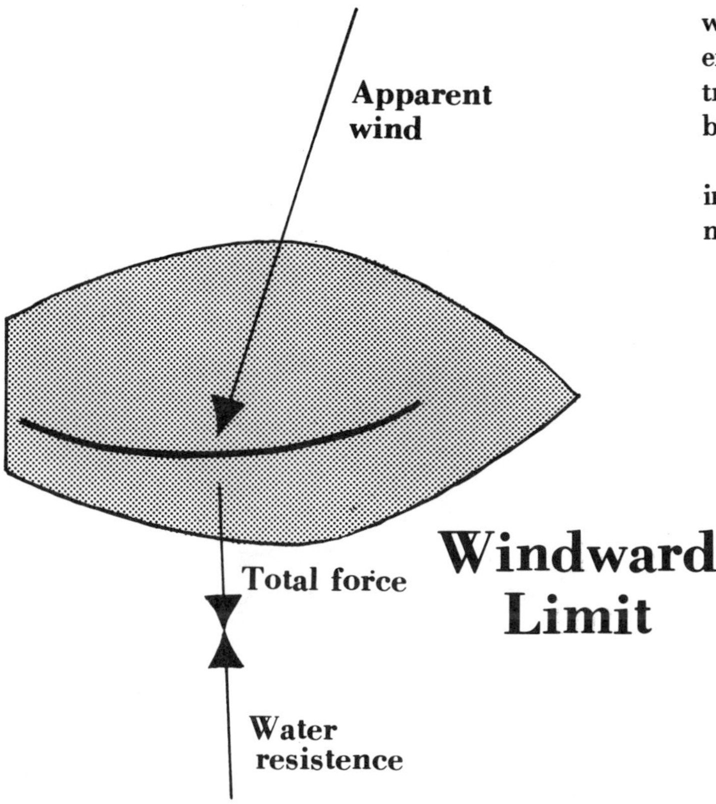

heading where the sail functions best, and the strongest total force still can pull the boat.

You don't reach the wind axis. You must come to the limit well short of it—later you will know exactly how short—because now you approach the basic reality that the boat can't actually sail against the wind it sails by. The limit would be the very end, except the sail comes here 5 degrees tighter than trim; so there still are these 5 degrees by which to go beyond.

Steer upwind, past the limit, and you keep sailing, but differently—still technically reaching but now with the sail lashed inflexibly to the boat. Boat

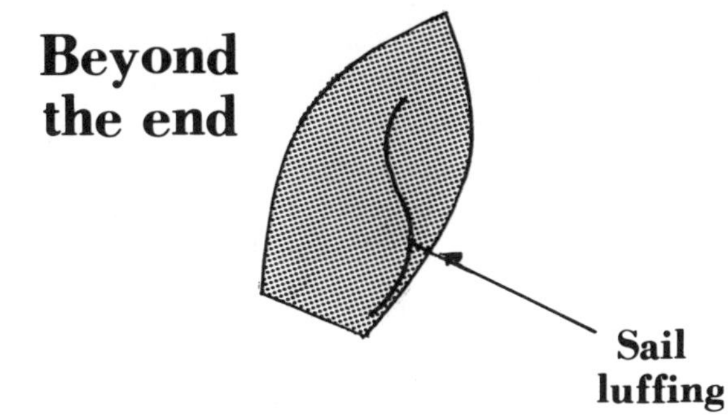

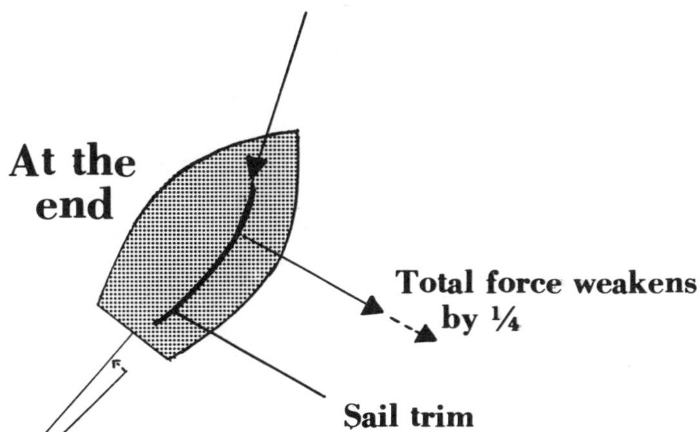

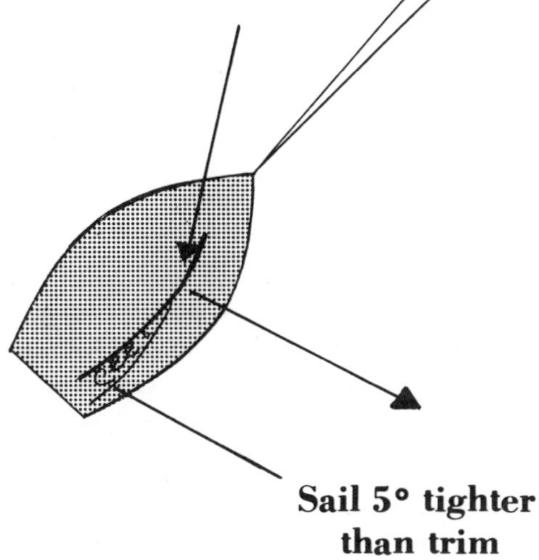

The boat comes to the windward limit of the reaches on the heading where it no longer can sail 5 degrees tighter than trim. The sail is all the way in. Boat and sail turn together upwind of here. The curve comes uncramped, and the sail loses power. Turning 5 degrees still higher, the boat comes to the end. Beyond the end, the sail no longer can hold the wind, and everything stops. *Drawing by Lana Cory Hall*

and sail turn together, as they must. They pinch into the wind. The curve of the sail turns up into the wind. Steer 5 degrees past the limit, and the curve comes uncramped in the wind. The two wind currents bend around the sail; the outer current holds to the full curve, no longer veering off. This is the state of trimness, aesthetic and imperfect.

This is just before the end. Because this is an imperfect state, the sail must lose power. Pulling forces that had been crowded forward in the cramped curve now become dissipated aft in the uncramped curve. Ungainly masses of forces are lost in the sail's after parts. That untidy lurch of extra power is lost with just this turn of 5 degrees, and the total force is weakened to about three-quarters strength. You feel this. The boat suddenly is enfeebled just when it most needs sail power to go against the wind. It labors, still moving but sailing with only marginal effect—just pinching into the wind, no more.

Then turn one more degree upwind, and the sail can't hold the wind any longer. It quivers and begins to collapse. The sail effectively is abandoned to the wind, the curve effectively blown off the sail. The collapse begins next to the mast and spreads aft, the curve sinking and rolling like a wave off the sail. For a moment a half remnant of the curve seems to hold in the sail's after parts, and some wind momentarily half turns on it, generating a fractional sort of sub-force. But then even the remnants are gone, and the sail is only flapping as the wind blows by. The currents are gone. The whole phenomenon is gone. Nothing is left to drive the boat.

This really is the end. The boat stops here, 6 degrees past the upwind limit and still far short of any alignment with the wind axis. It will begin to sail again when you steer back downwind. You know that.

There is a footnote to the physics lesson. There is the matter of weather helm and lee helm—the fore-and-aft balance of force and resistance. The total force, scaled down to its axis, becomes resolved upon its point on the sail: the center of effort. The resistance similarly becomes resolved upon a point on the centerboard: the center of resistance. If all the machinery were perfectly balanced, the total force axis could be projected over the boat to a point aligned exactly over the center of resistance; you could drop a hypothetical plumb line from the axis down to the center of resistance. Then the boat

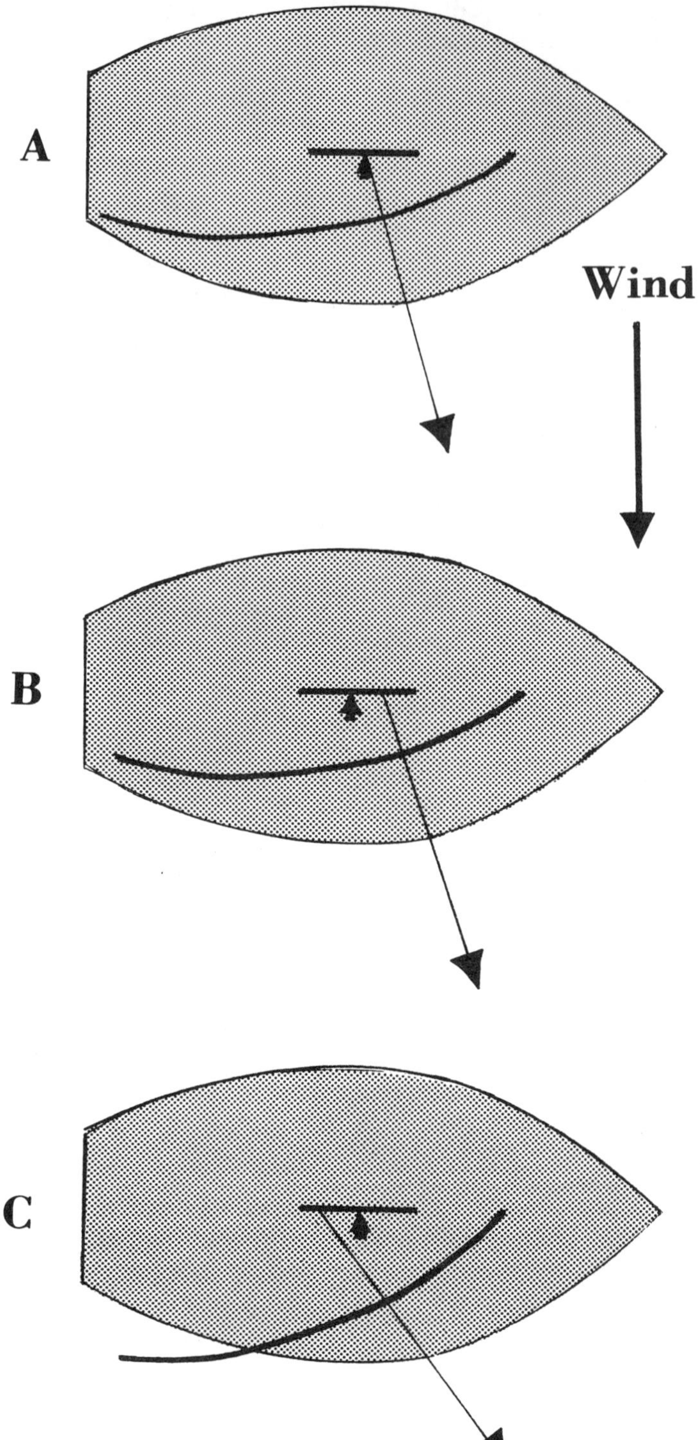

Weather helm and lee helm:
A. When all the machinery of the boat is perfectly balanced, the total force axis can be projected to a point exactly over the center of resistance.
B. The boat sails by a lee helm when the extended axis line crosses forward of the center of resistance.
C. The boat sails by a weather helm when the extended axis line crosses aft of the center of resistance. ***Drawing by Lana Cory Hall***

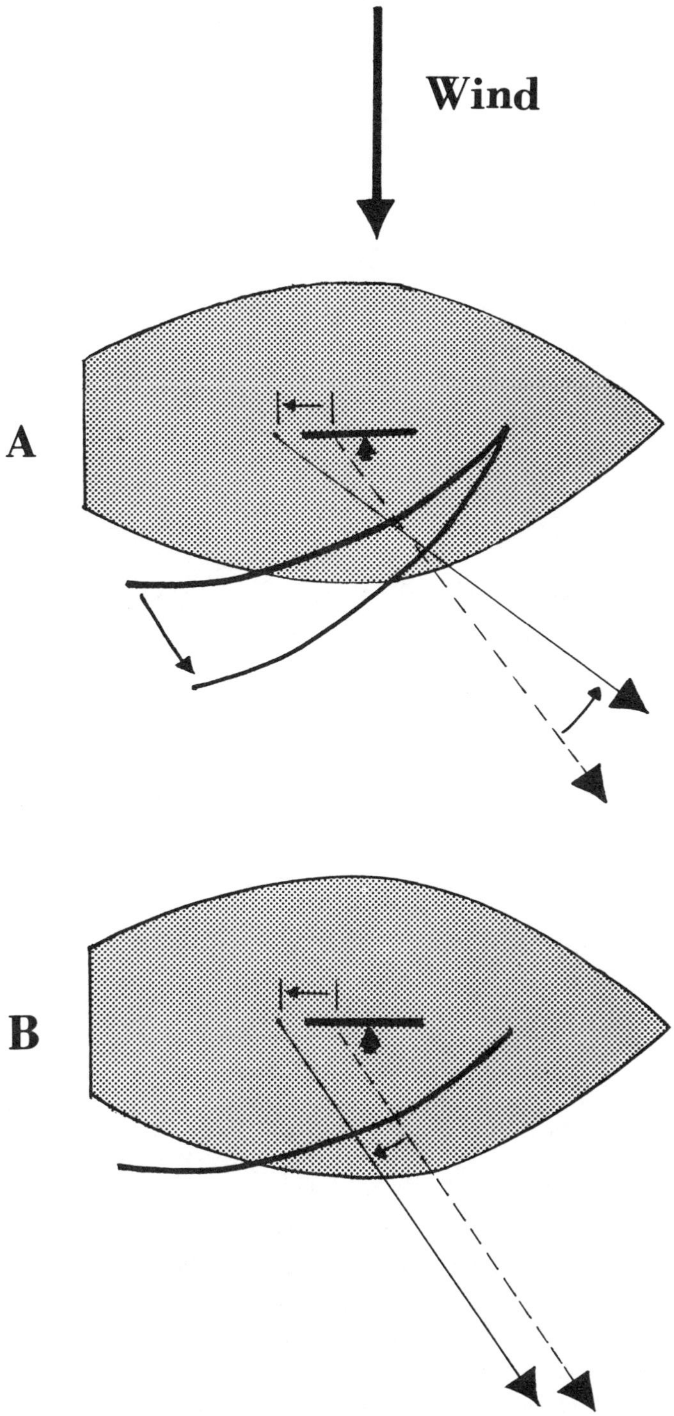

Weather helm increases:
A. The sail swings out; the projected axis line swings aft; and the forces pull with greater leverage on the boat's after parts.
B. The boat heels; the forces shift aft and again pull with greater leverage on the boat's after parts.
Drawing by Lana Cory Hall

would sail a straight line dead ahead, holding its course solely on the balance of its machinery. You never even would need to touch the tiller.

But small boats almost never can be such precision instruments, so ideally arranged and exactly aligned. The axis line may extend somewhere forward of the center of resistance. Then the forces in the sail pull harder on the boat's forward parts and pull the bow downwind; and so they turn the boat downwind, pivoting it on the center of resistance. You feel the boat bearing to leeward, and you have to keep steering it back, constantly nudging the tiller to hold the course. This is lee helm: this imbalance of machinery pulling the boat downwind.

Or more often the axis line may extend somewhere aft of the center of resistance. Then the forces pull harder on the boat's after parts and pull the stern downwind; and this time they turn the boat upwind, pivoting it on the center of resistance. This time you feel the boat bearing to windward, and you have to keep steering it back, now tugging at the tiller to hold the course. This is the weather helm: this imbalance of machinery pulling the boat upwind.

A sailboat, because of the ways it works, sails mostly with the weather helm and only rarely with the lee helm (which probably is good, because if occasionally you lose the tiller, then the boat usually is safer turning upwind than down). The boat sails, most generally, with greater and lesser weather helms pulling harder and not as hard to windward. The weather helm pulls harder when the sail is let out, because as the sail swings out, the projected axis line swings aft, and the forces pull with greater leverage on the boat's after parts. The weather helm also pulls harder when the boat heels, because heeling causes all forces to shift farther aft in the sail and so to pull farther aft on the boat. Of course the boat sails better, certainly easier, when the weather helm pulls less hard—when the machinery is more nearly balanced—though the boat still must encounter some conditions where it simply has to endure a weather helm pulling harder. (You will learn about this later.) But the weather helm, greater or lesser, must pull in any case. It is a trait of the boat, and this is what you need to know about physics.

6
The Extent Of The Phenomenon

Then this is the phenomenon. The wind and water are the elements, the boat a contrivance between them, and all the factors work because you hold the sheet and the tiller. The whole principle is there in your two hands: you can heft the weight of it; you can feel the forces in balance. This is the feel of the boat sailing.

And this is what you have. You grasp the phenomenon, and it is powerful. But now you need to be very deliberate with it because you don't know the extent of it. So here you take its measure. You set about trying its variables and finding its limits; you mean to come to a reckoning with it—to go where you can with it and know where you can't.

So now you begin to experiment once again: turning and trimming, now especially mindful of your involvements with forces moving and merging. This time you are intent on forces; you are feeling out their full range, testing them cumulatively, having considered them singly. You mean, very specifically, to reach a simultaneous and definitive understanding of all forces through all their shifts and changes: the forces that gather with you as well as the forces that gather against you. You intend to know them in all their permutations and combinations.

There is a way for you to do this. You acquire a particular set of insights into—and a particular sensitivity to—the speed of the boat. It is not the conventional sort of speed; it comes from an integral balance, not from a pressing urgency. You learn to think of it as a quality in sailing boats, not a quantity, like in motorboats. (Eventually you become vastly contemptuous of the crass velocity of motorboats.) You know speed as both cause and effect. It is a primal cause; it is the measure of that false wind which first merges with the true wind to make the apparent wind. And then it is the last effect: the

Extremes of speed under sail. ***Drawing by Don Raden***

ultimate gauge of all force and resistance brought to the final resolution and sailing the boat. The speed happens most conveniently for you as the manifestation of everything else; when you know it, you can know the rest.

You get the speed, with all other things being resolved, when the driving force, the forward component, pulls against the stable inertia of the boat. You know about the force; the inertia is more arcane. In one sense it is the basic structural character of the boat itself; in another it is a rigid discipline holding the boat to the rules by which things may move through water. It does this through complexities which you don't have to understand; you just need to know they are there—principles of flow, mass, drag, displacement, wetted surfaces, hull shape, and other things more complicated which marine architects dwell upon; you don't. The speed then emerges with forces exerted upon the boat in shifting mathematical proportions: if the driving force doubles, the speed may increase variously by a half or a quarter—or a tenth—depending on the inertia. This all works, rather imprecisely, according to asymmetrical hyperbolic curves plotted on charts. (It is essentially the same as a car burning more gasoline to accelerate from 50 to 60 miles per hour than to accelerate from 20 to 40 miles per hour.) But you don't dwell on this either. You just remember through all the intricacies that the speed of the boat depends equally on the forces shifting and changing and upon the inertia staying nearly always the same, the more constant factor. In time you come to know the inertia simply as the feel of the boat, the physical thing. Then you come to know the speed as the vital balance between force and inertia: the final manifestation.

Then you know with easy logic that each boat must have its own inertia and so its own speed. And each boat must perform in its own way, in its own apparent wind, and so must be different to a degree from all the rest; and any given boat is bound to be only slightly different from another while drastically different from yet another. This happens according to involved formulas. Big boats with long waterlines, sailing by the rules of displacement, should go faster than small boats with short waterlines. But with progressing technology comes a profusion of planing boats that can sail beyond those rules—skimming dishes built so light and slick that they actually rise out of the water they should displace, and they scud across the surface like hydroplanes, going far faster on certain courses than displacement boats ever could. Planing boats reach their radical fringe in the high-strung catamarans, which are subject only to the most uncertain disciplines: sailing on their two slender, shell-like hulls and flying without warning into great, erractic fits of speed. And then beyond the fringe, the last extremes of sailing craft are not boats but iceboats: severe, stiletto-shaped machines that stand poised over the ice on just three finely-honed hard-steel edges. The iceboats sail by the most extraordinary force patterns. They are limited only by abstruse aerodynamic extremes of airfoil drag. Virtually nothing else holds them, no inertia at all. And they go at speeds that are entirely bizzare—100 miles per hour and more, five or six times faster than the wind itself. (Iceboat speed is always miles per hour, while sailboat speed is always knots, for no reason except tradition.) Some day, if you do experiments in iceboating, you will know how very different indeed sailing can be from the experiments you do now in your little sailboat.

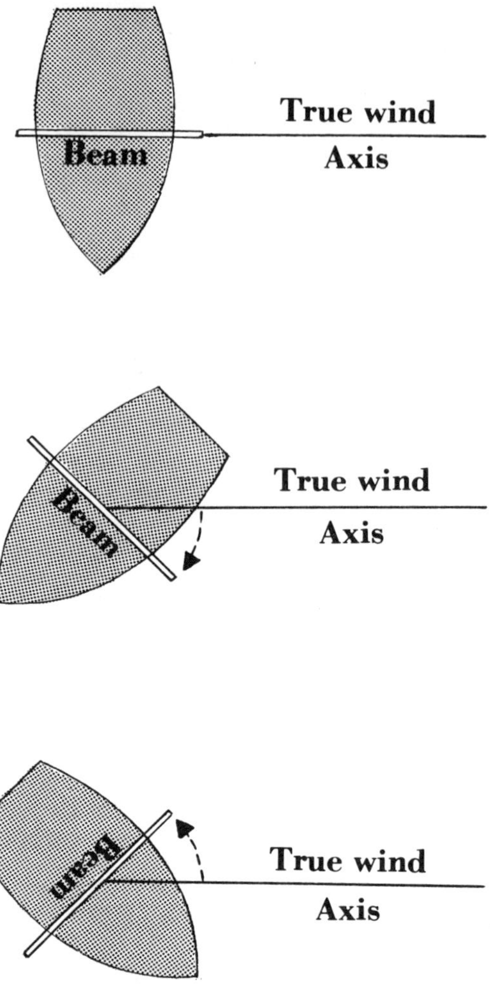

When the boat is on the beam reach (top), the beam is aligned with the true wind axis. As the boat turns downwind (center), the beam pivots forward of the axis. As the boat turns upwind (bottom), the beam pivots aft of the axis. ***Drawing by Lana Cory Hall***

So now in your boat you begin by sailing on a beam reach just because you have to begin somewhere. You go squarely across the wind: the true wind this time, the first line of reference. You sail at right angles to the true wind axis, so the true wind is aligned exactly upon the beam—the beam being for this purpose a second line of reference, a hypothetical but indispensable line set across the boat, always at right angles to the direction you are heading—and this is sailing on a beam reach. If you steered to leeward from here, however tentatively, you would sail down into the distantly indefinite sector of broad reaches. And in turning the boat you would swing the beam with it—the two pivoting together—bringing the beam forward of the wind axis, so on the broad reaches the true wind would always bear upon you from an angle measured aft of the beam. And if you steered to windward, you would sail up into the more certain sector of close reaches. Turning this way, you would bring the beam aft of the wind axis, so on the close reaches the true wind would bear upon you from an angle measured forward of the beam. But for this moment you go neither windward nor leeward. You hold strictly to the beam reach, the single, straight line of demarcation between all broad and close reaches. Just stay on the edge and keep your angles at 90 degrees. This is for reference.

Actually your boat sails at about its very best on this beam reach in a fair wind. Nearly all boats do; in light wind most boats sail best on close reaches, in heavy wind they are best on broad reaches, but those are special conditions which you learn later. Right now your boat drives powerfully across a fair wind. Its machinery is working hard though not straining. You can feel the forces: very strong now, almost palpable; you have them firmly under con-

All secure on the beam reach. The boat sails at about its very best. The forces feel strong but are firmly under control. *Drawing by Don Raden*

trol with a sure grip on the sheet and tiller. They would heel the boat, but you hike out on the edge and lean back against them, and the boat stays down, sailing flat. Then it is stable, steady; it holds its balance, riding on the waves, moving in tempo with them. It will not be shaken or slowed or dissuaded; it shoulders aside frivolous obstacles, keeping to its course. It is sailing at its best speed: maximum speed. Turn away from here—windward or leeward—and it can't do better than this; it must go slower. It is never as good heading anywhere else in fair wind.

You begin to see this when you apply hard specifics. (You have a license here: you can arbitrarily assume specifics of any size, so long as you keep them always consistent.) Assume your boat to be small and competent and quick enough to go 5 knots on a beam reach when the true wind blows 10; it is a boat of conventional inertia or less, probably more responsive than most but still a safely unremarkable boat, certainly not an uncommon boat. Its speed is entirely practical, even though it does sail by conveniently round figures. And when you see the forces becoming resolved upon it—the parallelogram forming—then you see it sailing in apparent wind blowing at 11.2 knots from an angle 27 degrees forward of both the beam and the true wind axis; the two still being aligned. You feel the apparent wind in your face; you trim for it. It is, as always, the wind you are sailing by: a distinctly oblique sort of headwind, substantially stronger than the wind you are measuring from—the true wind—and well ahead of it. Before you are done with all this, you come to know these two kinds of wind almost as if you really had measured them in degrees and knots.

This apparent wind has to be your own personal wind, unique just to your boat on this course in this

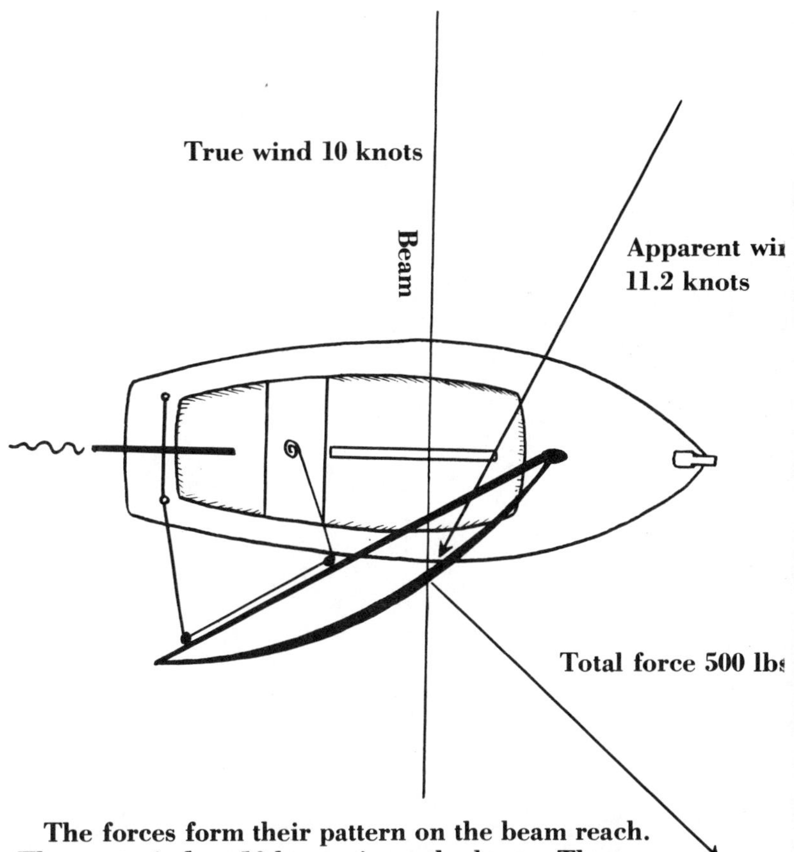

The forces form their pattern on the beam reach. The true wind, at 10 knots, is on the beam. The apparent wind, at 11.2 knots, is 27 degrees forward. The total force, at 500 pounds, pulls 48 degrees forward. *Drawing by Don Raden*

true wind. A faster boat going 6 knots here would sail in 11.7 knots of apparent wind 31 degrees forward; and a slower boat going 4 knots would sail in 10.8 knots of apparent wind 23 degrees forward. You encounter these boats and a thousand more, all sailing their different patterns in their different winds, and you have to be aware of them. They are the longer dimension of what you are doing.

But now you have just your boat on this beam reach. You sail it properly, keeping it flat and balanced, with the sail 5 degrees tighter than trim, and the apparent wind comes at its 11.2 knots and makes its turn upon the curve of the sail, and so it becomes—arbitrarily—500 pounds of total sail force. This is consistent. The rule says the total sail force must be somehow proportional to the square of the apparent wind speed, with the only variable depending on the sail area; so you assume a variable that is apt and easy. Assume for your small boat that the total force in pounds is four times the square of the apparent wind speed in knots; this is extremely apt and easy. Then you derive the 500 pounds from the 11.2 knots just for doing the arithmetic.

$$11.2^2 = 125$$

$$125 \times 4 = 500 \text{ pounds, total sail force}$$

Then you sort through the lines and angles from your place in the boat, and you see that the essential line of force comes in as the apparent wind axis—27 degrees forward on the weather side. In the curve of the sail, the apparent wind becomes the total force, resolved upon its own axis, bearing 75 degrees back against this same apparent wind. Wind axis and force axis meet at the dogleg angle at the sail's center of effort. Then the essential line of force goes out as the total force axis—the total force pulling 48 degrees forward on the lee side. With everything in place, you have 500 pounds pulling 48 degrees forward of the beam.

You need to see this in several ways. The total sail force pulling 48 degrees forward of the beam also must pull 42 degrees sideways from the bow—this being plane geometry: the same angle measured from both directions—and you have the advantage in the force pulling 6 degrees more ahead than aside: a slightly better than middling advantage. Then the whole arrangement of forces and angles is really a compromise you extract from the wind. The total force is considerable at 500 pounds, though still substantially less than others you will encounter. But such a force, directed at slightly better than middling advantage, is in fact the maximum arrangement by which the boat sails—the best of all compromises between you and a true wind of 10 knots. You would see all of the mobile logic of this if you had a perspective in higher mathematics: all the other arrangements must be less than maximum; all the greater forces must be directed at worse angles; all the better angles must direct lesser forces. This is the kind of compromise you get from the wind.

Then the total sail force is exerted at its angle upon the machinery of the boat and against the resistance of the water, and so it becomes resolved again into the two component forces that drive forward and press sideways.

The sideways component is now, in effect, 330

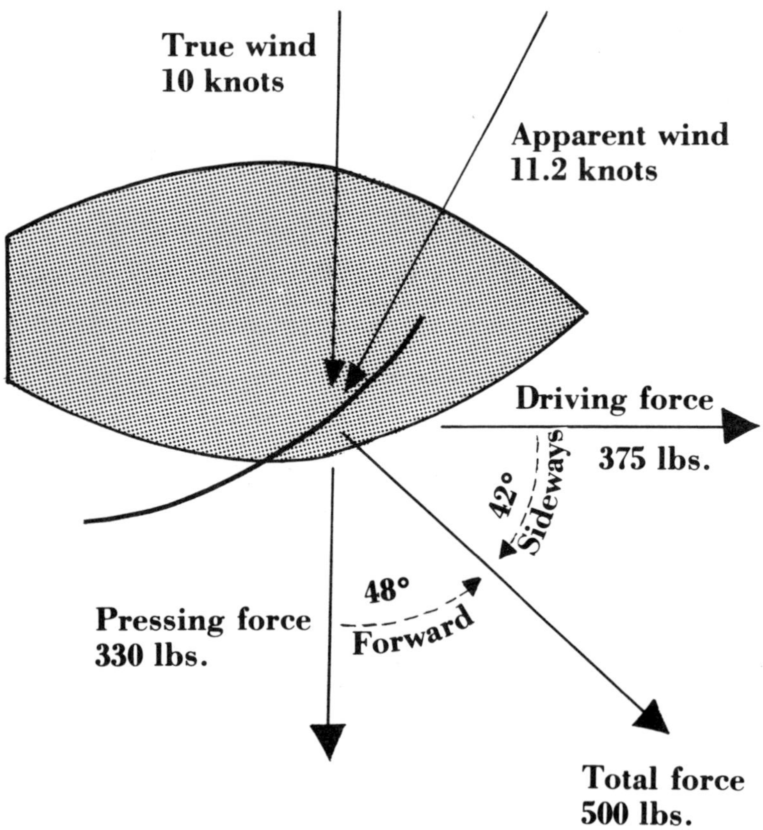

The boat sails the beam reach. The total sail force pulls 48 degrees forward of the beam—and at the same time it pulls 42 degrees sideways from the bow. The angle is the same but must be measured from both directions. *Drawing by Lana Cory Hall*

pounds pressing directly, dead upon the beam: at this it is the equivalent of the 500 pounds pulling obliquely, 42 degrees off the bow. You regard it as just a burden at first: something you must endure for making the compromise. It is unrelenting; it presses always at right angles to where you want to go. It would heel the boat, except you hike back against it; and then it just weighs heavily, both on the boat and on you. For a time you simply toil under it; then you slowly realize that the sideways component is actually the stable element in your universe. It has a very real and ponderable substance, and it holds always firm and still where everything else is rolling and heaving. You find yourself instinctively leaning on it for support, keeping the boat balanced and steadfast against it; and the boat can sail so smoothly this way that occasionally it might feel impervious even to the tossings of the waves themselves. You learn to feel good about the sideways component.

The forward component is more visible. It is the driving force. It drives the boat. On this beam reach it becomes 375 pounds exerted dead ahead: the equivalent of the same 500 pounds pulling 48 degrees forward. With the 6-degree angular advantage, it is the larger component by 45 pounds, the greater force by a 9 to 8 margin. The boat is driven forward this much harder than it is pressed

The boat sails at maximum speed as the skipper keeps a critical balance—maintaining maximum driving force: every possible ounce and fraction exerted dead ahead. ***Drawing by Don Raden***

sideways—at maximum speed it is: sailing at 5 knots with the true wind blowing at 10.

Then you hold the critical course: the boat still flat and balanced, the sail 5 degrees tighter than trim. You allow no deviation from the heading, no degree of heel, no variation in trim. You don't shuffle your feet or scratch your nose; you make no unwarranted move that might alter the balance. You keep feeling for any tilt or twitch or tiny deflection; you try to sense anything that might shift an angle or change a force, however minutely, and so disrupt the maximum arrangement, and you don't let any of this happen. You keep the arrangement as near as possible to mathematical perfection. Then you maintain maximum driving force—375 pounds: every possible ounce and fraction exerted dead ahead—the optimum compromise of all forces finally resolved together in the consummate effort of sailing the boat. And with this you have maximum speed, the manifestation of maximum force. The speed is arbitrarily 5 knots. You assume it is automatically adjusted for all the minor complexities and technicalities and imperfections which you probably do better not to know about: they number in the hundreds, and they might slow you a few thousandths of a knot for one reason and speed you a few thousandths for another. Never mind them now: you come to the overall reckoning with them later, and anyway you can't ever feel thousandths of knots. Just set your speed at 5 knots and sail with it. It is about 5¾ miles per hour, or as fast as you jog at a dog trot. Altogether a very good speed.

Somehow it seems faster. You don't realize this at first: this is a curious complication. The boat's speed, once you have it, becomes oddly deceptive. It always seems faster than it really is: or nearly always. This has to do with many things—the boat sailing, the wind blowing, the waves rolling, and the separate movements of the three being so intricately tied together that you must make a special, conscious effort at discerning them singly. Then other forces, partly extraneous, partly not, keep flying at your face, making noise, flinging spray, and generally getting in your way. They are small forces, but they are many, and as you sail harder they grow larger together and become their own illusion of something like speed. You tend just to grope at them for a while, until you can concentrate on seeing your way through them or around them. But through continuous exposure if nothing else, you do acquire a knack for all of this. You work at sorting out speeds: rejecting the wrong ones and selecting the right ones; feeling them or seeing them or sensing them, however you can. You practice by gauging speeds against fixed reference points, like buoys. Sail past the buoys very watchfully, perhaps a dozen times, perhaps two dozen, until you begin to get the real feeling for speed. The mechanics of speed really aren't so difficult after that. You begin to solve the problem when you just become aware that it is there to be solved.

But then there is one more thing: something essential that happens to you, an experience distinctly apart from the mechanics. Call it an emotion factor, if you are being scientific. It is the passion that seizes you, the exhilaration derived from the pure sensations of sails curving and forces pulling and water surging and all the rest; with the boat finally leaning and driving and sailing on its balance between you and the elements. This is powerful, even in a boat that doesn't go fast: it is transcendently awesome in one that does. (When you first reach 20 knots in a high-performance planing sailboat, you can barely withstand the sheer emotional strain; you feel as if you are tearing asunder yourself, the boat, and even the seas themselves.) The passion is indeed this magnificent, and you must be glad for it; it is the truest reason for doing any of this. Except now it has its full hold on you when you mean to be completely dispassionate, so you must allow once more for the boat feeling faster than it really is. You probably have to sail past the buoys some more, trying to find the way to measure exhilaration, but in time you get a feeling for this too. After a certain point you begin to feel rather amazed at yourself, that you keep getting these feelings for intangible things.

7 Downwind

Now turn the boat. You have made your reckonings: now steer to leeward, slowly and deliberately; go this way first just because the other way, windward, is better to go last. But turn: start the forces shifting and the angles changing; set in motion all the logic you have established. This is where you mean to have the definitive understanding.

Turn 5 degrees. Make the first move small and cautious. Ease the sheet: keep the sail in its one position in the apparent wind—finely adjusted, 5 degrees tighter than trim; the apparent wind axis and total force axis both held in place overhead—and turn the boat beneath. The boat and the beam turn together, always at right angles. The boat comes off the beam reach and swings 5 degrees downwind, toward the total force axis. The beam comes out of its alignment with the true wind axis and pivots 5 degrees ahead, toward the apparent wind axis. The apparent wind axis stays in place, 27 degrees ahead of the true wind axis or only minutely less now: a difference too inconsequential to measure. (In time the apparent wind must shift appreciably, but not now.) Then the total force axis also stays in place, being fixed at the dogleg angle to the apparent wind axis, still bearing 75 degrees back against it—the two axes meeting at the sail's center of effort and holding there. So with all the lines in perspective, the true wind is now 5 degrees aft of the beam, the apparent wind 22 degrees forward. The total force pulls 53 degrees forward, 5 more than before, and the boat sails 37 degrees askew to it, 5 less than before; the angle narrowing this much between the boat and the force that pulls it. You are 5 degrees to leeward.

But there are adjustments. There is a sequence of causes and effects which you don't see objectively; you have to learn the feel instead. The apparent wind is first. It is partly self-determined; it must change as the boat turns and the parallelogram slants and the true and false winds meet at different angles. And now if it doesn't change in direction, it must change in force. It must chase after the boat turning downwind—chasing very obliquely since it still comes from ahead of the boat, but chasing nonetheless—and it must expend a part of itself in the pursuit, and so it must weaken. And it does; its line shortens inevitably in the progression of parallelograms. It was an 11.2-knot wind on the beam reach; now it overtakes the boat as a 10.8-knot wind. It expends 4 tenths of a knot chasing across the 5 degrees.

Then as the wind weakens coming into the sail,

the force, in turn, must weaken going out—being proportional, as always, to the square of the apparent wind speed. The total sail force on the beam reach was 500 pounds pulling 48 degrees forward; now it is 467 pounds pulling 53 degrees forward. It is 33 pounds weaker and 5 degrees ahead: the pounds are lost; the degrees are gained. And now the boat sails by a new arrangement, a lesser force, better directed: a weaker force at a more potent angle.

It isn't the maximum arrangement: it has to be something less. The 467 pounds pulling 53 degrees forward—exerted against the water and resolved into components—become 372 pounds driving dead ahead: a driving force 3 pounds weaker than the 375-pound driving force of the beam reach. With this, the boat sails a scant few hundredths of a knot slower than the 5-knot maximum speed: in the final balance the loss is this much more than the gain. The arrangement is this much less than the maximum one.

Drawing by Don Raden

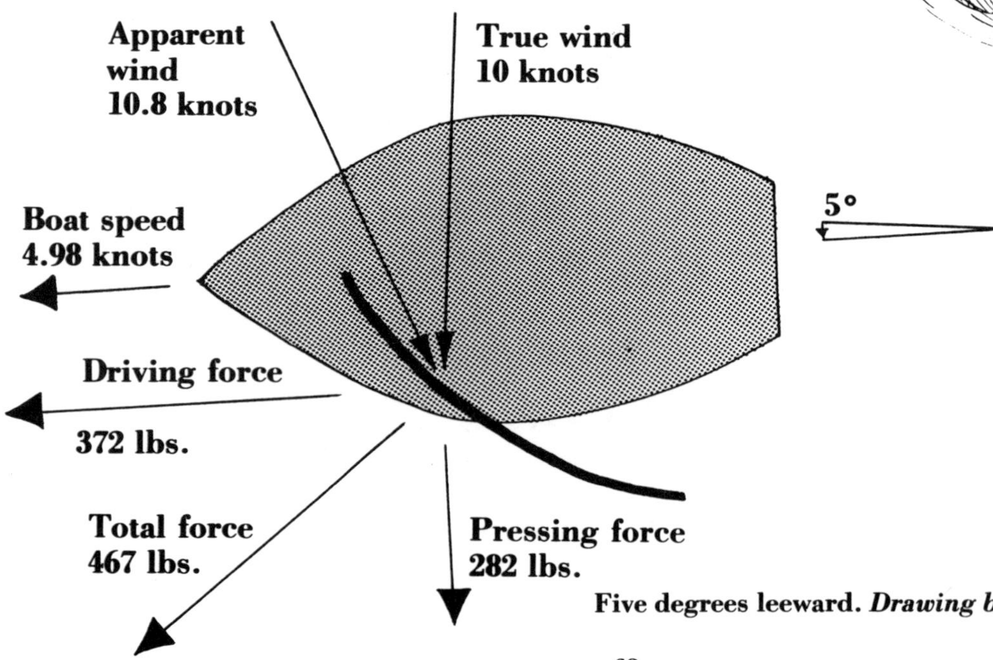

Five degrees leeward. *Drawing by Lana Cory Hall*

You see some of this happening: the obvious things. You feel more things. And you have notions about the rest, but you can't be sure yet because this is only the first move, and so many adjustments are so small. You may notice a sensation of sorts in the backs of your ears when the wind slackens by 4 tenths of a knot. Or you may wonder if the tension in the sheet eases slightly when the total force weakens by 33 pounds. But you don't feel the boat slowing by scant few hundredths of a knot—and you aren't about to until you acquire an exquisitely fine edge of expertise. What you do feel is mostly indistinguishable from what you felt before: the boat sailing ahead, strongly and straightforwardly. Except suddenly it feels significantly lightened: it isn't working so hard. You notice this now; you didn't at first. The boat just seems to go more easily over the water, as if in some way it has come unburdened. You feel this most definitely. There is a special reason for it.

This is the same arrangement from the other side. This is the total force adjusting as it pulls sideways—not like it adjusts as it pulls forward. It is the same force: still a lesser force at 467 pounds, still being 33 less than the 500 pounds on the beam reach. And it pulls 37 degrees sideways: 5 less than the 42 degrees sideways on the beam reach. From this side it is less force worse directed: a weaker force at a less potent angle. The 33 pounds and the 5 degrees are both lost in this direction. Nothing is gained.

Then this force exerted this way at this angle becomes resolved into a 282-pound component pressing sideways; it is 48 pounds less than the 330-pound sideways component of the beam reach. And you feel this if nothing else: 48 pounds stop pressing. The boat lightens just this much, or it seems to; it relaxes slightly but perceptibly, settling beneath you just a little. You don't hike out quite so far. You sail just a trifle more easily.

Then you begin to see how it all happens. You go with what the forces give you, but you sail to leeward by the angles. The forces become less as you steer away from the wind coming into the sail, but the angles become better as you steer toward the force going out. The forces falter, but the angles direct them forward: the forces lose; the angles gain. To leeward, from now on, the forces must lose more, and the angles must gain less. Together they must work this much against you. There must be this net loss between them.

Then the boat has slowed perceptibly and lightened ponderably, turning downwind the first 5 degrees. And its first net loss has been 3 pounds forward, 48 pounds sideways, and a scant few hundredths of a knot of speed. Now it is going to turn

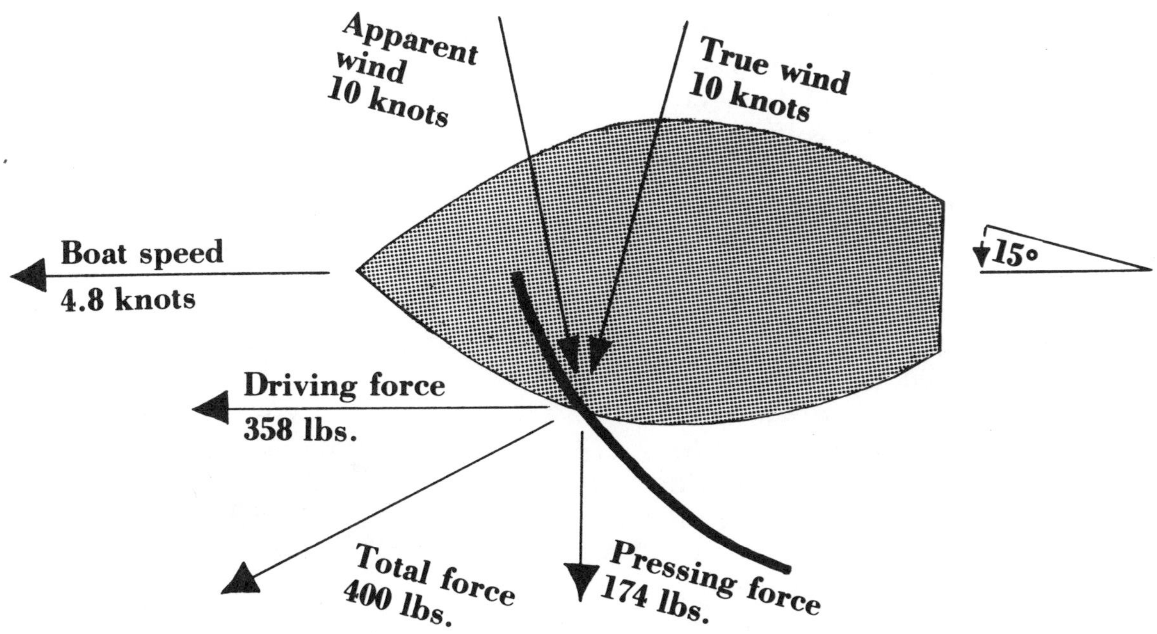

Fifteen degrees leeward. *Drawing by Lana Cory Hall*

much farther and lighten and slow much more, sailing by the angles.

So keep turning the boat. Keep easing the sheet; make all the fine adjustments. Steer 10 degrees farther to leeward. You come to a course 15 degrees below the beam reach; you hold the sail 5 degrees tighter than trim. And the rest keeps happening. The true wind holds steady; you still presume it steady. The apparent wind still doesn't shift appreciably; eventually it must, but not here: it still is very nearly 27 degrees ahead of the true wind. The boat turns 10 degrees still farther from the apparent wind, which sails it, and so it comes 10 degrees nearer to the total sail force, which pulls it. The angle between boat and force narrows this much. And the beam, at right angles to the boat, pivots 10 degrees farther ahead of the true wind, and so it comes 10 degrees nearer to the apparent wind. And as the boat turns away, the apparent wind again expends a part of itself chasing after—still obliquely, and now across 10 more degrees—and now it comes into the sail at exactly 10 knots, which is 8 tenths of a knot less than before. (For this one moment it becomes the equal of the true wind and gets passing notice as such: it has been more until now and will be less from now on, and none of this is important when you sail the boat.) Then the total force, weakened with the wind, goes out of the sail at 400 pounds, which is 67 less than before. It is once again the lesser total force, still pulling at the same proportion to the square of the apparent wind speed, still bearing the same 75 degrees back against the apparent wind. The lines are in place.

You are on a broad reach, sailing 15 degrees to leeward. The true wind, at 10 knots, is 15 degrees aft of the beam: you measure from it. The apparent wind, at 10 knots, is 12 degrees forward of the beam: you sail by it. The total force, at 400 pounds, pulls 63 degrees forward when the angle is measured from that direction—and 27 degrees sideways when the angle is measured in *that* direction. And you exert the total force both ways against the water, resolving it again into components. The driving force, the component of the total force exerted forward, becomes resolved at 358 pounds dead ahead. The pressing force, the component of the total force exerted sideways, becomes resolved at 174 pounds dead abeam. The boat's speed, with force and inertia in their mathematical balance, is 4.8 knots.

This is 2 tenths of a knot less than maximum speed. This is the first increment gone, the first perceptible gauge of loss over gain. You lose all but a trifling fraction of the 2 tenths as you turn the last 10 degrees, coming here to this broad reach, 15 degrees to leeward. You already had lost the fraction—the scant few hundredths—turning the 5 degrees just before. And you lose 14 more pounds of forward driving force in this turn of 10 degrees, and 108 more pounds of sideways pressing force. This time you do feel it all, or you begin to. Everything starts to happen largely and ponderably enough.

You feel the sideways pressing force going first. It goes the most; it lightens as it goes; it is the kind of force that would lighten rather than weaken. Now it lightens most drastically, losing the 108 pounds. This is a loss of nearly 40 per cent: all of it

Sailing 15 degrees to leeward, the boat feels distinctly less powerful; it is palpably lightened. The wind blows more tranquilly. The sail pulls more gently. *Drawing by Don Raden*

gone when you sail 15 degrees to leeward—all neatly and geometrically vectored out of existence like the 42 pounds just before. This is a greater burden lifted off, a more substantial element precipitously gone from the weight pressing upon the boat. And you know abruptly when it is gone. You are hiked and braced against the sideways force; you are at grips with it, enduring it: then this much of it gives way. It seems to go out from beneath or behind, where you aren't watching. It leaves you out on the edge, overbalanced. And it just drops you a little, with a sudden, sinking sensation. The boat leans under you. The mast sways over you. Everything heels to windward, the wrong way. For an instant you even may lose the sense of balance; you recover by sheer reflex—sliding your body off the edge and down into the cockpit, finding the right place and reestablishing the balance. You level the boat again; you steady it and sail it, adapting by instinct to its lighter feel.

Then you feel the rest: it all follows. Turn your face toward the apparent wind blowing at 10 knots, and indeed it blows more tranquilly past your ears than it did at 10.8 knots. Hold the total sail force at 400 pounds, and it definitely pulls more gently on the sheet than it did at 467 pounds. And concentrate finally on the driving force and the speed together—they are always together—and now most certainly they make a tangible difference in the way the boat moves. This time you begin to sense it all. The boat with 358 pounds driving is distinctly less powerful than it was with 372 pounds driving. And at 4.8 knots it is slightly but discernibly slower than it was at nearly 5 knots. You simply feel it slowing when you feel everything else; you even learn to see it slowing as you pass the bubbles in the water. It all happens this way: you sail easier but slower, going to leeward with the angles. From now on you lose your speed like this: increment by increment.

Then on: you must continue.

—27 degrees leeward; true wind is 27 degrees aft. Apparent wind is 9 knots and aligned upon the beam: 0 degrees forward, 0 degrees aft. Total sail force is 324 pounds, 75 degrees forward. Forward driving force is 316 pounds dead ahead. Sideways pressing force is 72 pounds dead abeam. Speed is 4.5 knots.

You steer 12 more degrees downwind to here—from 15 degrees leeward down to 27 degrees leeward; still easing the sheet and making the fine adjustments, still turning away from the apparent wind and toward the total sail force—and so you bring the boat down to this very specific heading, 27 degrees leeward, where it sails squarely across the apparent wind. It is on a beam reach of sorts in the apparent wind: an unacknowledged beam

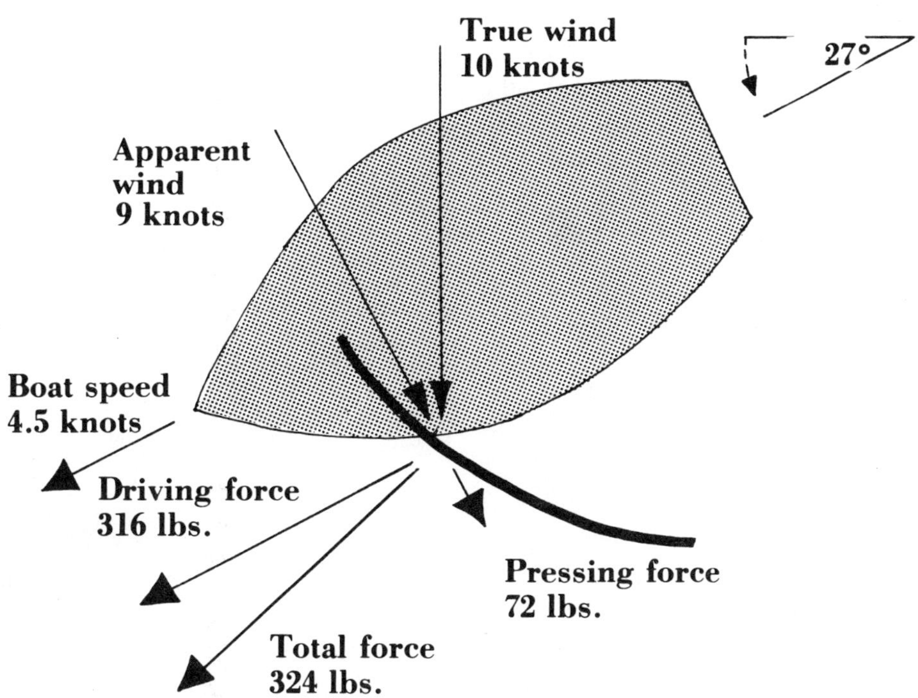

Twenty-seven degrees leeward. *Drawing by Lana Cory Hall*

reach, more tactile if less authoritative than the definitive one across the true wind. The apparent wind is no longer a headwind, not even obliquely; it is not yet a tailwind. It is on the line between, on the beam; it is at right angles to the boat. Call this the other beam reach, just because it never had a better name or a real name, and remember you come to it 27 degrees to leeward of the real beam reach. Later you will need to know it is here.

You unburden still more, steering the 12 degrees down to this other beam reach. The boat unburdens. The rest unburdens. There is a most precipitous and fundamental unburdening. The apparent wind slackens by a knot as you steer farther from it. The total force weakens by 76 pounds as you steer nearer to it, and it pulls 12 degrees farther forward; the angle between boat and force narrows this much. Then the sideways component lightens by 102 pounds—going out from under you again, dropping you a little—and only 72 pounds remain, still pressing, and they are no weight to hike against. You simply ride with 72 pounds, hardly feeling them. You hold the sheet with an easy grasp, and you let the sail hang out over the side, just keeping it 5 degrees tighter than trim. And you steer the boat like a toy; there is no effort at all. This is the easiest kind of sailing, 27 degrees to leeward. You are entirely comfortable. You begin to feel almost euphoric.

Except now, as the sideways component lightens, you feel its stable element shrinking away—a phenomenon that is vaguely disquieting, though not actually disruptive. You feel more of the burden going and less of its substance remaining; and now burden and substance together decline to just the 72 pounds pressing sideways: the last component force left for you to lean against when you balance the boat. You instinctively sense the delicacy in this. Where once you had braced your full weight solidly against 200 or 300 pounds, now you only touch very gingerly against these 72; altogether they would give you only figurative support—rather like the support you would get grasping twigs if you stood teetering on a sapling over a creek—with perhaps a disproportionate measure of reassurance. You touch against the 72 pounds just to keep a perspective that is in fact more faith than substance, and from now on you sail the boat feeling the balances in it more than the forces upon it. You realize now that the stable element is about to shrink completely and precipitously out of existence, and when it is gone, you are going to balance with your own unsupported sense of equilibrium. You feel new responsibility.

But here, 27 degrees to leeward, the total force is 324 pounds pulling 75 degrees forward, and against the resistance of the water, it becomes resolved into 316 pounds of driving force exerted dead ahead and moving the boat at 4.5 knots. The driving force loses 42 pounds in the turn of 12 degrees. The boat slows 3 tenths of a knot: another increment gone. Altogether it has slowed half a knot since sailing at maximum speed. The boat now sails only 15 degrees from the direction the total force pulls, and it is about to turn still closer.

And on:

—38 degrees leeward; true wind 38 degrees aft.

Sailing 27 degrees to leeward, the boat rides effortlessly with the wind. This is the easiest kind of sailing. *Drawing by Don Raden*

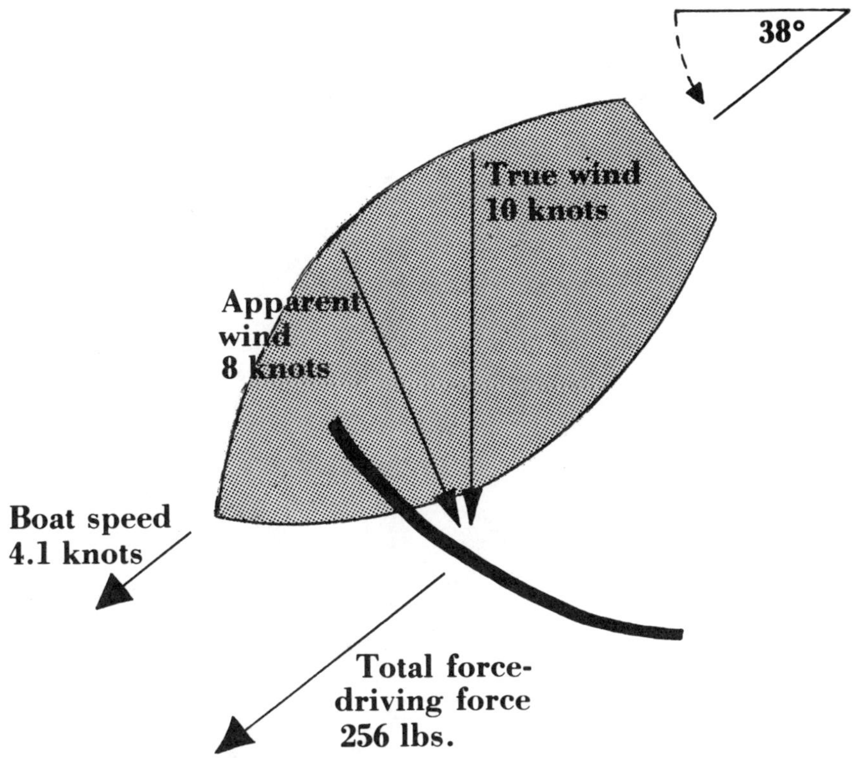

Thirty-eight degrees leeward. *Drawing by Lana Cory Hall*

Apparent wind is 8 knots, 15 degrees aft. Total sail force is 256 pounds, 90 degrees forward. Forward driving force is the same: 256 pounds dead ahead. Sideways force is 0: no weight, no direction; it no longer exists. Speed is 4.1 knots.

The apparent wind shifts. This is the first time.

It veers 4 degrees toward the true wind while the boat turns 11 degrees away. It shifts now for all the reasons it didn't before—because it is a resolution of forces and partly self-determined; because it is both a cause and an effect of the way the boat moves. Now, as the boat slows and turns, the forces slide and shrink and are restructured into new parallelograms, more sharply slanted—this being, like always, the ongoing process of cause and effect. And this time the forces make a parallelogram slanted beyond a critical point, and upon this they become resolved in a new direction: on a new diagonal, moved 4 degrees. And this is the shift of the apparent wind. It must happen inevitably, and now that it finally does, it is simply a trigonometric function.

Then this heading, 38 degrees leeward, is where you bring the boat and the total sail force together. You steer 11 more degrees down to here, turning the boat away from the apparent wind and toward the total force. You play out the last few feet of the sheet, letting the sail go out nearly all the way, so it hangs nearly upon the beam, nearly at right angles to the boat—and so it sets here, 5 degrees tighter than trim. And here the boat must come into alignment with the axis of total force. The boat and the total force had been 15 degrees apart; now the boat turns 11 of those degrees, and the force shifts the other 4. The total force shifts with the apparent wind, as it must, because the sail stays 5 degrees tighter than trim, and the force still bears 75 degrees back against the wind, holding tenaciously at the dogleg angle: force and wind pivot together as if their separate axes were welded together at the sail's center of effort. So while the apparent wind shifts 4 degrees away from the boat, the total force shifts 4 degrees toward it. And the boat turns its 11 degrees toward the force, and they meet on this broad reach, 38 degrees to leeward. They align here and go forward together. All of the total force pulls dead ahead: it becomes its own driving force. It does not pull sideways. There is no sideways force.

From now on you balance alone except for the innate structural balance and integrity of the boat

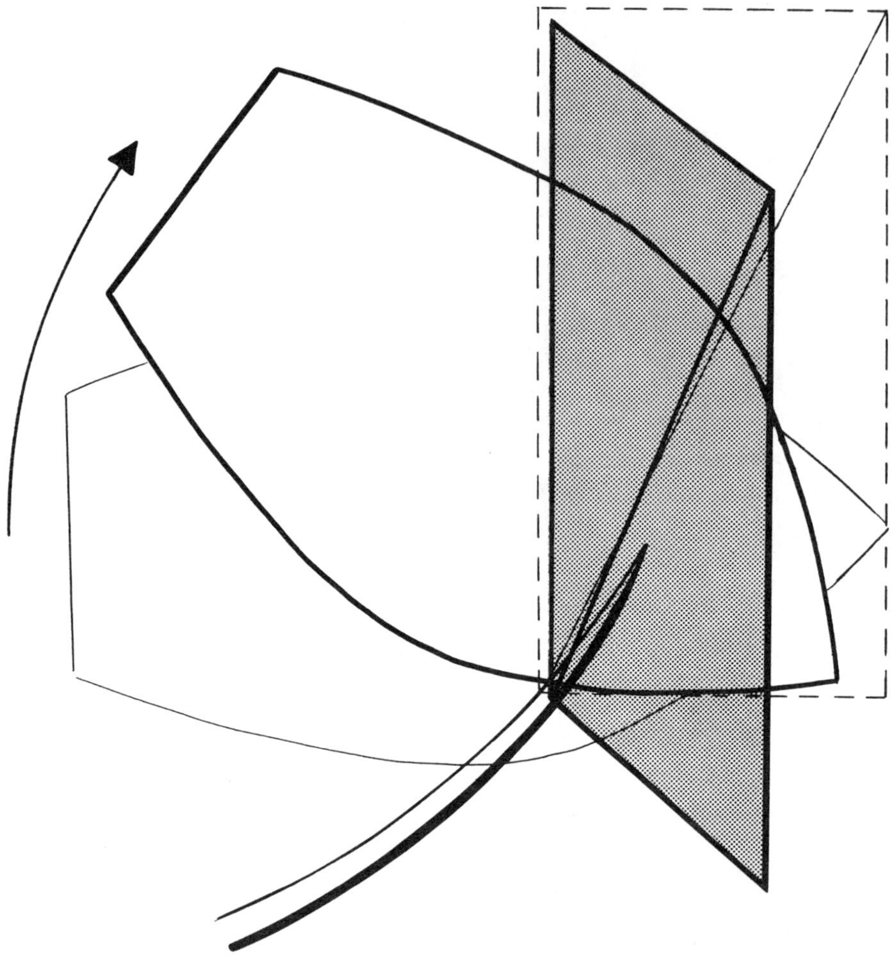

The apparent wind shifts. The boat turns 38 degrees from the beam reach—where the apparent wind axis is the diagonal of the parallelogram with hyphenated edges—down to this heading where the axis becomes the diagonal of the gray parallelogram, more sharply slanted. By simple cause and effect, the parallelogram is slanted beyond a critical point, and the apparent wind becomes resolved on a new diagonal moved 4 degrees. This is the shift of the wind: a trigonometric function. ***Drawing by Lana Cory Hall***

itself. You have no component support pressing from the side: no stable element. You sail down in the cockpit, keeping a low center of gravity, often crouching on your toes and teetering on your bare reflexes, trying to roll with the rhythm of the waves just beneath. They are the same waves as before, routine waves; they were of no special consequence only a moment ago, when you did have substantial support; you simply leaned back and sailed straight through them, and they easily gave way—too easily, perhaps; they seemed so smooth and pliant and totally attuned. But now that you are alone with the waves, they aren't really like that. They are beginning to move in ways you haven't felt before. One wave abruptly lifts the stern for no apparent reason. Another drops the bow. A third nudges the boat lightly but pointedly as it passes by. You suddenly sense waves all around, all of them pushing and prodding in odd new ways. They don't actually hinder the boat, nor threaten it, nor even jostle it; they just commit these subtle but unprecedented little effronteries upon it, where once they never would have dared. They are beginning to toy with the boat, now that they have you alone in it.

stant too late; you tend to overbalance too often. But you do keep the boat sailing. It wobbles, but it works well enough so that you can see you are essentially right in most of what you do. You see also where you are going to learn the skill in this. From now on you are going to practice balance and timing, and when you are done with the science, you continue to refine the art. And you refine indefinitely.

Meanwhile, the apparent wind has slackened by a knot, and the total force has weakened by 68 pounds. And the driving force, which now is also the total force, has weakened by 60 pounds. Force and component, both directed dead ahead, have joined and become a force alone (the "total-sail-driving force," a name far too cumbersome to use), which both pulls the sail and drives the boat. With this force, the boat has slowed another 4 tenths of a knot. Another increment is gone.

Sailing thirty-eight degrees leeward and becoming more tenuously balanced, the boat is nudged pointedly by a wave. The waves are beginning to toy with the boat. *Drawing By Don Raden*

Then the boat sailing 38 degrees to leeward is driven at 4.1 knots by a 256-pound force. It sails at slightly more than three quarters of maximum speed, powered by slightly more than two-thirds of maximum driving force. The balance between force and inertia thus begins to emerge mathematically—to show itself for the first time.

You respond, of course: not perfectly but more or less adequately, knowing by feel alone that this is not the same kind of sailing. You have an acute new awareness of waves: of being alone with them and feeling accountable for them. They swell, and you must shift; they push, and you must pull. You have to move with them and keep the balance on them and be very smooth and quick and coordinated all the while. You need to control the boat less forcefully but more sensitively, to work less strenuously but more adroitly. You try all this, beginning with just half a touch and half an intuition. You oscillate; you fidget between port and starboard; probably you are a little too frantic at first. You balance *here* an instant too soon and counterbalance *there* an in-

Things are necessarily different after this. You come to this heading—38 degrees to leeward, where boat and force align—and this turns out to be the downwind limit of the reaches. You are going a good way farther than this, but not reaching, not with the sail 5 degrees tighter than trim. You can't trim the sail any more. It is nearly at right angles to the boat; it is trimmed all the way out to the end. It presses against the shroud now, or it is only a millimeter away. If you tried to let it out farther, the shroud would stop it. And you wouldn't let it out much farther anyway, even if you could in one of those uniquely potent little boats without shrouds, because then you would deflect its full force completely out of bounds—across the bow and off to windward, beyond the leverage of the machinery that must contain it. (Then at a certain point the sheet and tiller would lose effect in your hands; the boat in sudden frenzy would wrench itself out of control and pull back to windward, spinning around with an overpowering and rather grotesque weather helm; and you would know the feeling of awful helplessness: the sentiments of an egg taken unawares on a turn through the beater.) Just believe this: you have come as far as you can with the sail in its most functional state, 5 degrees tighter than trim. You go from here down into the area where it must work at less than its best. You go beyond the limit.

Then you stop working the sheet. You abruptly cease everything you had done incessantly—all the fine adjustments: pulling in the sheet, easing it out, keeping the sail constantly in its one position in the apparent wind, however the boat turned beneath. You stop all of that. Past the limit you can only grasp the sheet at its very end and keep the sail fixed nearly at right angles to the boat—holding it rigidly in its one place on the boat, turning it with the boat, however the wind blows after. This is once again a different kind of sailing, going beyond the limit.

This time steer very experimentally to leeward, just a trifle at first: turning the boat and now bringing the sail around with it. The boat swings away from the wind once again; and the sail, nearly at right angles, now slides across the wind—just this far: this trifle. So the curve comes this much more across the wind; the bend cramps this much tighter; and the outer wind current can't hold as long to as wide an arc of the curve, cramped tighter. The current contorts to its limit, trying to make the tighter turn around the convex surface, but now it must veer away this much sooner, off an arc this much shorter. And this time it must separate forward, past the critical point in the flow and force patterns; it peels just this far into the forward third of the sail, the power sector, the area of dynamic forces. In effect the outer current siphons away this much of the sail's pulling power. It leaves this much less sail area under pulling force and this much more under eddies and uncertainties. It makes the total force this much weaker going out—now relatively weaker than the apparent wind coming in—because the sail can't be 5 degrees tighter than trim any more.

Then complete this. Steer just 5 degrees more to leeward—6 to be certain: a modest, momentary turn. Hold the sheet at its very end; keep the sail in its one place on the boat. The rest happens. The boat and the sail keep turning as one, still fixed nearly at right angles. The sail comes slowly across the wind; the bend cramps inexorably tighter; the outer current can't hold to it. In 6 degrees the current separates completely from the convex surface. It peels swiftly across the sail's forward parts; directly through the sail's strongest pulling power; then it is gone. It leaves the sail in full stall: the wind blowing bluntly against the concave surface, spilling around the edges and dissipating itself in the chasm of eddies and turmoil behind. The sail, stalled, functions at three-quarters power from now on. The total force survives at three-quarters strength—a slower, simpler, very different force. It is more push than pull after this; essentially it is little more than a dull remnant of plain pushing force. All of its dynamic pulling energy has been abruptly siphoned away.

(In stronger wind this doesn't happen quite yet. Stronger wind, by sheer momentum, still holds for the moment to some part of the outside of the sail cramped this tight; the current bends with the curve and sustains some effect of laminar flow and exerts some element of pulling force. It won't peel away until the boat turns farther downwind. But that is a different condition.)

After a while you learn to feel when the total force weakens. The sheet eases slightly but rather abruptly in your hand. Tensions slacken here and there. The boat just seems to relax a little and settle into the water, slowing palpably, though not drastically. The whole sensation is subtle but unique. For the first time the boat doesn't seem lighter as it slows. It just slows. The total force, if no longer the same, remains at least a force exerted forward. It does this much for you as you sail on to leeward: no matter how or where the wind comes; the total force—whatever happens to it, whatever remains of it—goes straight ahead regardless, fully engaged in driving the boat.

Turn one more degree. You come to a halfway point.

—45 degrees leeward; true wind 45 degrees aft. Apparent wind is 8 knots, 24 degrees aft. Total sail

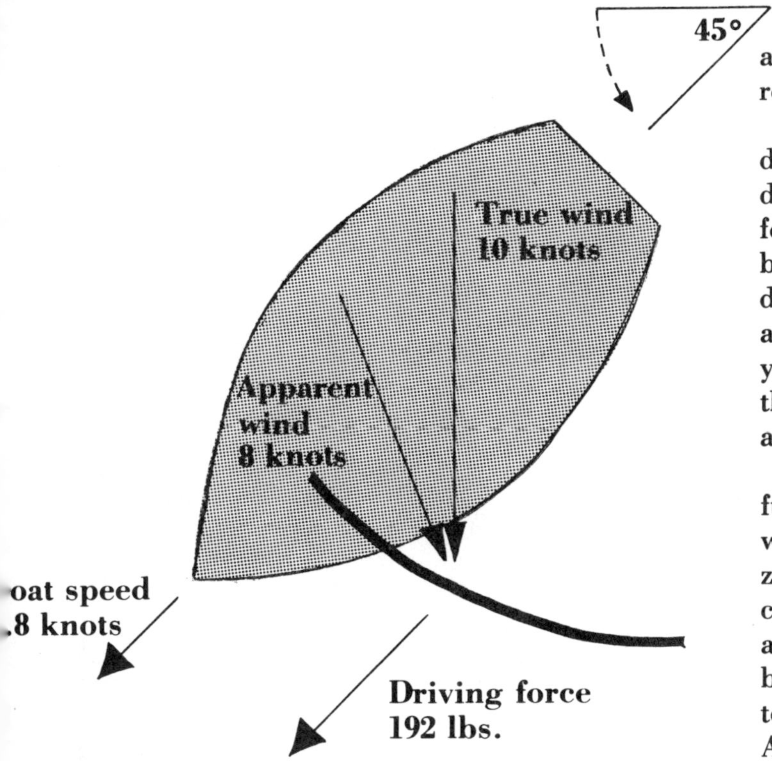

Forty-five degrees leeward. *Drawing by Lana Cory Hall*

force is 192 pounds dead ahead. Speed is 3.8 knots.

Ostensibly this would seem the classic broad reach: sailing exactly upon the mid-diagonal, half across the true wind, half down it. Except now this becomes yet another kind of sailing: definitively impure and imperfect. By the strictest principles it shouldn't be broad reaching at all, nor reaching of any sort if the sail can't be trim or 5 degrees tighter. Yet in the very practical sense it still is broad reaching. It has to be at least an extension of broad reaching, if only for the moment: perhaps a surrogate of sorts, just because it isn't yet running either. Running is what you will do next, after you really are done with broad reaching—running before the wind; sailing finally downwind with everything spread wide and full and grand. You are coming presently to a place where you stop reaching and start running, but it is a highly subjective place in the apparent wind. You can't calculate it or fix objectively upon it; you don't even find it the way you find other places. You can only go past it rather indeterminably and decide for yourself, rather intuitively, that it is there and once you are past it, the boat is running. Each time you go past you decide this just a little differently, and each time the place shifts slightly. But wherever it is, wherever you do begin running, you are not there yet. You are going there. You are going to get there by reaching beyond the reaches.

(Then understand where you are, sailing 45 degrees to leeward. With the apparent wind 24 degrees aft, you sail about 7 feet across it for every 3 feet down it. You are not even close to running before it; you won't come close until you sail more down than across. With the true wind 45 degrees aft, you sail equal distances across and down it, and you would be quite near to running before it, except the true wind of course is for reference. You don't actually sail the boat with it.)

There is something more. As the sail comes into full stall, the small eddies behind it swell to large whirlwinds—you remember this—and the stall zone widens abruptly from the narrow cavity to the churning wind chasm, and you bring the boat around to the very edge of this. Now you actually begin to veer into the chasm: to sail very obliquely toward the aerodynamic heart of darkness itself. And you feel the first effects. The boat begins to move in ways it never did before; it does odd things, or odd things are done to it. You can't be sure. The forces that burdened it are gone. The remaining forces are wavering, as if they might come unstuck or do something irrational. You suddenly want to grope after forces, just for reassurance that they still make the boat go. It does go, but it doesn't seem fully directed. The timing is off. You keep balancing the boat against waves, but it keeps sliding out of phase with them. Little waves keep catching it at illogical moments, nudging it and rolling it gently but incongruously, and you are balancing elsewhere, anticipating larger waves that miss narrowly and leave you hanging. You correct constantly, adjusting to disrupted rhythms. You still have good control when you need it, but your touch isn't quite so sure. Everything somehow feels more remote. You have certain forebodings about what is going to happen when you steer in even closer to the whirlwinds.

The boat slows 3 tenths of a knot turning the last 7 degrees on the way to this heading, 45 degrees leeward. This time it slows solely because of faltering sail power; it slows abruptly enough so that the apparent wind still overtakes with undiminished force; it is still an 8-knot wind, even as the boat turns away. (The apparent wind does shift 2 degrees nearer to the true wind, but with no change in force.) This only happens here.

Meanwhile, if the water were ice, the needle-

Sailing forty-five degrees to leeward, the boat begins to veer into its own stall zone, the chasm of whirlwinds and turmoil behind the sail. ***Drawing by Don Raden***

pointed little iceboats, the last extremes of sailing craft, would be sailing this course at 50 miles per hour or better—five times faster than the true wind—and the apparent wind still would be a headwind for them. Iceboats always sail in headwinds, even when they go nearly down the axis itself. Iceboats have their own ways with the wind.

You, however, keep going.

—60 degrees leeward; true wind 60 degrees aft. Apparent wind is 7.2 knots, 45 degrees aft. Total force is 156 pounds dead ahead. Speed is 3.6 knots.

The apparent wind in effect comes 21 more degrees aft of the beam; it shifts 6 more degrees toward the true wind, while the boat turns 15 more degrees away. Now it is 45 degrees aft, and you sail equally across and down it, and you can decide any time from now on that you have come to the place where you stop reaching and start running; you come quite close just in these last 15 degrees. So say you are running already if the sail seems spread wide enough. Or say you aren't running yet if the boat still doesn't feel like it. It doesn't matter. You

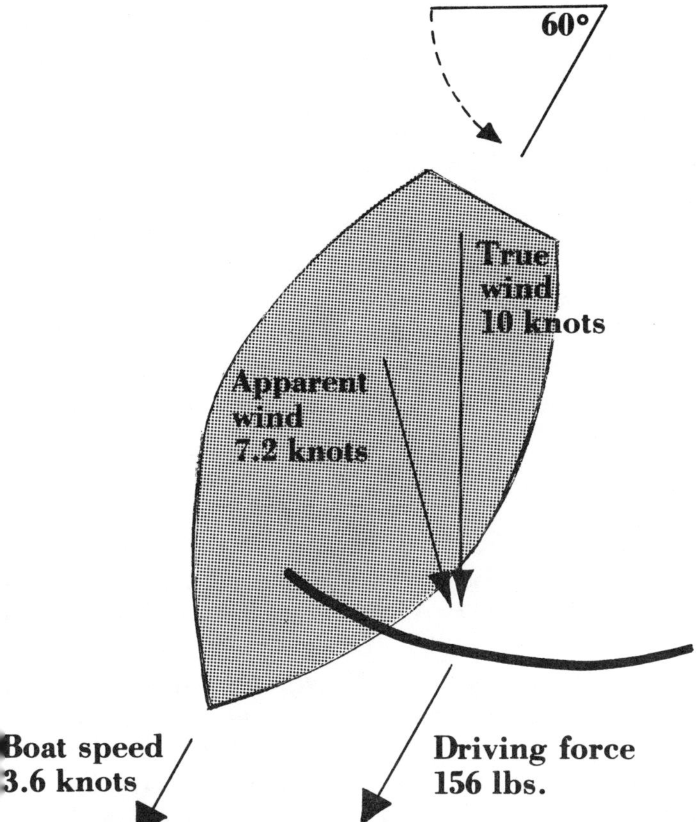

Sixty degrees leeward. ***Drawing by Lana Cory Hall***

decide this when you are ready.

The boat feels slow now, and not altogether functional. It keeps going, but it seems less driven by definite forces than spirited by indefinite ones. It keeps edging into mood: it has small, erratic fits, reeling and plunging in the waves, becoming almost giddy sometimes, even as you steer and balance. Then it suddenly goes placid, almost sluggish, just drifting along with no discernible purpose. You begin to doubt your part in this. You still maintain sufficient control, making the boat go where you mean it to. But you wonder if you should be doing things you don't know about, or sensing things you don't feel. You don't really seem to be doing much at all any more. You just feel detached, riding in the boat and letting the wind push. You don't feel comfortable.

The true and apparent winds are 15 degrees apart and still closing. The apparent wind slackens by 8 tenths of a knot; the total force weakens by 40 pounds. The boat slows by 2 tenths of a knot, losing an increment significantly smaller than the one lost just before.

Then on:

—75 degrees leeward; true wind 75 degrees aft. Apparent wind is 6.7 knots, 67 degrees aft. Total force is 135 pounds. Speed is 3.5 knots.

You sail about 5 feet down the apparent wind for every 2 feet across; so you probably decide you are running here. Most people decide somewhere near here. This just seems like running before the wind.

You still don't feel much. The boat is in its mood and has its remote non-feel. You keep riding uneasily, holding the sheet and tiller. This all does seem too easy.

The apparent wind slackens by half a knot and shifts 7 degrees nearer to the true wind. The two winds are only 8 degrees apart. The total force weakens by 21 pounds. The boat slows by a tenth of a knot. You just steer past this heading, barely noticing.

And on:

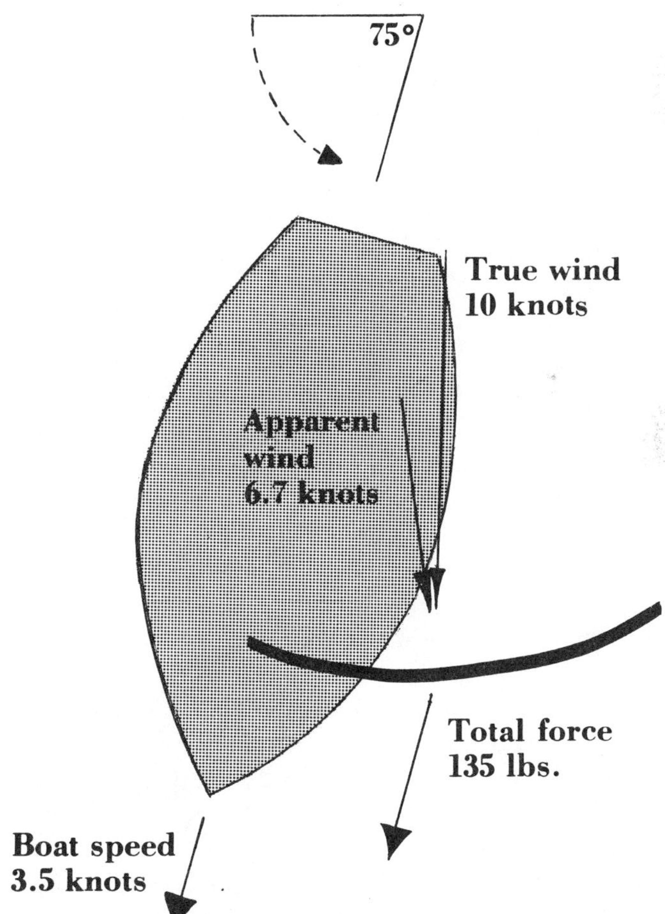

Seventy-five degrees leeward. ***Drawing by Lana Cory Hall***

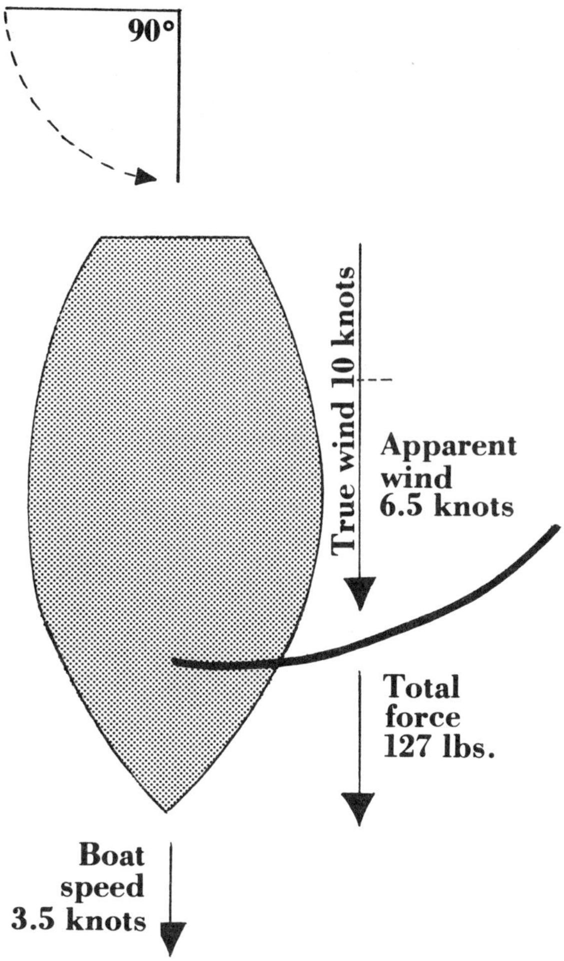

Ninety degrees leeward, dead before the wind. All forces are aligned on the true-wind axis. *Drawing by Lana Cory Hall*

—90 degrees leeward; true wind 90 degrees aft. Apparent wind is 6.5 knots, 90 degrees aft. Total force is 127 pounds. Speed is 3.5 knots.

You stop turning now. You can't steer farther to leeward. You are all the way there, running. The boat sails exactly upon the true wind axis, the line of reference. The sail sets almost squarely across it. The true and apparent winds come together at the true wind axis. The total force aligns with the true wind axis. All the lines of force merge upon the axis like an umbrella folding. Then there are no more angles. There is only the axis, one line, and everything—boat, sail, wind, force—goes straight down it.

The apparent wind, at 6.5 knots, is now the minimum wind; it slackens by 2 tenths of a knot as you turn the last 15 degrees. The total force, at 127 pounds, is the minimum force; it weakens by 8 pounds. The boat, at 3.5 knots, sails at its minimum speed downwind, its last increment gone; it slows by an imperceptible fraction from the 3.5 knots of the heading just before, and now it sails at 1.5 knots less than the 5-knot maximum speed. In the balance of force and inertia, the minimum speed of the boat running downwind turns out to be a little more than two-thirds of the maximum speed of the boat reaching across the wind—the boat being pushed at minimum speed by slightly more than one-third of the force that drove it at maximum speed. Such is the way the mathematics work out. The true wind speed now is simply the sum of the lowest boat speed and the lowest apparent wind speed, both measured downwind along the same axis line. With this you sail dead before the wind.

This is an especially strange way to sail. It seems completely simple, almost blissful, like nothing at all, as if there are no more forces and you are not even moving any longer. You could be just suspended here, weightless, tranquil, and—ostensibly—terribly secure. Running before this kind of wind, you hardly feel anything.

But in fact the boat is completely into its mood now. It is running straight toward the depths of its own wind chasm, directly at the invisible ragings of the whirlwinds themselves. And it goes most uncertainly, encountering things you can't know about. It overtakes small warps and spins in the wind, sudden twists among the eddies, or just voids in the air. It slides against the tails of the whirlwinds gently lashing back; the whirlwinds come spinning around the mast, then around the sail's trailing edge. They swing by turns behind the convex surface, one veering in, another veering out. They swing rhythmically in and out, first from one side, then from the other. The boat only begins to rock with them, almost imperceptibly. The sail quivers slightly. The mast may sway a few degrees. You hardly notice.

You need perhaps twice as much wind before you really can understand what is happening; just for this you presume twice as much wind—momentarily, if arbitrarily—just because sooner or later you have to *experience* what is happening. With twice as much wind, you sail into a vastly larger wind chasm. The whirlwinds swell and spin and lash back much harder; this time you know they are there, swinging in and out. They set the boat reeling in its mood. The boat is giddy once again but no longer gentle. It lurches suddenly into quick, hard fits of rebellion. It leans over; it pulls convulsively; it surprises you. Then it goes slack. Then it wren-

Sailing on the dead run, the boat is completely into its mood—utterly tranquil one moment, then wrenching convulsively in open rebellion as it sails directly toward its own wind chasm. *Drawing by Don Raden*

ches again, trying to pull off course. It really means this; it is fighting you. And then it just floats again, utterly docile, as if nothing had ever happened. You never can sense a workable logic in this; you have to develop combat reflexes instead. You learn to be deeply mistrustful of the boat in its mood, to fight it quicker than it fights you. You become adroit at balancing and very fast at tiller handling and extremely watchful all the while. And you are urgently persuaded that the boat indeed is not stable when in its mood, and you are not terribly secure. You realize very soon that if the boat ever does have occasion to turn on you or overpower you or do anything violent, it will do so here, dead before the wind, where it seems most ethereal.

So you sail most cautiously, perhaps savoring the risk—knowing it at least, whether you actually feel it or not, whether it is actually there or not—but trying not to do this for long. You don't press your luck with the wind dead behind your back. (This would be different another time, on a larger scale, in bigger boats with greater substance. Then you would run downwind with a grand audacity, flying full spinnakers into incalculable ferment—and flaunting the risks as you go, like fire engines flaunting sirens. Another time you would.) Now, on the small scale, you mean only to get your little boat off the wind axis and out of this as soon as possible—to steer it out, just as you steered it in.

The ways out are to windward. All ways are windward from here; all turns are windward when you are dead before the wind. There is no other direction for you to steer. There is no more leeward from here.

8
Upwind

There are two ways to turn: there are two ways to windward. One is *back* to windward: turning the boat back from the axis line and back the way it came—steering it upwind where it came downwind. That way is called heading up. The other way is *on* to windward: turning the boat on across the axis line and then on still farther—steering it upwind the way that had been downwind until now. That way is complicated.

(You will learn about this. Once the boat crosses the axis line, it suddenly is sailing by the lee, and this clearly constitutes a state of transgression. The wind is on the wrong side of the sail, the sail on the wrong side of the boat; and the boat, in effect, is now on the wrong side of the wind. The whole arrangement is wrong; it feels wrong. You can sense intuitively that everything is ominously misaligned, and the consequences will be abrupt and drastic. In another moment the boat will jibe. It has to jibe to go across the axis and on to windward. And you don't know how to jibe yet.)

Then go the other way. Turn back to windward. Head up. This feels right.

You sail toward the wind as you had sailed away from it: steering the boat in a long, smooth, deliberate arc across the water. But now you reverse the arc—as if you came here tracing half of a figure *S*; now you go back tracing the other half. And you go back more swiftly and certainly because you know the way. You go up where you came down. You sail against the angles, losing the forces. To windward you simply undo whatever you had done to leeward. And you redo whatever you had undone. This is the way.

Then start this way. Steer the boat back off the wind axis and out of the dead run. The angles reopen; the lines of force come apart from the true wind axis—like the umbrella starting to unfold. The apparent wind veers away from the true wind; the total force pulls askew to both. You turn farther, opening the angles wider. You keep turning, and at a certain subjective point you stop running and begin reaching. The boat heads by degrees toward the wind, driving very obliquely at it. The forces gather slowly in the sail, growing with the combined impetus of boat and wind starting to come at each other. And you begin to gain more in the forces than you lose against the angles; you go perhaps a tenth of a knot faster. You pick up the first increment of speed on the way to windward—the last you left behind on the way to leeward.

Drawing by Don Raden

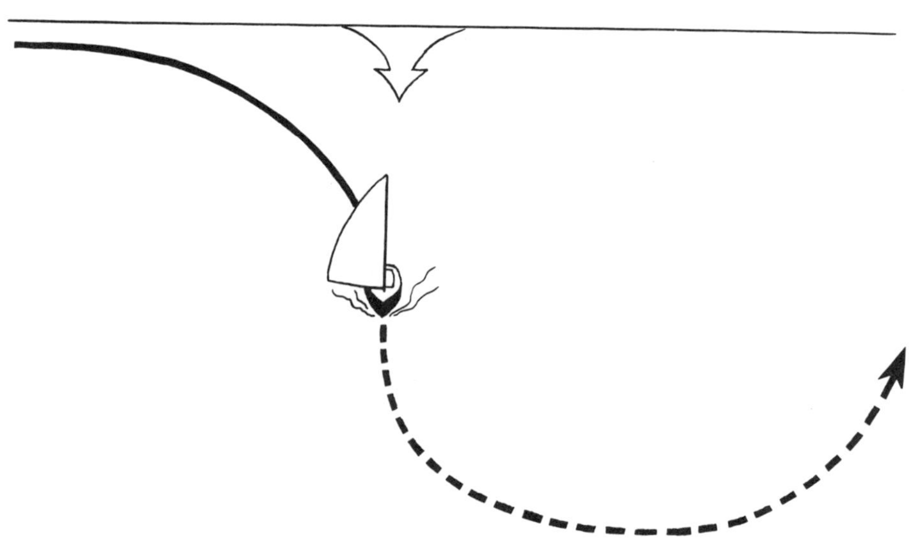

Having come downwind on a solid curve, the boat now turns upwind to follow a hyphenated curve, as if tracing the second half of a figure *S. Drawing by Don Raden*

You steer 30 degrees toward the wind to regain that 10th-of-a-knot increment. And with the turn, the apparent wind strengthens by 7 tenths of a knot and shifts 15 degrees away from the true wind, and the total force strengthens by 29 pounds. Then you steer 15 degrees farther and regain the next 2 tenths of a knot, and the apparent wind strengthens by another 8 tenths of a knot and shifts 6 degrees still farther from the true wind, and the total force strengthens by 36 more pounds. With this you are halfway back to the beam reach, sailing once more on the 45-degree mid-diagonal, half across the true wind, half down it. The apparent wind is 8 knots, 24 degrees aft, just as it was when you sailed here on the way to leeward. The total force is 192 pounds dead ahead, driving the boat at 3.8 knots. You come this far with the sail in full stall and functioning at three-quarters power, the wind simply blowing into it and spilling around the edges, into the turmoil of the chasm behind. So far you have effectively sailed in this chasm. Now you are about to come free of it.

Steer 7 more degrees to windward, holding the sheet at its very end, turning boat and sail together, nearly at right angles to each other. With this small turn, you bring the sail out of full stall and around to its most functional setting, 5 degrees tighter than trim in the apparent wind. The curve becomes the catalyst once again; the inner and outer wind currents make the critical turn forward, exerting their weight and non-weight upon the sail's power sector. And the total force regains its pulling power—64 more pounds of sail power, driving the boat 3 tenths of a knot faster, even with the apparent wind still at 8 knots. (The apparent wind shifts 2 degrees farther from the true wind, but with no change in force.) The boat gains as much speed turning these 7 degrees as it had gained turning the entire 45 degrees before. Now you sail it at 4.1 knots, 38 degrees below the beam reach—back at the downwind limit of the reaches.

Now begin sailing up through the reaches. Begin sheeting in where before you stopped sheeting out; keep the sail adjusted once again to its one place in the apparent wind; keep the apparent wind axis and the total force axis fixed at the dogleg angle, and turn the boat beneath. You steer clear of the wind chasm—as you must now—and you bring the boat out of its alignment with the total force. You reopen the angle between boat and force, deliberately turning the boat awry to the direction the force pulls it. The boat turns to windward. The apparent wind shifts farther from the true wind. And the total force, at the dogleg angle to the apparent wind, pivots to leeward. So it goes. The force, again exerted obliquely upon the boat and against the water, becomes resolved once again into its forward and sideways components. The forward component emerges logically enough and drives the boat. It is the driving force again. The sideways component simply materializes out of nothing, the first vestige abruptly resurrected where the last vestige had been vectored out of existence. It begins to press, lending its first element of support. You lean tentatively toward it, testing for the feel and balance. You begin to hold the boat steady in the waves.

Then keep steering toward the apparent wind and now away from the line of total force—where on the way to leeward you had steered away from the wind and toward the line of total force. The wind and the force both grow stronger: the wind as the boat drives nearer to it, the force as the boat turns farther from it. The angle just reopened between boat and force now widens by degrees; the force begins to pull against the way the boat turns. The total force becomes a greater force at a less potent angle, gradually pulling more sideways to make the boat go forward. And for now the force has the advantage over the angle. The force gathers mightily while the angle is still small; the force drives more impetus into its forward component than the angle deflects aside. It gains more than the angle loses. So the boat goes faster as you steer to windward—being driven harder in the overall resolution of losses and gains. For now it goes faster, and the wind and force grows still stronger. And the angle keeps opening wider as the boat turns. Inexorably wider.

The sideways component, the pressing force, is less obtrusive, still the far smaller component but now the more certain one. It gains steadily from now on; it increases with both force and angle, pressing harder as the force gathers and harder still as the angle widens. It just keeps gaining for as long as you sail to windward. Inexorably.

Steer 11 more degrees upwind, to the heading 27 degrees to leeward—to the other beam reach, the one squarely across the apparent wind: the beam reach that is more tangible but less definitive than the acknowledged one across the true wind. The apparent wind strengthens by another knot and shifts another 4 degrees as the boat turns, and now the wind, aligned exactly upon the beam, comes into the sail at 9 knots. And the total force goes out at 324 pounds pulling 75 degrees forward: 68 pounds stronger but now 15 degrees askew to the boat; the angle opens this much. So the force gains, the angle loses; and the losses and gains are weighed and balanced and manifested in the two components. The forward component gains 60 pounds; it is now 316 pounds driving the boat. The sideways component gains its first 72 pounds and begins to press upon the boat. And the boat holds steady in the waves and goes 4 tenths of a knot faster: the first margin of gain over loss.

You sail at 4.5 knots, half a knot less than maximum speed.

Then steer 12 degrees higher. You turn the boat this far up and into the apparent wind; with the turn the apparent wind becomes a headwind, this far ahead of the beam. The apparent wind itself does not shift appreciably this time—just because of the ways it is determined—but it gains another knot as the boat turns another 12 degrees nearer to it. And the total force gains another 76 pounds as the boat turns 12 degrees farther from it. The angle between boat and force widens this much; this much advantage is lost. With losses and gains resolved, the forward component strengthens 42 pounds more with the force than it weakens with the angle. The sideways component presses 102 pounds harder with both. The boat drives 3 tenths of a knot faster and tries to heel. You hold it down, beginning to shift your weight back toward the windward rail. You are 15 degrees from the beam reach; the true wind is this far aft.

Then 10 degrees still higher: 5 degrees short of the beam reach. The apparent wind gains another 8 tenths of a knot, the total force another 67 pounds, and the angle opens 10 degrees wider. Losses and gains are resolved. The forward component gains 24 more pounds than it loses; it keeps driving the boat ahead. The sideways component gains 108 pounds and just presses harder. The boat sails almost 2 tenths of a knot faster—just a scant few hundredths less. You are nearer to the edge, keeping the balance.

And then steer the last 5 degrees back to the beam reach: the real one, squarely across the true wind. The apparent wind gains 4 tenths of a knot; it is now 11.2 knots, 27 degrees forward. The total sail force gains 33 pounds; it is now 500 pounds, 48 degrees forward. And the angle between boat and force opens 5 degrees wider; the boat now sails 42 degrees askew to the force that powers it; this much advantage is lost. So set the gains against the losses; resolve them all in the two components. And the forward component is now 375 pounds; it drives the boat ahead with 3 more pounds of impetus, and with this it becomes maximum driving force. The sideways component is 330 pounds. It presses 48 pounds harder, and you begin to lean a little more seriously against it. You are almost on the rail now, holding the boat down, keeping the sail still 5 degrees tighter than trim. And you go just a scant few hundredths of a knot faster—the last margin of gain over loss. You sail at 5 knots: maximum speed.

You remember this. You started like this: sailing the boat at its very best, with all the lines and angles in their optimum arrangement. Now you are back to this, and it still is the best. You hold the balance. You have forces directed and working, the boat driving strongly ahead, completely attuned; it is powerful. You bring it back to this, trading losses and gains, picking up increments by tenths of knots. Now you are at the place where loss and gain intersect mathematically. You have all the increments here. You gain them when you steer to here. And now you must lose them when you steer on from here.

You do this last. You steer again to windward, and now you go above the beam reach and sail upwind, into the sector of close reaches. From now on you sail with both true and apparent winds forward of the beam; you deliberately turn the boat against both winds, against all the winds it sails by. You pull in the sail and gather the forces, however oblique; now you are out on the edge, sailing the boat flat and driving it against the angles, however obliquely. And you go for the limit, and then for the end. You know the end has to be there to windward; it is the final reality—the purely physical place where you can't sail farther because you can't actually sail the boat in violation of the wind it sails by. But you mean to go a long way upwind before you come to such an end. It is going to be at least a very distant place.

Then turn very slightly against the wind, just a degree at the start to be sure the boat really is going to do this. It should keep sailing almost as if nothing had changed. (If it doesn't, if it falters, stalls, or sails crabwise, it is a very bad boat, and you must abandon it. It has to be a rare and most

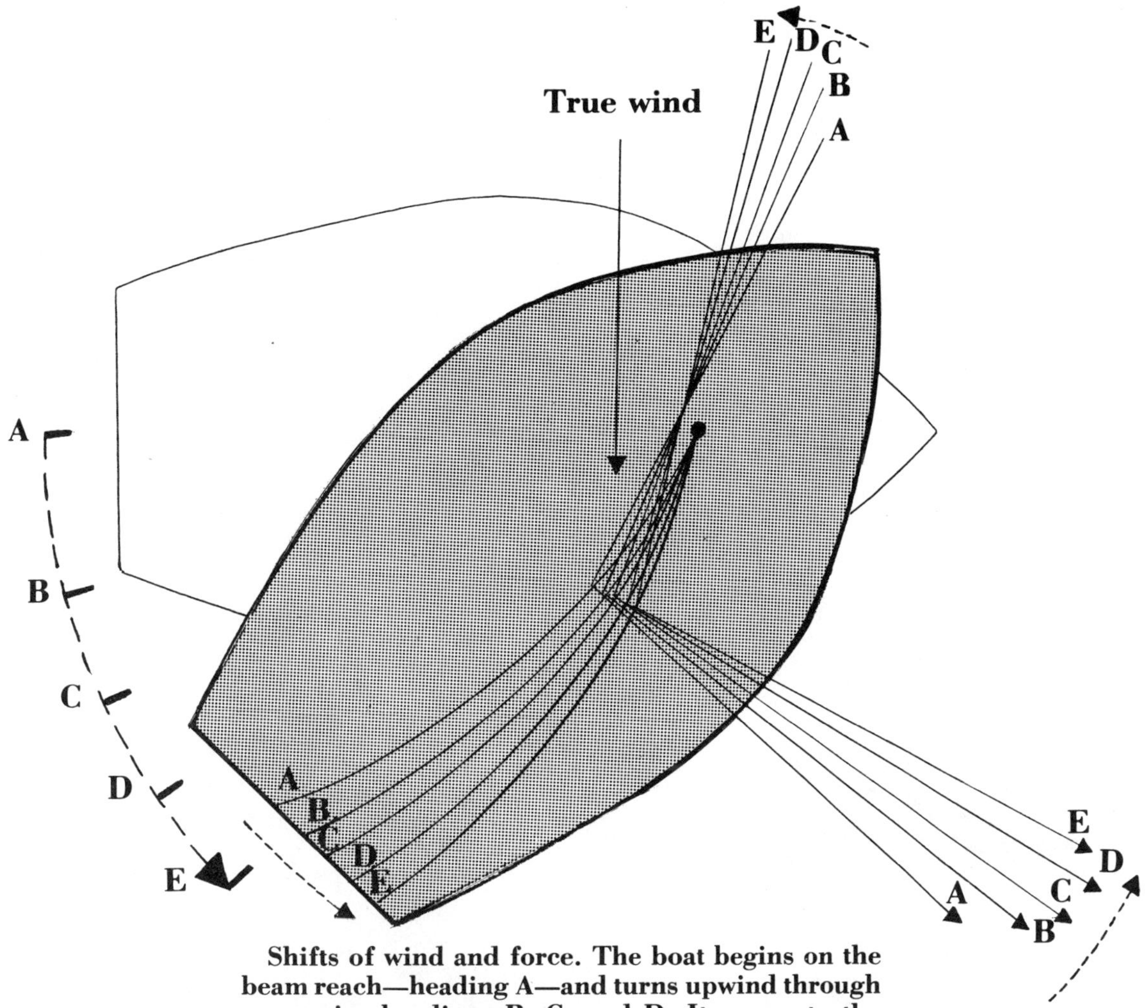

Shifts of wind and force. The boat begins on the beam reach—heading A—and turns upwind through successive headings B, C, and D. It comes to the windward limit at heading E, sailing 45 degrees into the wind. As the boat is turning, the apparent wind is shifting; at each successive heading the wind is resolved on a new axis and is blowing with a different strength. The total sail force, holding at the dogleg angle to the apparent wind, similarly shifts to new angles and pulls with different strengths. For each heading, the sail is adjusted to a different setting to hold 5 degrees tighter than trim. ***Drawing by Lana Cory Hall***

uncommonly bad kind of boat—typically a treacherous toy hacked out of plastic packing foam and sold for box tops—a dangerous boat in any case just for its being unable to go above the beam reach. Destroy it. Don't ever let it sail again. It is that bad). A good boat actually attains its most resourceful state when it sails against the wind. It works harder, even as it begins to lose speed—now losing more against the angles than it gains with the forces, but still rising to the challenge, feeling stronger than ever. Your boat is like this, a good boat now beginning to sail at its very best upwind. You know just by feel: it will keep going for as long as the sail can hold the wind.

Then on:

—5 degrees windward; true wind 5 degrees forward. Apparent wind is 11.5 knots, 30 degrees forward. Total sail force is 529 pounds, 45 degrees for-

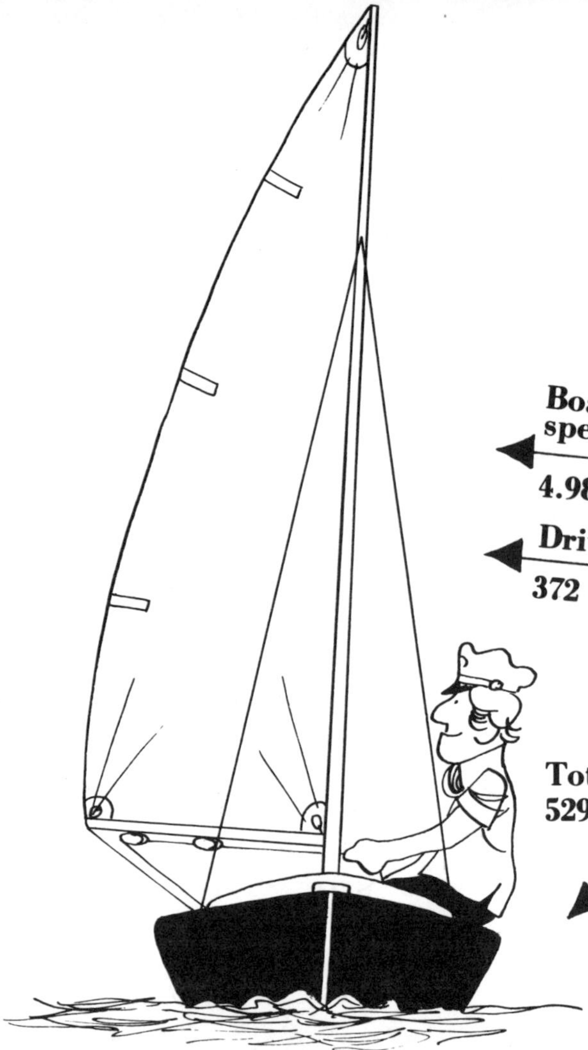

As the boat sails 5 degrees to windward, the sideways component can be felt pressing harder. It has been the lesser of the two components; now it is going to be the greater. ***Drawing by Don Raden***

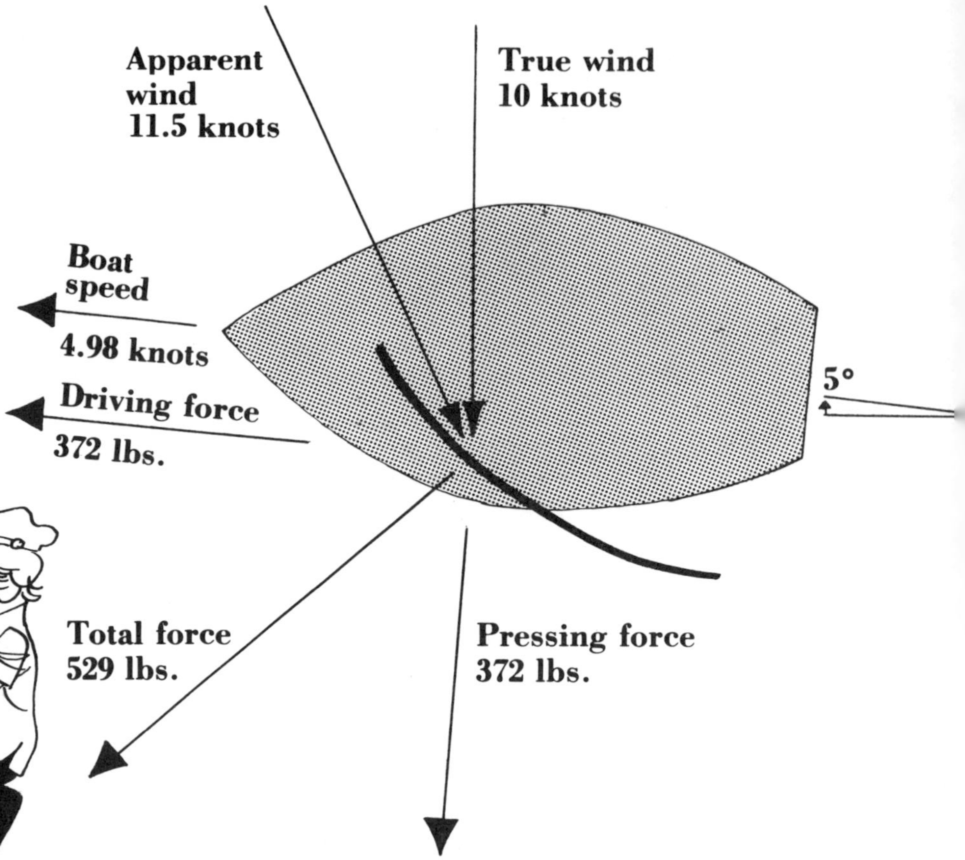

Five degrees windward. ***Drawing by Lana Cory Hall***

ward. Forward component force is 372 pounds. Sideways component force is 372 pounds. Speed is slightly less than 5 knots.

You gain and lose. The apparent wind is 7 tenths of a knot stronger than on the beam reach, and the total force pulls 29 pounds harder. The apparent wind begins to move once again, veering the first 2 degrees back toward the true wind—where it must go after this, because of the ways it is determined. So the apparent wind axis shifts 2 degrees aft on the boat's windward side, and the total force axis, at the dogleg angle, pivots 2 degrees forward on the boat's lee side: a 2-degree gain. But the angle still widens 3 degrees between where the boat goes and where the total force pulls—opening 5 degrees with the turn of the boat and closing 2 degrees with the shift of wind and force—so now the angle between boat and force is exactly 45 degrees. And the total force, 29 pounds stronger than at maximum speed, pulls exactly half ahead and half abeam upon the boat; but now it pulls 3 degrees farther sideways to make the boat go forward. The pounds are gained; the degrees are lost; the components are resolved forward and sideways, and the line of total force becomes the mid-diagonal between them. Now the components measure the same: 372 pounds driving forward, 372 pounds pressing sideways, and the forward component is 3 pounds weaker than the 375 pounds that drove the boat at maximum speed. The boat now slows a scant few hundredths of a knot—the same scant few hundredths it slowed earlier, turning the first 5 degrees to leeward. This is the first margin of loss over gain, sailing above the beam reach, against the angles.

The sideways component gains 42 pounds. You feel it; it is quietly unrelenting. After this you become very serious about it. It has been the lesser of the two components; now it is going to be the greater. It is going to be immensely greater than any forward component ever could. It is going to gain steadily while the forward component loses; it

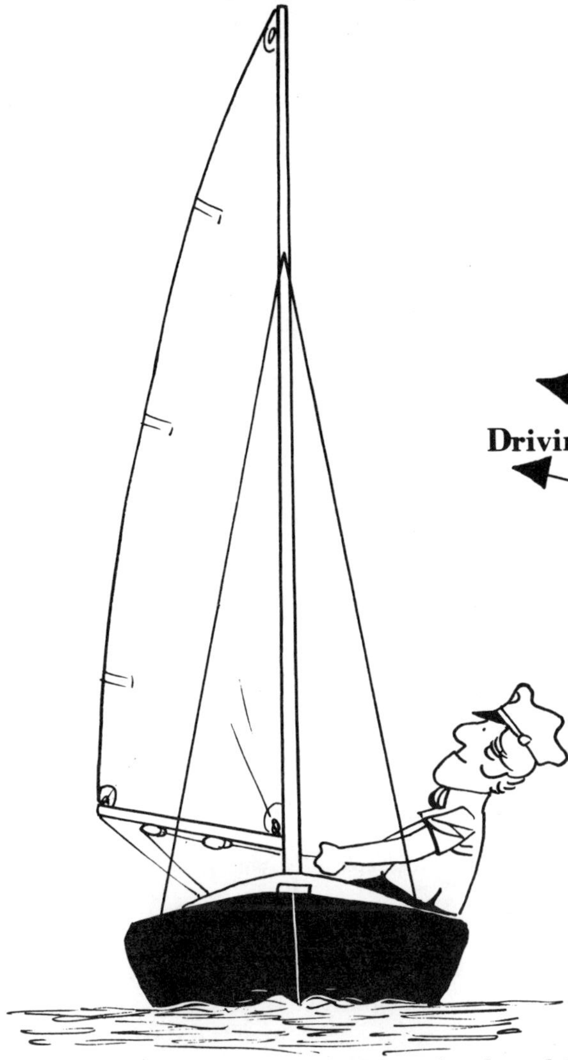

Sailing 15 degrees to windward, the skipper begins to lean against sideways forces—not leaning hard yet, just applying steady leverage. *Drawing by Don Raden*

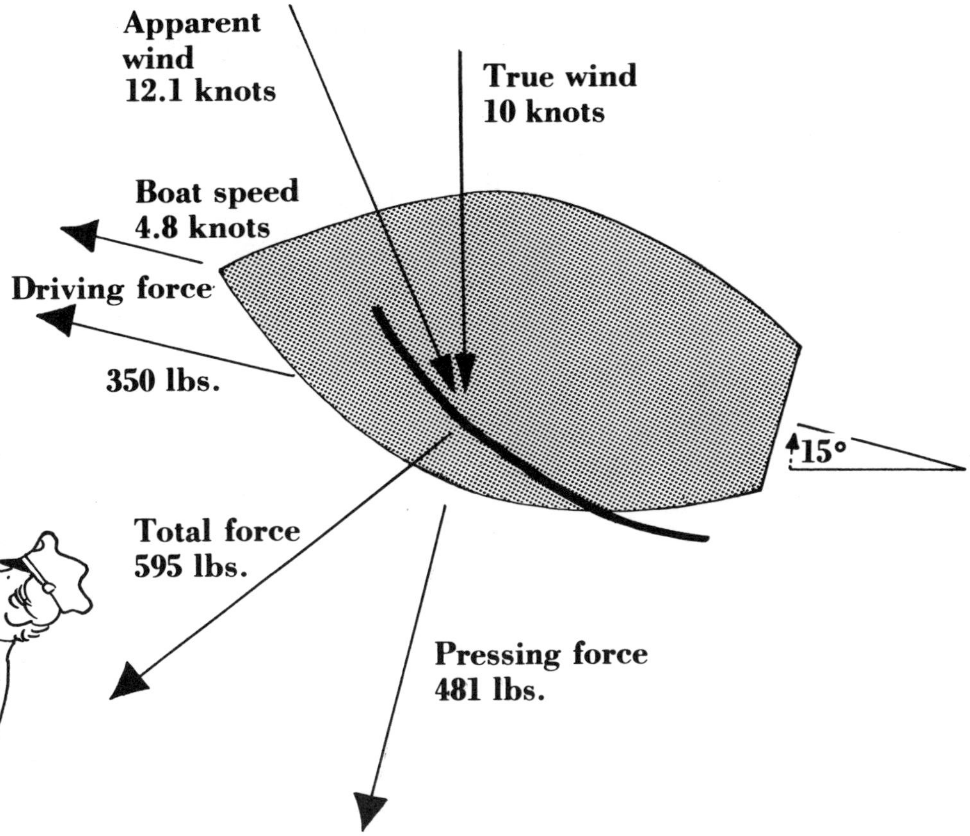

Fifteen degrees windward. *Drawing by Lana Cory Hall*

is going to press with a weight that increases far beyond even the full impetus of maximum driving force. Because the sideways component is going to keep growing and gaining with both forces and angles: growing as the total force does, with the square of the apparent wind speed; and gaining inexorably as the total force pulls more abeam than ahead. You are coming to a confrontation with the sideways component. From now on you are going to learn just how good you and your boat really are, to keep sailing forward under its weight.

Then lean harder against the heeling force. And steer higher:

—15 degrees windward; true wind 15 degrees forward. Apparent wind is 12.1 knots, 38 degrees forward. Total force is 595 pounds, 37 degrees forward. Forward component is 350 pounds. Sideways component is 481 pounds. Speed is 4.8 knots.

The apparent wind gains 6 tenths of a knot and shifts 3 degrees aft. The total force gains 66 pounds and shifts 3 degrees forward. And the boat turns 10 degrees upwind. The angle between boat and force closes 3 degrees with the shifts but opens 10 degrees with the turn: so now it is 7 degrees wider, and the total force, 66 pounds stronger, pulls this much less forward and this much more sideways. The forward component loses 33 pounds and drives the boat 2 tenths of a knot slower: the first increment gone. And the sideways component gains 109 pounds and heels the boat under its sheer weight: 481 pounds on this heading. The sideways force simply keeps pressing, and you lean back against it—not leaning hard yet, not in this kind of wind—just applying steady leverage. You bring the boat down from its heel; it comes easily. You level the deck and hold the balance, and the boat drives forward.

You sail at 4.8 knots, close reaching, 15 degrees to windward. When you last sailed at 4.8 knots, you were broad reaching, 15 degrees to leeward. The sideways component pressed less than half as hard then as it presses now. You simply reclined on it

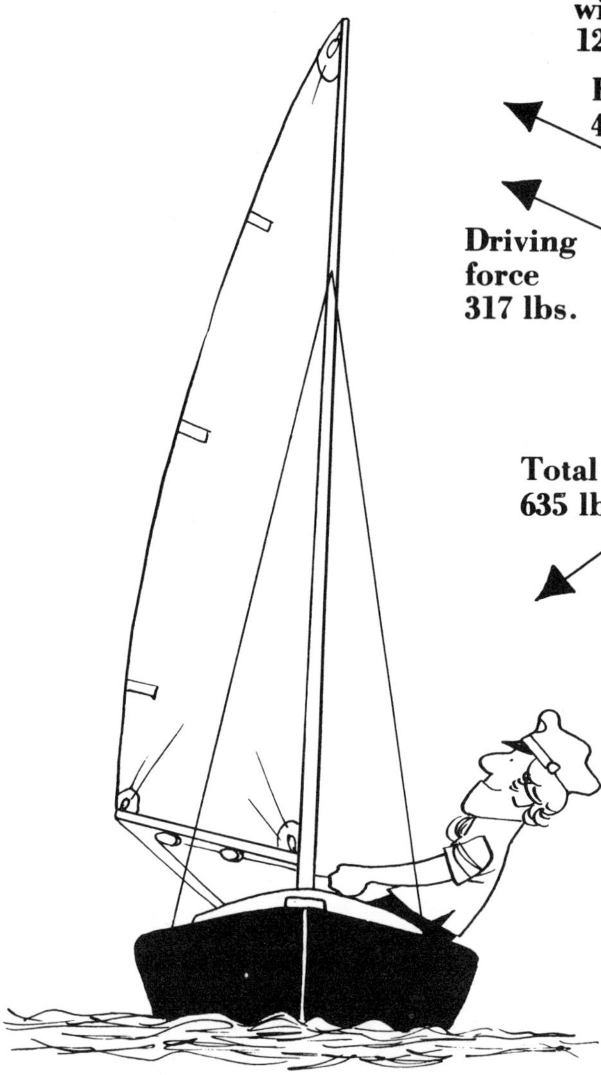

With the boat sailing 25 degrees to windward, the skipper begins to hike over the side, leaning a little harder against pressing forces. *Drawing by Don Raden*

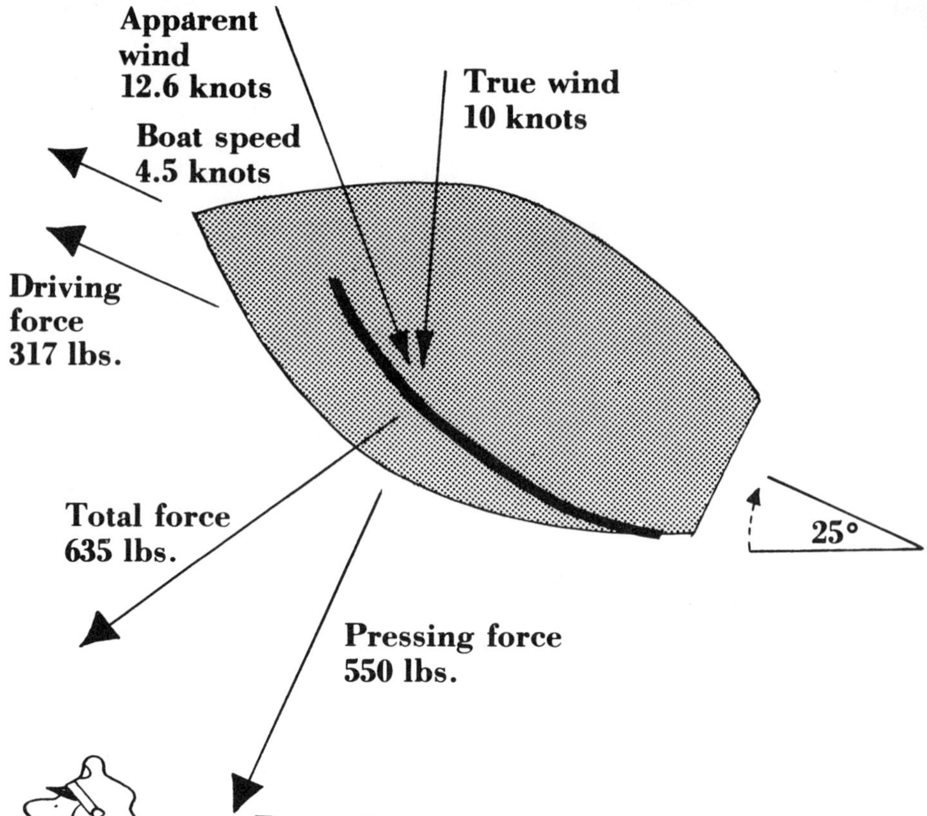

Twenty-five degrees windward. *Drawing by Lana Cory Hall*

and rode along with it while the forward component drove the boat. Now you work more than twice as hard sailing the boat above the beam reach as you then worked sailing below it, and the boat goes the same speed here that it did there. You lose and gain.

For this moment the apparent wind comes into the sail at very nearly the same angle that the total force goes out. The boat is halfway between the two axes, bisecting the dogleg angle. So the geometry progresses.

Then on:

—25 degrees windward; true wind 25 degrees forward. Apparent wind is 12.6 knots, 45 degrees forward. Total force is 635 pounds, 30 degrees forward. Forward component is 317 pounds. Sideways component is 550 pounds. Speed is 4.5 knots.

The phenomenon continues. The apparent wind gains half a knot and shifts 3 degrees as the boat turns 10. The total force gains 40 pounds and shifts 3 degrees. The angle between boat and force widens another 7 degrees. The forward component loses 33 pounds. The sideways component gains 69. You begin to hike over the side, leaning a little harder against the pressing force, and the boat drives upwind 3 tenths of a knot slower.

The apparent wind, 45 degrees forward, is now on its mid-diagonal—half ahead, half abeam; you go half across it, half against it. You came this far sailing more across than against, and you must go on sailing more against than across. But right here you are halfway to sailing dead into the apparent wind, and you keep steering diligently toward it, knowing you aren't going to get through the other half.

And on:

—35 degrees windward; true wind 35 degrees forward. Apparent wind is 13 knots, 51 degrees forward. Total force is 676 pounds, 24 degrees forward. Forward component is 275 pounds. Sideways component is 622 pounds. Speed is 4.2 knots.

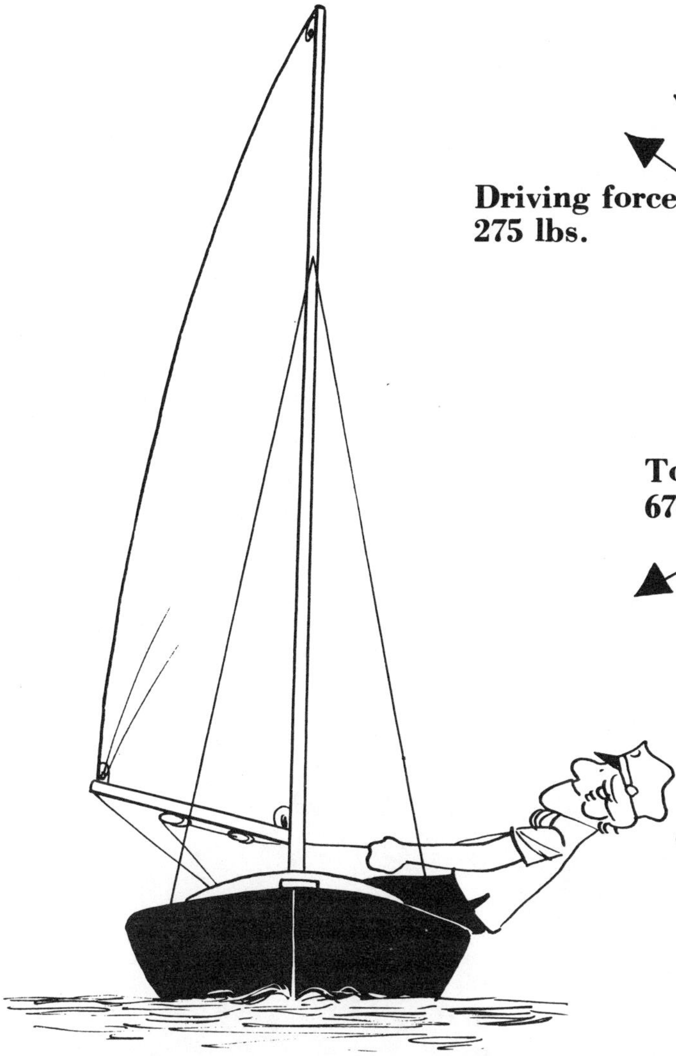

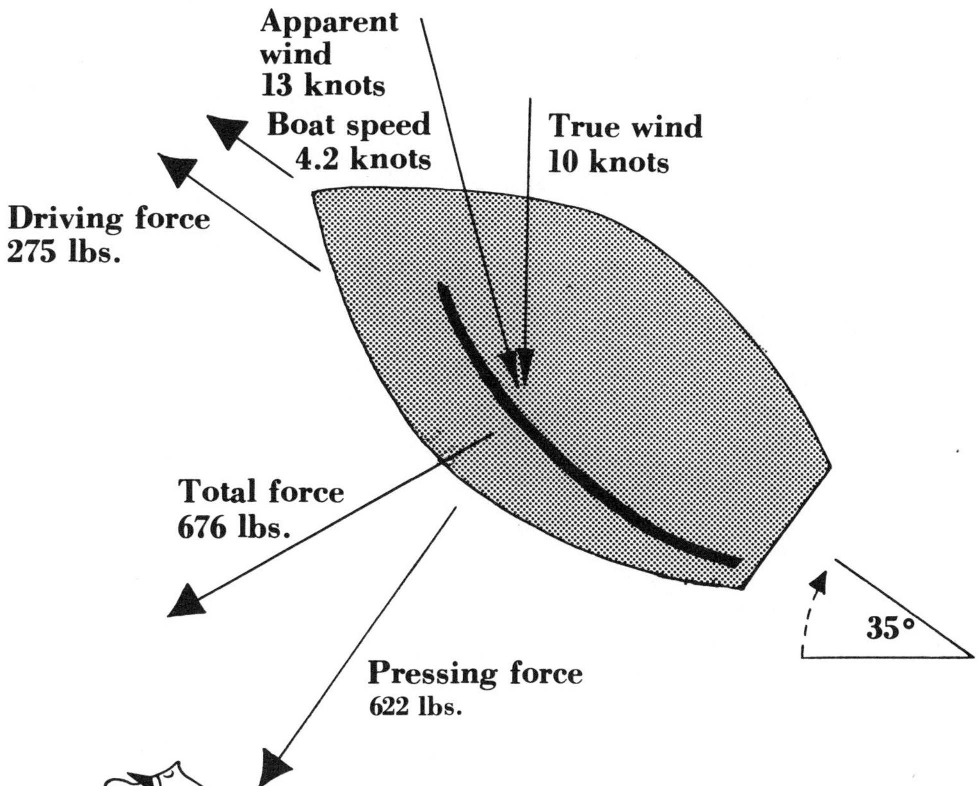

Thirty-five degrees windward. ***Drawing by Lana Cory Hall***

Sailing 35 degrees to windward, the skipper hikes beyond the edge, applying more insistent leverage to keep the boat sailing flat. ***Drawing by Don Raden***

The boat turns. The wind shifts. The force gains. The angle widens. And you slow 3 tenths of a knot. Another increment is gone: the logic is inevitable. You lose what speed you must, and you strive to maintain the speed you still have. You pull harder on the sheet, keeping the sail trimmed and working. You trim incessantly now: trimming becomes the most critical thing. You keep the curve constantly true and rigid, always at the precise setting: the sail 5 degrees tighter than trim in the apparent wind, the two axes fixed at the dogleg angle. Now especially you need the turn of the wind on the curve; you need every possible force you still can get from it—every last ounce and fraction that still can push the boat, or pull it, or in some way drive it against this same wind. You can't ever afford to squander forces when you sail upwind in a fair wind.

So you do everything right. You apply a tight grip on the sheet; you keep the sail finely adjusted, 5 degrees tighter than trim in the 13 knots of apparent wind, 51 degrees forward. And you generate 676 pounds of total sail force pulling 24 degrees forward and 66 degrees sideways—still pulling both ways as it must, but now 42 degrees more abeam than ahead—and so you have the best force at the worst angle so far exerted upon the machinery of the boat. The forward component, at 275 pounds, still drives the boat, which is essential. But the sideways component, at 622 pounds, is fully upon you for the confrontation. It generates 9 pounds sideways for every 4 pounds forward: It is 247 pounds more than the greatest driving force, which drove the boat at maximum speed. And now it presses with all its real and considerable weight upon the boat. The boat leans. You lean back. You are hiking out beyond the edge now, applying a more insistent leverage. You bring the boat down, but it comes more grudgingly this time. It is work-

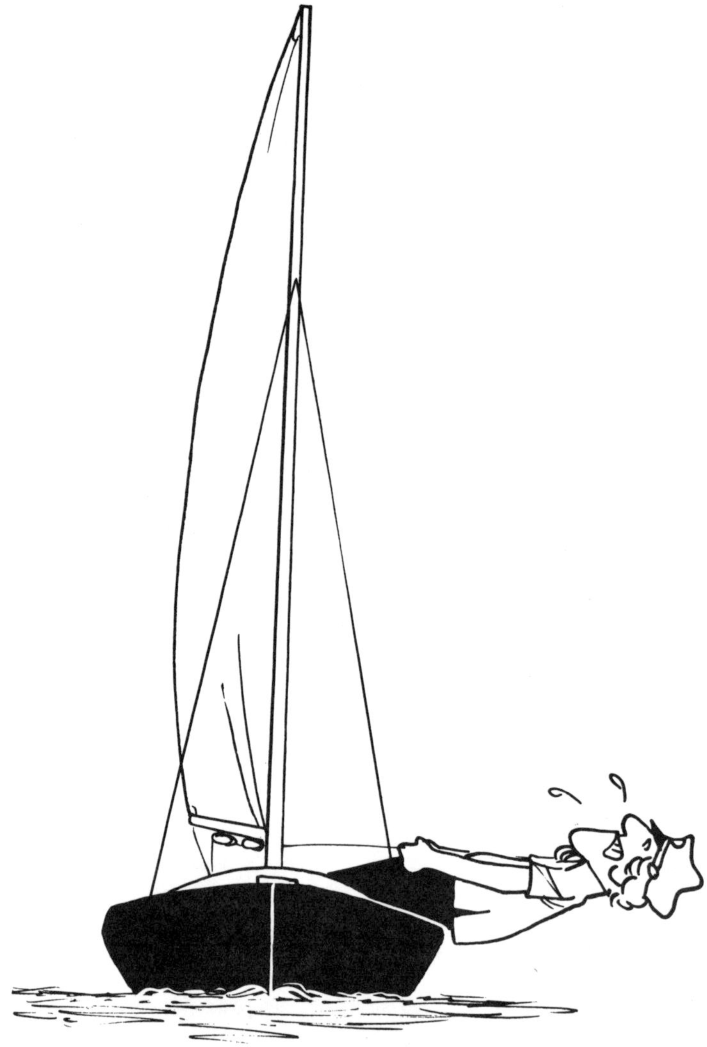

When the wind blows twice as hard and the boat sails 35 degrees to windward, the skipper hikes to the last extreme, holding nearly horizontal above water—just to keep the boat sailing flat. *Drawing by Don Raden*

ing doggedly, still driving ahead, though more heavily burdened.

(Here, once again, you need a larger understanding before you really can know what is happening. You have to experience all this—momentarily, if arbitrarily—in perhaps twice as much wind, with the sideways force grown to a truly awesome weight pressing upon the boat. With twice as much wind, the boat heels precipitously to leeward, and you hike with your very soul to windward. You hook your toes under a thwart or under the hiking straps, and you stretch your body to its last extreme, extending two-thirds of yourself out beyond the weather rail. You become a radical cantilever, holding nearly horizontal above nothing but water, taking all the strain in your stomach muscles; you call this gut sailing. You keep the boat level if you are strong enough, or heavy enough, or, in the final excesses, just determined enough to withstand the pain. Otherwise you do better to let the boat heel and sacrifice a measure of force and speed—which in fact is far more sensible; you find that a slight degree of heel relieves a significant degree of suffering. Here in any case you come to the real confrontation with the sideways component. You don't pretend to dismiss it after this: you are pitted directly against the pressing force, wholly committed to holding it back so that some driving force—whatever elements you still can get from the total force—still can make the boat go forward.)

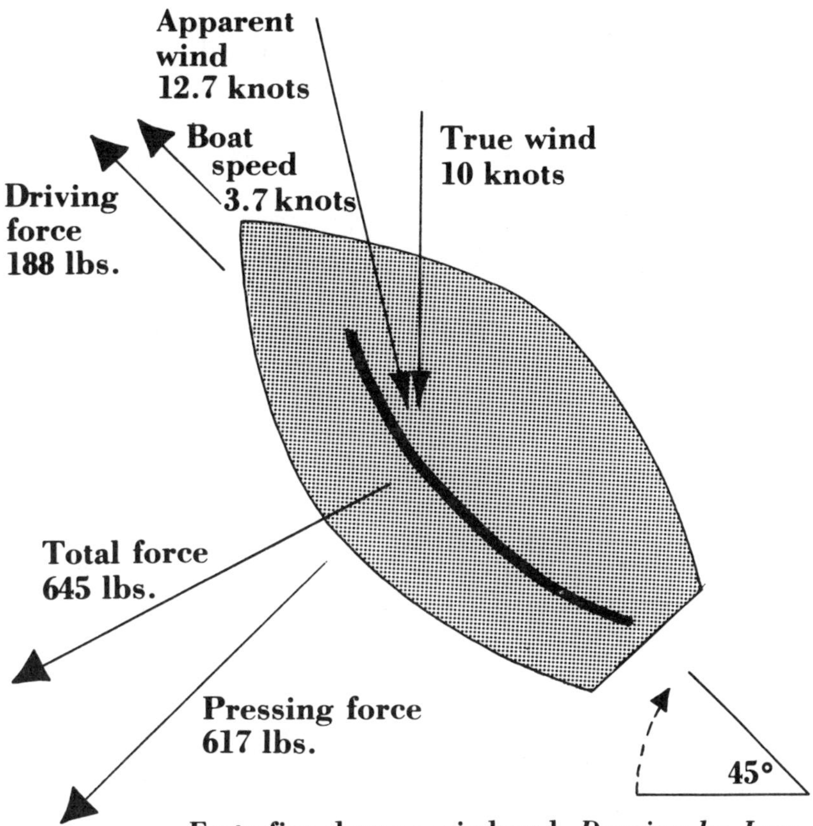

Forty-five degrees windward. *Drawing by Lana Cory Hall*

Then you know, within limits, that you are going to be essentially equal to the sideways pressing force. It need not overpower you so long as the wind is less than gale force. You and the marine architects will see to that.

You find yourself sailing resolutely up through the close reaches. You look squarely into the weather and steer the boat at it—against the waves, through the spray, shipping water. You get wet. You begin to ache. But you realize that this is real sailing. It is harder than any other kind of sailing, but you need it more; you are better for it. You were a dilettante on the broad reaches, a mystic running before the wind. Until you came upwind, you were an innocent. Now you are sure and steadfast. You have had your confrontation. You have paid your dues.

On:

—45 degrees windward; true wind 45 degrees forward. Apparent wind is 12.7 knots, 58 degrees forward. Total sail force is 645 pounds, 18 degrees forward. Forward component is 188 pounds. Sideways component is 617 pounds. Speed is 3.7 knots.

You come to the limit: the upwind limit of the reaches. This is as far as you can go with the sail 5 degrees tighter than trim. The true wind is now on the mid-diagonal, half ahead, half abeam; and you sail equally across and against it. The apparent wind is forward to the point where you sail 8 feet against it for every 5 feet across. And now you are about to stop sailing altogether.

Make the limit definitive here, a limit of convenience on the mid-diagonal, even though it probably is conservative for good boats. Good boats should turn past here and stop somewhere beyond; your boat will go readily past. But no boat will go much farther than this. Even for good boats, this is the beginning of the end.

You pull in the last inch of the sheet as you reach the last degree upwind to here. The apparent wind shifts again; the wind slackens even as the boat turns against it—just because of the ways it is determined: because the boat finally slows this much with so many forces pressing sideways and so few driving forward, and the parallelogram slants past a critical angle, and the boat slows still more, and the apparent wind slackens still more. The boat slows half a knot, with all things eventually resolved, and the apparent wind slackens by 3 tenths of a knot, and the total force weakens by 31 pounds. The forward component loses 87 pounds as the weakened force pulls farther sideways. (It pulls 7 degrees farther sideways: The force shifts 3 degrees; the boat turns 10.) The sideways component loses as the force weakens and gains as the force pulls sideways—and lightens 5 pounds between loss and gain. Even the unrelenting pressing force must lose now, in this final turn of the phenomenon. This is how the end comes.

Then you are close-hauled. You have brought the sail all the way in. If you pulled it still tighter you would only flatten the curve, and then nothing would work. You would kill the whole phenomenon. So you restrain the final tension just enough to hold the curve, but otherwise you pull the sheet hard against the spars and stays and even the chain plates themselves. Steer to windward from here, and the sail must turn with the boat. There is no more room to adjust the sail to its one position in the apparent wind while the boat turns beneath. Boat and sail go together from here—and die together in the next 5 degrees.

The boat does keep sailing up through these extra 5 degrees, if only as an aftereffect, just beyond the limit; it still may be reaching in a very technical sense, though you do better to consider it to be pinching now. The sail comes finally out of its most functional state, 5 degrees tighter than trim, and into the pragmaticaly imperfect state of trimness itself—the pure physical phenomenon tangled in the boat's structural machinery—this just before the very end. You steer higher and abruptly lose power, turning the sail more into the wind and less across it. The curve comes uncramped. The outer wind current—the fitful current—bends after a fashion around the full convex surface, and the air flows across the curve's after parts. But now forces that had been concentrated forward are dissipated aft, out of the power sector. And the pulling force weakens precipitously; the extra lurch is lost; the total force weakens by as much as a quarter in this turn of 5 degrees. So the speed drops; the apparent wind slackens with more impetus lost; the angle widens between boat and force. The boat suddenly is a feeble thing, trying to pinch against wind and waves with just a vestige of its old driving force, and it can't go upwind on a vestige like it went downwind: everything is against it this time. It heaves spasmodically, only theoretically better than mere flotsam. Now it comes to this.

But it still moves. It slides down one wave and into the next. It can't push through, as it once would have; it is almost pushed back, but something holds it, and it rises up unsteadily, and the wave rolls beneath. It falters nearly powerless at the next wave but gets past; it somehow goes over the next. The boat has grave doubts at each succeeding wave, but it keeps going. It no longer has any real speed; it is doing well enough just to maintain headway—pinching upwind, right to the end. It is not about to die until the very end itself.

You almost never try to push the boat this far: it sustains such an appalling loss to gain the extra 5 degrees, and even that gain is effectively wiped out by the waves pushing back. But the boat is still a very good one just to come here. Its final measure is the way it sails at the end, close hauled and pinching—coming back, as it always must, from the broad reaches and runs. (Those hyperdynamic catamarans can't do nearly as well: Most of them can't—except for a few machines of such advanced design and such extraordinary tolerances, tuned to such critical pitches that they can work only for a few precocious technicians. The small, typical catamarans usually fail long before for lack of substance, often becoming grotesquely inept outside their narrow element on the broad reaches; they come crabbing and muddling wretchedly back to windward, as if this were some ignominious atonement for their phenomenal speeds to leeward.) Your boat, presumed to be a good boat, just keeps making its way, indefatigably and quite incredibly. It sails 50 degrees into the true wind, and even this is conservative; any number of boats will go farther. But you have to bring yours at least to here, just to know that it can do it.

Then you steer even higher upwind, and you want to pull the sheet still more, but you know you can't. And so you come to the end.

The sail softens. It quivers next to the mast. The curve slowly collapses. The boat bobs up on one more wave, hesitates on the crest, shuddering, all its lines going slack. It comes erect, rising uncertainly from its angle of heel. And it slides into an awful descent, still shuddering, sinking into the trough between this wave and the next. It pushes with fading forces into the next wave, but its impact is gone; it halts again. But the wave gets under the

The end. ***Drawing by Don Raden***

boat and shoulders it past; and the boat moves once more with just half a curve still hovering in the after parts of the sail. It half lurches, half sails over the wave just beyond. And then with the curve gone altogether, the boat somehow musters up one last spasm of its old momentum and climbs past one last wave. Then it stops. It is done. It lies adrift, rocking in the waves. The sail flaps. The forces are blown away.

It dies hard. It is a good boat.

9
The Polar Diagram

You come to the end, as you expected, against the ultimate physical reality that, having done all the rest, you still can't sail against the wind you sail by. Not really: not directly. You just wonder for a while if you might, and you aren't surprised when you don't. At the end you still sail only obliquely against the wind: no better. At best you extract only a momentary if meaningful compromise from it. You go every place where the sail can hold the wind, and you stop only when you come to the place where it can't.

Theoretically you would have gone perhaps another 12 degrees upwind and stopped only at an absolute mathematical end, where the total force would have pulled dead abeam and merged into its own sideways component—and the forward component would have been vectored out of existence, and nothing would have remained to drive the boat. Everything would have frozen in place: the wind and water deadlocked against each other, the boat paralyzed in a seizure of absolute mathematics. But the boat can't ever come to such an end because its machinery can't ever work as perfectly as the theory that would take it there. Even as a good boat, it still must be a practical boat with inevitable flaws and discrepancies—sags, slippages, misalignments, complexities—all minimal things, mostly microscopic in effect, but they gather one-by-one against this boat or any boat going to windward. And at the end, the practical end, they add up to a most ponderable amalgamation of imperfections, all aligned specifically against the boat's further progress. Altogether they become manifested as the 12 theoretical degrees where the practical boat can not sail—these 12 degrees measuring the difference between a good boat and the bounds of utter possibility.

So you cross out the 12 degrees beyond the end, where a real boat doesn't sail, and you shade the 5 degrees before the end, where a good boat does better not sailing. And then you draw your limit on the mid-diagonal, 45 degrees to windward. Sail to the limit, and you come 45 degrees above the beam reach, and the true wind axis, the first line of reference, remains still another 45 degrees upwind, unnavigable and inviolate. So you stop here, having failed to conquer the wind but having come close enough to take liberties with it. The wind compromises with you on everything except the last 45 degrees, and so it yields enough for you to sail the boat handily. But in the final accounting it still retains the better part of all this. It sets the limit, and you sail by it.

The limit, once established, is the same on port tack or starboard. The boat is symmetrical and sails by the same principles on both and turns toward the same axis on either. The distinction is solely which side of the axis it approaches—which way it turns toward this line it can't reach. On port tack it turns to port; the line lies off the port side. On starboard tack it turns to starboard; the line lies off the starboard side. On both tacks it stops 45 degrees short of the line; it leaves two sectors, each this wide, one on either side of the line. The two sectors together make a definitive quarter circle: a quadrant bisected geometrically by the wind axis. This quadrant is where the boat does not sail. It is the eye of the wind.

Then you see the full circle, and you take out this one-quarter segment where the boat doesn't sail, and you are left with a three-quarter segment where it does sail. Then your limits are defined.

Now reassemble the circle. Put the segments back together and fit a navigator's compass around them. You need the compass as a calibrated scale to measure upon; a clock face could do as well, but the compass is more traditional. The sail's center of effort becomes the center point of the compass. The boat becomes the compass needle, slightly offset from the center point but pivoting functionally if hypothetically upon it. Then the other things come in turn—winds, forces, lines, angles—all the factors beginning to show on the face of the compass, where you begin to see them together. This is where you get the full perspective.

Start with the true wind: still the same 10-knot true wind. Make it a north wind (arbitrarily once again; you retain your old license to be arbitrary)

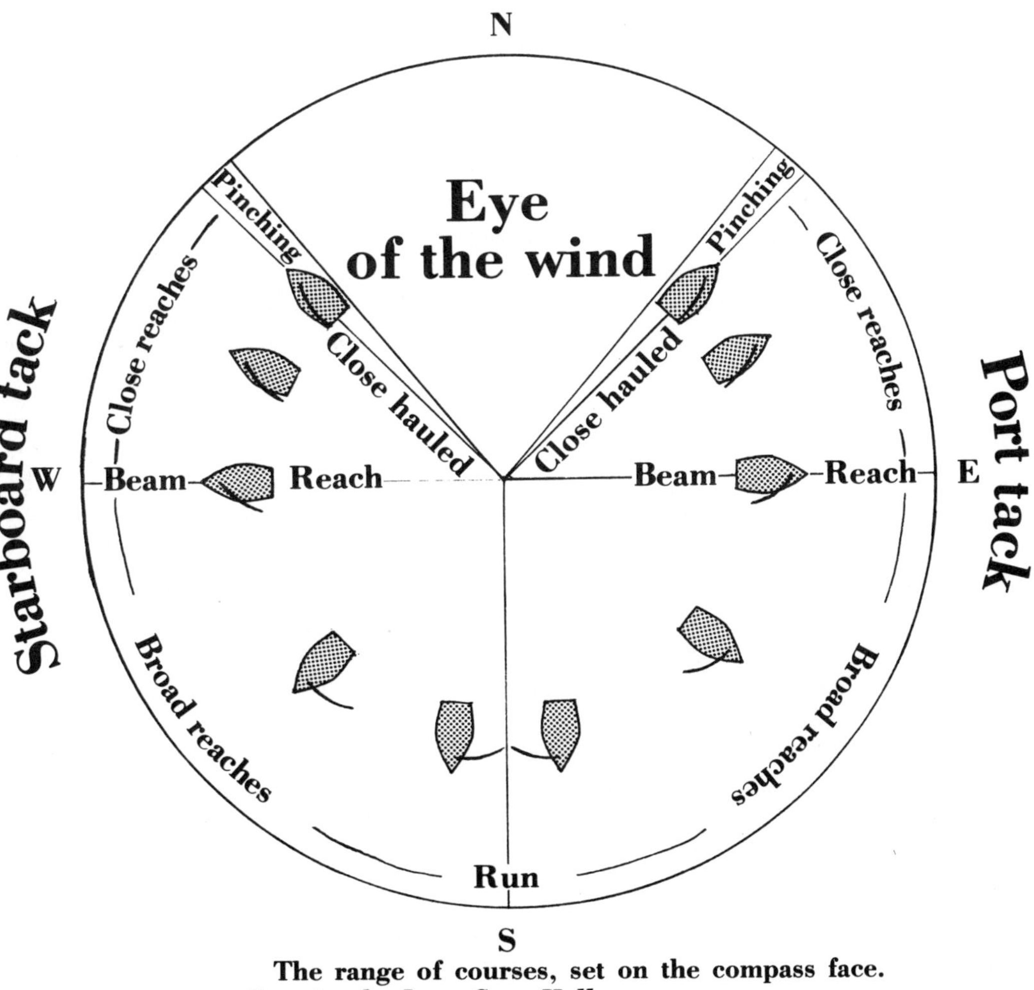

The range of courses, set on the compass face.
Drawing by Lana Cory Hall

for no reason except that it has to blow from somewhere, and it usually is allowed the most authority from the north. Run its axis due south, straight through the middle of the compass—one delineative line dividing the circle into eastern and western halves. On port tack, the boat sails into the eastern half; the needle points into the eastern half circle. On starboard tack, the boat sails into the western half; the needle points into the western half circle. On the axis itself, the boat runs due south, dead before the wind, sailing in neither half but on either tack. It runs on port tack when the sail hangs out over the starboard side and on starboard tack when the sail hangs out over the port side. The needle lies all the while on the line between half circles—though this is academic because the boat runs the same way before the wind, regardless of tack. There are no tacks of any sort for heading due north, up the wind axis. The boat doesn't sail up the wind axis.

Then draw a second line, equally delineative: this line going east and west through the middle of the compass, dividing the circle into northern and southern halves. The boat sails upwind, close reaching, into the northern half; the needle points upwind into the northern half circle. The boat sails downwind, broad reaching, into the southern half; the needle points downwind into the southern half circle. The boat sails on the beam reach on the line between half circles: on port tack going east and on starboard tack going west. On the line the boat goes in either direction, and the needle points either way.

Then the two lines meet at right angles at the center of the circle—the center of effort—and as each line singly halves the circle, the two lines together quarter it. Now there is the northeast quarter, where the boat sails to windward on port tack; the northwest quarter, where it sails to windward on starboard tack; the southeast quarter, where it sails to leeward on port tack; and the southwest quarter, where it sails to leeward on starboard tack. The boat sails all its courses within the permutations of the four quarters. Before deducting for the limits, this is everywhere the boat would go.

Then draw the limits, two radial lines 45 degrees to windward: one line northeast from the center, the other northwest. The northeast line divides the northeast quadrant into equal sectors—a lower sector measured from east to northeast, an upper sector from northeast to north—and the northwest line similarly makes equal sectors of the northwest quadrant. The entire northern half circle now becomes these four northerly sectors. The boat sails upwind through each of the lower sectors—on port tack and on starboard, each in turn. It comes reaching up 45 degrees to each of the two limit lines, and it sails there, close hauled, northeast on port tack, northwest on starboard. When it goes beyond either line, it turns past the limit and into the upper sector; and it slows abruptly, pinching through the extra 5 degrees. And then it stops at the end. North of here lie points to which the boat can't sail.

Then the two northernmost sectors—the two upper sectors, the wind axis between them—together make the quadrant that is the eye of the wind: the limit. The end is just inside the eye, 5 degrees within either edge. The eye of the wind becomes simply the short arc of the circle: 90 degrees between northeast and northwest. And the rest of the circle is the long arc, the long way around: 270 degrees between northeast and northwest. From the middle of the circle, the boat sails toward any point in the long arc and toward none in the short. The long arc is vastly greater: three quadrants of the horizon, as wide and free and open to the boat as any compromise with the wind will allow. But the short arc remains the fourth quadrant: the limit, uncompromised.

Now chart the courses—the headings, the speeds—all on the face of the compass. The courses are lines radiating outward at specific angles and scaled to specific speeds: the long lines are fast courses; the short lines are slow ones. The longest lines become the beam reach. Draw it due east from the center for port tack and then due west from the center for starboard tack; and measure it off each way at 5 knots for maximum speed. It looks like a single 10-knot line across the circle, but it really is the pair of 5-knot lines aligned end-to-end and balanced over the center point. It is the beginning of the symmetry in this.

The next course is the pair of lines drawn 5 degrees to leeward and scaled to a scant few hundredths less than 5 knots. These two lines also radiate outward from the center point: they balance upon it; they are symmetrical upon it—but they don't align on it. They radiate at their 5-degree downward rake and so meet at a very broad angle, rather like cat's whiskers. And each pair of lines thereafter meets at a slightly sharper angle. Away from the beam reach, all lines must meet at angles. The beam reach is the only alignment in all the courses the boat sails.

Then chart the rest of the courses. Draw balanced pairs of lines radiating outward: progressions of lines meeting at sharper angles; the lines growing shorter as the boat goes slower. You have been through this. The boat slows as it turns farther from the beam reach; it slows turning both above and below the line: upwind and downwind, north and south. And as it slows, it makes its pattern. The lines radiate at their significant intervals and shorten by their significant increments—the intervals being close though uneven (as you have seen them calculated), the increments small though varying: both being the inevitable causes and effects of factors shifting and changing. Each successive pair of lines must radiate farther from the beam reach: an interval past the pair before and an increment shorter. As the boat turns south, the lines radiate that way, and you measure the intervals and lop off the increments. Until you come to the dead run, and the last increment is gone: then the last two lines merge into a single abbreviated remnant of a line, the shortest line to leeward. You set this line dead upon the wind axis and scale it to 3.5 knots, the minimum speed downwind.

And as the boat turns north from the beam reach—upwind—the lines radiate that way, and you mark them at their intervals and trim away their increments. Until at the limit you draw the lines northeast and northwest: both lines hard against the eye of the wind, the two meeting at a right angle at the center point. You scale the lines to a speed of 3.7 knots, which would be minimum speed upwind, except the boat then goes past the limit and pinches the extra 5 degrees up to the very end. There you must draw the last pair of lines and scale them to about 2.5 knots: roughly half of the maximum speed. These are the shortest lines of all, though they only measure pinching speed, and you don't really count pinching speed; you don't actually notice it when you sail the boat. But here you come to pinching speed, and for what it is worth, it is the boat's minimum speed. It completes the symmetrical framework.

After this you fill in all the embellishments of the pattern: the progressions of curved sails and apparent winds and total forces and component forces. The sail in its different settings becomes a series of precise little curls attached like the tails of commas to the ends of the lines you have charted. The apparent wind is refined down to a series of specific little axis lines attached like sharp accents to the little curls. For each course the boat sails, port tack and starboard, a little axis line is set at a particular angle and scaled to a particular wind strength and so fixed in position with a specific little curl. You draw all of this: the full range of winds, forces, lines, angles; all of them fitting into the pattern on the face of the compass. You see everything the boat has done, everywhere it has gone.

Then at the very last you draw the line tying the whole phenomenon together—a single line linking the end points of the charted courses, tracing the outline of the entire pattern; you draw it like a child draws a picture connecting the dots. And you see a shape materializing: an ovoid of sorts, like the profile of a fat football. But the upper side of the ovoid precipitously collapses into a deep *V*-gash, as if the football just then had been fearfully wounded. And the underside shows two slight distortions: two small but distinct soft spots, as if the football were deflating rapidly. This shape emerges. It is a meaningful shape when complete, not complicated but curious, an interesting shape like an ink blot, to conjure up images. If you see it first as a distressed football, then you might watch it evolve into a bat or butterfly with wings outspread, then perhaps into the overstuffed cheeks of a chipmunk, or possibly into a mashed valentine. It can work even as an abstractly erotic shape, if you remember it better that way. But this shape is definitive by any image. It is the form of the whole pattern, the overall gauge of the speed of the boat. It spreads widest on the beam reach to chart the boat at maximum speed there; then it narrows both windward and leeward, bending nearer to the center of the circle to chart the boat at all lesser speeds. To leeward the shape distorts slightly on the broad reaches—at the two soft spots on the underside—where the sail goes into full stall, and the boat abruptly loses an increment of speed. And to windward the shape descends suddenly and momentously into the deep *V*—the boat pinching and slowing, the sinuous line sinking like a spent shell into a radical downward trajectory—and there it marks the course where the boat stops sailing. This deep *V* is not the eye of the wind; it is the end within the eye. The eye is 5 degrees wider on either side, the full quadrant marking the practical limit. This *V* is where the boat finally comes, having passed that limit and pinched still

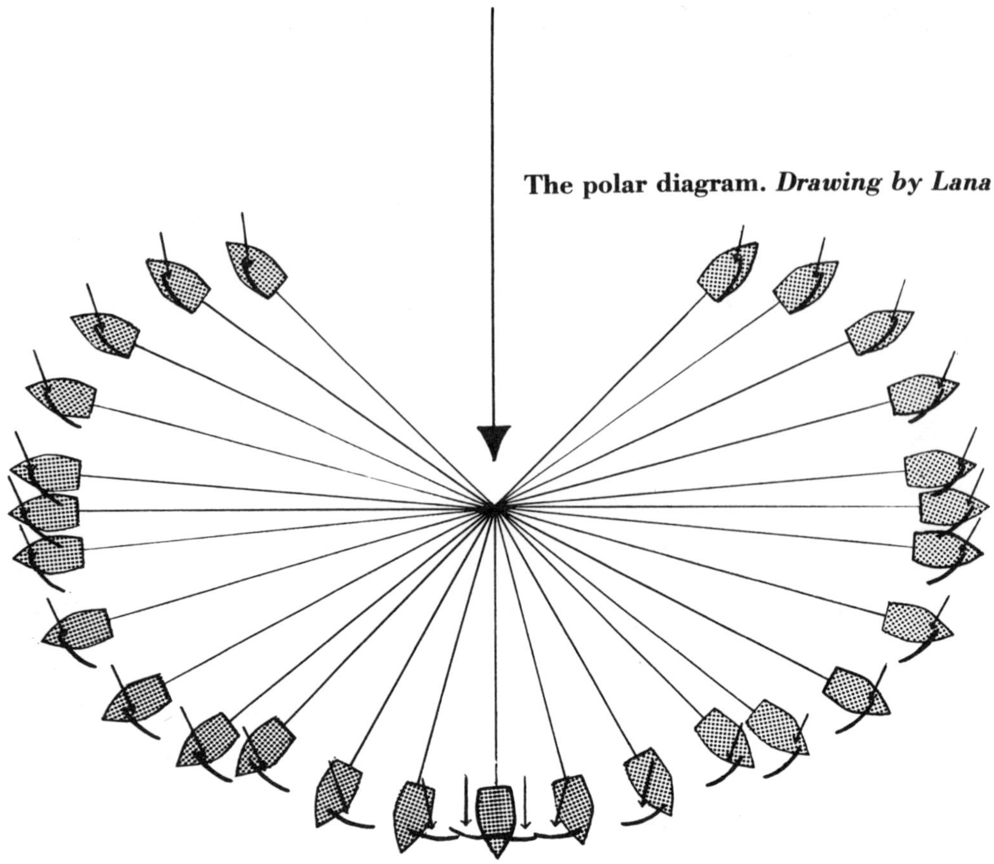

The polar diagram. *Drawing by Lana Cory Hall*

The polar diagram becomes an extension of the boat. It goes where the boat goes. It is the ultimate manifestation of everything that sails the boat. *Drawing by Don Raden*

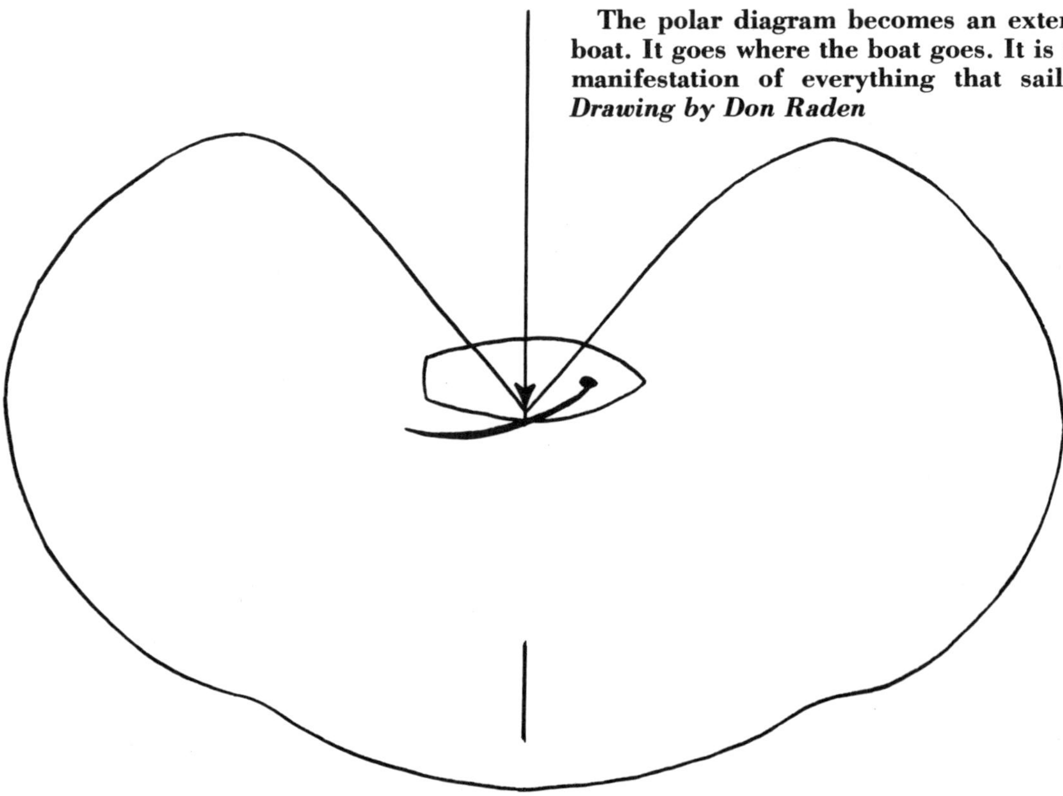

higher, up through the extra 5 degrees. This is the very end.

Then the completed shape, set on the compass, is the polar diagram: a thing fundamental enough to go by a scientific name. Once drawn it defines everything just by the form it takes, and it is this configuration just for this boat. It would be a rounder, more compact diagram for a slower boat. It would become nearly circular for the heaviest, beamiest, deep-keel slug of a boat, sailing mostly at the same plowlike pace in all directions (except, of course, into the eye). It would extend its utmost to near-grotesque widths for some of the more frenzied catamarans—which, in their seizures of high velocity, could stretch the diagram out to a shape vaguely but appropriately like an infinity symbol. (Stretched beyond that, the diagram would become only an uncertain, hypothetical shape at best for the frenetic little iceboats sailing by their bizzare force patterns at their near-transcendent speeds). The polar diagram spreads wider to leeward, acquiring a more bilious look, for a boat in heavy wind or a boat flying a spinnaker: both boats being driven hardest on the broad reaches, sailing in special conditions that alter the very basic force patterns. The polar diagram is plainly an ultimate thing: the ultimate measure of the boat and the ultimate manifestation of everything that sails the boat—the ultimate constant in any one boat and never the same constant in any two. Resolved and refined and now fixed in place, the polar diagram becomes the definitive understanding you meant to reach.

You see the polar diagram as an attachment to the wind axis and as an extension of the boat. It is both. It goes where the boat goes, carried like the soul with the body—as indeed is the axis itself, the boat's very lifeline—but it remains always oriented to the axis, whatever the boat's heading. The boat turns always upon the axis and inside the polar diagram and remains always integral to both; it can never sail away from either. The polar diagram is a pendant on the true wind axis. The boat is the instrument set within, turning there like the needle on the compass.

10 Coming About

Then you cross the wind axis itself. Finally you do the real maneuver that so far you only have presumed—all this while setting yourself hypothetically on either side of the line, on port or starboard tack, as you needed. But this time you make the actual transit between tacks; you steer to the line and turn past it. You sail the boat out of starboard tack and onto port, or out of port and onto starboard. Both ways you come to the crossing.

The crossing is radial. The boat *turns* past the axis: crossing radially over the line like the compass needle crosses radially over a white-etched base line. The boat is *fixed* to the axis; boat and axis join at the center of effort, the critical point on the sail. And just upon this very specific geometry of line meeting point, the boat would pivot hypothetically—figuratively—on the center of effort. Then as you steer upwind, the boat would pivot upwind toward the axis. Or as you steer downwind, the boat would pivot downwind toward the axis. Turning upwind or down, the boat pivots, in effect, like the compass needle. This time you mean for the boat to turn all the way to the axis, align with it, and turn past. To cross.

Then the crossing is both upwind and down. You come to it either way: to the same line, the same crossing in principle, even though the maneuvers are different. Crossing upwind is coming about; it is easier than it looks. Crossing downwind is jibing; it looks easier than it is. Coming about is deliberate. Jibing can be dramatic. Coming about is the more certain way across the axis. Jibing can involve uncertainties. You learn coming about first—now—and you are wiser for it. Later on you jibe.

Then come about. Or bring the boat about. You just abruptly do it, the first time you do anything really abruptly. Say "Ready About!" the traditional forewarning for hundreds of years. (Make this a habit: say "Ready About!" always loudly and clearly, even to yourself when you are alone in the boat.) And push the tiller. Until now you only nudged it minutely; now push it hard to leeward, swing it across and say "Hard Alee," the second warning, and the last one, also traditional for hundreds of years. And pull in the sheet as fast as you can.

The boat swerves sharply to windward, turning hard on force and impetus suddenly redirected. It drives up through the close reaches, then quickly beyond the limit and past the end—the wind spilling from the sail, the curve sliding off the edge, the forces disengaging—and into the upper quadrant, the eye of the wind. The boat keeps going on a loose

Drawing by Don Raden

but persistent momentum: jolting and pitching with all lines slack but never hesitating, just heading upwind. It simply heaves itself, mass and inertia, up through the last windward sector, turning the last 40 degrees to the wind axis. There for a measureless microsecond it points dead into the wind; then it turns past. It crosses the line.

The sheet hangs slack through the traveler blocks. The wind just blows by the sail now, buffeting it randomly on both sides; the sail writhes and whips and makes a half-worrisome din above. And now with the turn of the boat, the sail comes swinging and flapping across on an arc of its own, passing overhead like a great gate rattling on its hinges. The boom sweeps low over the cockpit, shuddering across at the level of your ears—and you learn the essential reflex of dodging beneath before it drubs you on the skull. (The boom is notorious for a long tradition of skull drubbing; it could derive its name from the endless hollow reverberations.) And all the while the boat still turns on its momentum: past the axis now, it keeps going, heading down through the last windward sector across the line. Having come up to the line through one windward sector, it now goes down through the other. Like this it crosses the eye of the wind.

The boat turns 40 degrees down through the last sector, and the sail and boom swing clear, dragging the sheet and traveler blocks across the deck. The

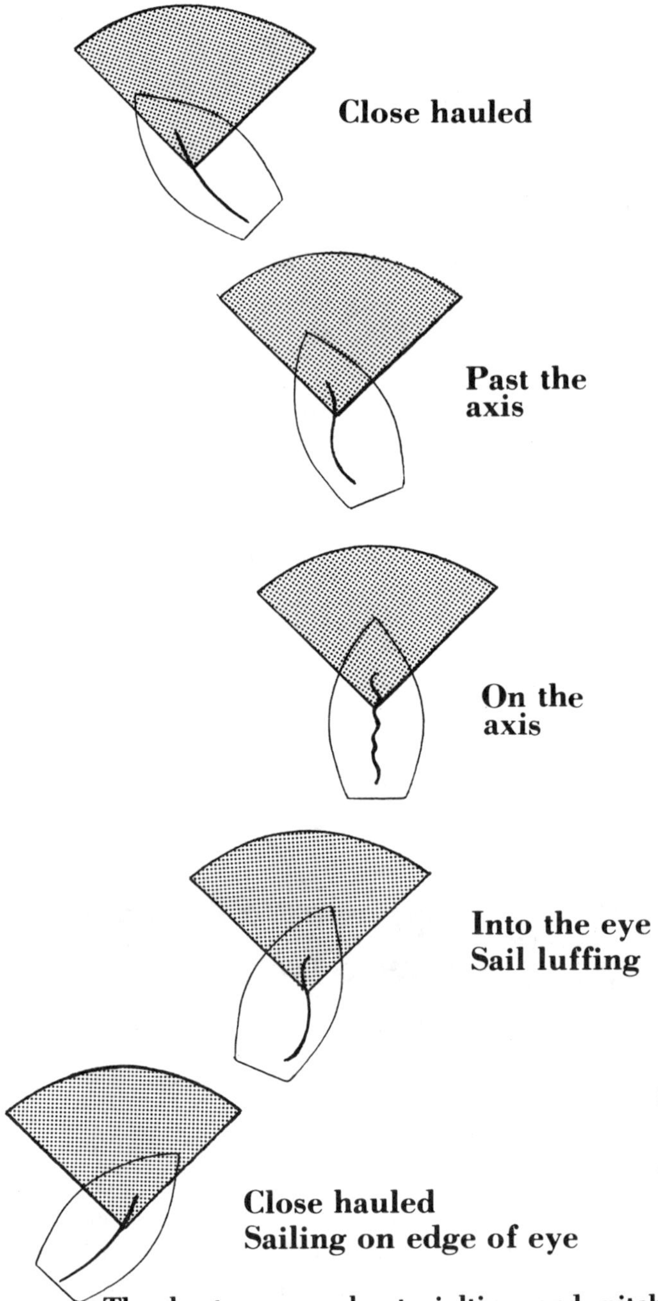

Coming about

The boat comes about, jolting and pitching, riding the loose but persistent momentum up through the eye of the wind. ***Drawing by Lana Cory Hall***

blocks strike the stops at the ends of their tracks; the sheet tightens slightly; the sail stiffens tentatively along the trailing edge, then begins to fill. This is across the axis. This is the other tack. The sail is on the other side of the boat now, the wind on the other side of the sail, the boat on the other side of the wind. This time the sail fills the other way—with an apparent wind at the same angle but from the other side—and the curve turns the exact reverse of the curve that was there before. The surface once outside now turns inside; convex turns concave; windward turns to leeward. The wind currents turn on the reverse curve. The outer current grows larger and moves faster; the inner current grows

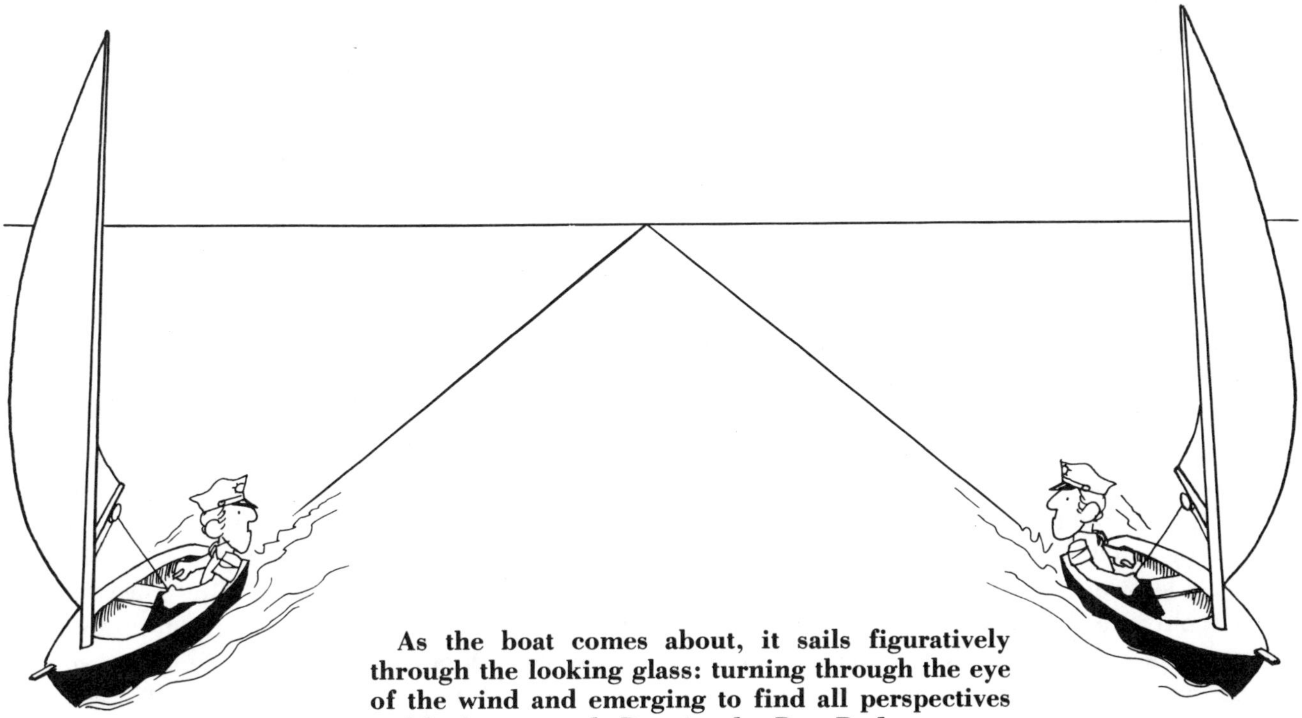

As the boat comes about, it sails figuratively through the looking glass: turning through the eye of the wind and emerging to find all perspectives suddenly reversed. ***Drawing by Don Raden***

smaller and moves slower. The pressures weigh upon the sail; the forces gather and pull. The boat drives forward. It all still works. But now the boat heels the other way; the side that was high sinks low. And you move across to hold down the *other* side—the one that was low, now rising high. You cross over like everything else does. The boat on the new tack becomes the once-turned mirror image of the boat on the old. You bring it about, and in crossing the axis you steer it through the looking-glass.

The maneuver is easy. You don't force it. You just start it, and it happens as a logical sequence: it is plain mechanics. The boat comes about readily enough in three or five or eight seconds, depending on how urgently you are sailing it. You hold the tiller hard alee for just about that long, and the boat is around and driving again: it loses perhaps a quarter of its speed going through the eye of the wind, but it quickly regains that coming out. You sail on into the looking-glass, a little surprised at the sheer competence of it all.

Afterward you have the problem of perspectives. Everything functions like before; except now the boat sails as a mirror image, and all its perspectives are once-turned. You look out from the cockpit and see a world once-turned. Wind and waves go in the same directions, but now on the other side; lines meet at the same angles, but now turned the other way. The shore itself somehow turns about in the distance: all the landmarks—trees, buildings, hills—become reordered and realigned, though fixed to the earth. Even the numbers on the sail read backward. And you come sailing for the first time into this world once-turned, never even hesitating at the edge, just riding in on the boat's momentum. You are all right for a moment—until you look up and try to see your way. And you can't. You are suddenly disoriented. Your own perspectives are the only ones not reversed, going through the looking-glass.

You can only start over. You have to establish the very basic directions, like at the beginning—the true wind first; then the true wind resolved down to its axis, the line of reference; then the line coming across the water to the point on the sail; and then the line holding to the point as the boat turns. You construct the geometry, like before, except it is once-turned, but this time you have surer insights, and you are much quicker to see it all together and functioning. So with the lines coming into place, you straightly recover your bearings. You begin to see where you are, then where you have come, and where you are going. You see where the boat turns across the axis, then how it sails on either side. And you don't have the problem after this. You just fix upon the new order of landmarks and sail on into the looking-glass, and you know the way out is the other way, back over the axis. It becomes simple: from now on you have all perspectives, the full set of perspectives. You turn them either way. You come about both ways.

It is good this first time, but it is much too good. You presume everything right, and so, presumably, you do everything right. You are allowed to take this liberty only this one time. After this you don't presume, and you don't do as well. Now you have to learn to do everything right by learning not to do everything wrong.

Actually, in coming about, you can do only a few specific things that *aren't* right, but you still have to do them at least once, just to learn not to, because coming about is really the best maneuver you make, but it remains a singular maneuver that in fact you must do wrong in the eventual process of doing right.

You come about with the tiller. This is the lone fundamental. You do everything right or wrong with the tiller, and the rest of the machinery follows. You put the tiller hard alee when you start about; you hold it there when you turn about; and you put it back amidships when you are about. Those are the right things you do. Anything else, anything different, is wrong.

So now, again—for real—say "Ready About!" and "Hard Alee!" and swing the tiller abruptly to leeward. You swing it *far* to leeward, impulsively, almost violently this time, like a fighter punching. You go clear across the cockpit pushing the tiller to its limit, setting the rudder almost at right angles to the boat, nearly flat against the stern transom. You mean just to blast through the eye of the wind, to drive the boat into immediate frenzy, spinning it up and around on that instant, and in that same instant to be gone from there, sailing away on the other tack, leaving the very elements stunned by the impact. Such is your first impulse: simply to hit hard and be about and away. It is the wrong thing.

It doesn't work. It only seems about to. The boat reels and lurches, but the rudder at right angles doesn't really turn it. The rudder just drags in the water, and the boat swerves heavily sideways against more water; it pushes around a lot of water; the water makes a great sloshing noise, being pushed. The boat dissipates all its momentum pushing water. It goes sluggish and loses its impact on the instant you had meant for it to hit hard. It does get through the eye of the wind, just because it is a good boat, but it comes out swashing sideways and just stalls rather absurdly, mired in all the water it has pushed. The centerboard holds the boat sideways; the rudder at right angles holds it fore-and-aft. You have to drift and muddle with the boat dead in the water, working the sheet and tiller, trying to get the forces pulling. And the boat begins to move and gather way, but it makes a toilsome recovery. Once it stops, it is always slow starting again.

Then that way is wrong, probably more chronically so than all others, though now and again you keep trying it out of sheer determination—wanting too much, pushing too hard, and so dragging down the boat. You are bound to try it every so often, even when you know far better. But now you do the right thing and try deliberate restraint instead. You push the tiller only halfway to its limit, and you stop it there and hold it, so the rudder is 45 degrees to the boat—half across it, half along it, half the right angle—and you call *this* hard alee. And this is just about right; it surprises you. The boat turns sharply, not on a corner as you would have wished, but at least on a tight arc: swerving sideways very slightly because boats do swerve in a turn, but riding easily over the water, sliding on it, rocking with it, not pushing it. The boat comes almost rhythmically around to windward, its momentum intact; it goes without effort through the eye of the wind. The sail shakes twice swinging across—just perfunctory little shrugs, as if it were only shedding flies—and simply turns itself out the other way, filling with a soft, sudden "thump." Then you sail away on the other tack, the boat driving forward, never even inconvenienced. You do come about in three or five or eight seconds, and if you are exactly right, you lose and regain only a quarter of the boat's speed; and even if you aren't exactly right, you lose and regain only slightly more, which still is right enough.

So from now on you are right enough just setting the tiller hard alee at about 45 degrees, halfway to its limit—just puting it there and holding it there and bringing the boat about. Do it once, and you can do it again; it works so long as you maintain the discipline. Later you can even refine this further, down to a single sensitivity for setting the tiller exactly right. This remains always the best maneuver you can make with a sailboat.

Except you still can do it wrong. After you have

the boat and machinery working right, you are the last remaining element. And now you have to work right. And you probably don't at first. Hardly anybody does.

It seems unlikely. You need only set the tiller and hold it; there shouldn't be anything to do wrong in that. But watch yourself now; see how you do this. Say "Ready About" once again, and "Hard Alee" and push the tiller across and bring the boat up into the eye of the wind. The boat stops driving on forces and starts rocking on momentum. The sail flaps overhead. The boom swings across, sweeping low, toward the soft spots in your skull. You dodge beneath the boom, but not handily; you are off-balance in the rocking boat, and you are bothered by the urgency of the sail rattling in your ears. Suddenly you feel beset by too many things happening—all the machinery letting go and moving about, shifting and crossing as if everything were coming apart and back together again. For a moment, contemplating this in the eye of the wind, you are powerfully dissuaded from any thought of the tiller in your hand, and in that moment you abandon that hand to bare, unguarded reflex. Then amid the rocking and rattling and coming apart, the hand betrays you. It pulls the tiller back.

You don't notice. You don't realize until too late. It is like picking your own pocket. As you are dodging under the boom, or trying to balance, or whatever—being preoccupied in any case—your own hand and arm, with an insidious contraction of muscles, bring the tiller sharply but unobtrusively back to windward, delicately setting it amidships once again: in the accustomed place where it steers dead ahead. Then the rudder aligns, and the boat stops turning and just points up the axis. And while you still are dissuaded and unaware, the boat stops; it jettisons all its momentum and dies in the eye of the wind. You eventually rise up from under the boom, finally clear of it, your skull undrubbed, and you look about in amazement. The boat is lying completely inert on the wind axis, bobbing and flapping, dead in the water, like flotsam.

It has been dead before, just within the edges of the eye of the wind, but this time it is dead at the very center; it is dead in the extreme. Pull the sheet, push the tiller, and you have nothing: no stirring, no response, no feeling; there is nothing at all. The sheet is only slack rope in your hand, the tiller a stick. The sail just blows lifeless in the wind; the rudder flaps in the water, a meaningless appendage. Push or pull, you have no effect; you only flog the dead boat with its own dead machinery. You can't make it move. You can't steer it. With all the wind blowing, you can't sail the boat out of this. It is in irons. It is dead and entombed in the eye of the wind.

Be steady. Hold firm. You are at least very secure with the boat in irons. In the eye of the wind, you occupy the safest refuge from the wind. You are pointed up the axis. The boat's narrowest edges are to windward; only its minimal forward configuration is in the way of the wind blowing and the waves rolling. And the wind just blows past, and the waves roll by, both carrying away their essential weight and force, neither having much significant effect on the boat. The wind does make the sail flap, but that is only noise; and the waves do make the boat pitch, but that is only motion. The boat simply shrugs all that away. It is a good boat and just bobs in place, passively, like a bubble, staying upright with its own innate integral stability. It has a stable, peaceful death in the eye of the wind.

Now there is time. You can pause and consider this. You lose and gain—like always. You put the boat in irons, and in this state it dies. But in this state you bring it so very safely into the shelter of the eye of the wind. And even though you do this by mistake this time, the state itself, however unwarranted, still is valid and necessary. In all other states the boat must sail; in this state it must stop sailing. And this boat, like all boats, eventually must stop. Sometimes it must stop to take refuge, sometimes for special reasons; eventually it just must stop because you are done sailing. This is to remember for later.

So having come to this, now you come out.

The boat begins to move; imperceptibly at first, and backward this time—aft—and not because of you or anything you do It just floats like this because this is the way the wind and waves push. It still is dead, like flotsam; it floats like a ghost boat. You sit in the cockpit and let the sheet hang slack, which is all you need to do: just keep it slack. The boat, floating aft, veers randomly off the axis and begins to drift around very slowly: a hulk simply awash, turning gradually sideways in the combined forces of wind and waves. It finally comes squarely across the wind and just lies there, wallowing in the troughs of the waves. You pull the sheet and fill the sail and set it 5 degrees tighter than trim, and the boat hesitates, goes tense and begins to drive ahead.

A boat can be steered backward, out of irons. The trick is to remember to push the tiller in the direction the bow is meant to point. *Drawing by Don Raden*

It gathers way, sailing on the beam reach. You resurrect the boat, riding it out of irons.

But you can do better at this. When you know that the boat really does come out of irons, you can take the tiller and steer out quite handily: the trick being that the boat floating aft must be steered aft—backward—and you probably never thought a sailboat would be steered aft; the notion would seem to transgress its very design. But this does work, much better than you expect. The boat needs only to start drifting, just to be moving somehow; and you set the tiller very gingerly and turn the rudder very conservatively, applying no leverage, only hopeful guidance. Then as the boat floats aft, lifeless but nonetheless moving, the rudder gets a hold of sorts on the water: an element of steerageway, however intangible. And suddenly the boat just swerves backward and out of irons, coming sharply around and lying squarely and passively across the wind. You pull in the sheet, genuinely impressed. Everything works so quickly and easily that at first you aren't even sure you made it happen.

You do have the problem of reverse steering. You push the tiller one way, and the boat, floating aft, backs around and heads that way; it turns, in effect, where the tiller points. But you intuitively reject this because you are conditioned from the first just to steer ahead: to push the tiller one way so the boat, driving forward, heads the other way—turning where the tiller doesn't point. You first try reverse steering only as a very doubtful experiment, understanding in principle that it works but knowing by feeling that it can't work, or at least shouldn't rightfully work. Nevertheless it does work, and you have to adapt to this. You push the tiller to starboard, and the boat backs smartly around, turning starboard; push to port, and it backs around, turning port. You have to try this several times before it doesn't feel wrong and you can begin to accept it. You work at getting the touch. Try reverse steering just within the eye of the wind, turning first toward one edge, then across toward the other, coming close enough to cross each time but purposely veering back. Then try steering strictly on the axis itself, floating aft and guiding the boat precisely down the line. The touch is different, but you learn to steer either way out of irons, onto port tack or starboard. There is this much control, even over a dead boat.

So steer out of irons and sail away, and when you next bring the boat about, you put the tiller hard alee and hold it there, and this time you make your hand stay firmly in place. But you make another mistake. The boat comes around on its momentum, rocking and flapping through the eye of the wind, then emerging close-hauled on the other tack, scarcely slowed, the sail filling, the forces pulling. The boat heels, and you hike out to the edge, then beyond, leaning far out over the water, bringing the boat back down. But just as everything works, suddenly nothing does. The boat comes unbalanced. It stops heeling. It drops beneath you, too abruptly; it almost dunks you as you hike too far past the rail. You do frantic contortions, pulling yourself back into the cockpit. And then you see the boat is not driving ahead. It still is turning around; it has come through the eye of the wind and just kept turning as if somehow disoriented—down through the close reaches, past the beam reach; and now it is through the broad reaches and heading rapidly toward the dead run, down the axis itself—while you are preoccupied: still trying to trim and balance to sail close-hauled. You are in fact dissuaded once again, and the boat turns because now your hand keeps the tiller rigidly in the place where you first set it hard alee. This time your tiller hand betrays you by *not* moving, by *not* setting the tiller back amidships when the boat comes through the eye of the wind. You are wrong after coming about even though you do it right.

Just in time, you set the tiller back amidships, and just in time the boat stops turning; before it would have crossed the wind axis and gone into a flying jibe—which you aren't ready to do yet, and don't ever want to do without meaning to—so this time you get out of it easily enough, just by steering. And from now on you do everything right with the boat and machinery when you come about. You set the tiller hard alee at 45 degrees. You hold it there through the eye of the wind; everything crosses over. Then you emerge from the eye and set the tiller back amidships. You arrange your perspectives in the world once-turned; and you fix upon a course and set the sail 5 degrees tighter than trim; you level the deck and hold the balance. You sail the boat, having brought it cleanly through the looking glass.

Then you have almost all of it. You do this much with the boat and machinery; you do the remainder with yourself. You resolve the complications caused by your own presence: your arms, legs, hands, feet, and the rest—all getting involved in the mechanics of coming about. So now as you steer through the eye of the wind, and the boat rocks, and the sail flaps, and everything else happens—while you still are balancing in the boat and dodging beneath the boom, and watching where the boat turns, and how the wind blows and where the sail fills; and as you keep yourself undissuaded all the while, holding the tiller hard alee through the eye of the wind—now you must get up from one side of the cockpit, move across to the other side, turn around, and sail from there. And as you move and turn, you must exchange sheet and tiller between your two hands. Your tiller hand must give up the tiller and take the sheet; your sheet hand must take the tiller and give up the sheet. So as you cross the cockpit; and the boat crosses the axis, your tiller hand becomes your sheet hand, and your sheet hand becomes your tiller hand; and like this you come out of the eye of the wind and sail on the other tack.

(It is somewhat as if you sat in a chair, holding a stick in one hand and a rope in the other. And you got up from the chair and traded stick and rope between your hands and sat down in a facing chair. Except it can't be that easy.)

So what you really have is an exercise in coordination. You need to do several things in a single move: a very particular move, your own personal move. And you don't learn such a move, you have to invent it. You can only try it and refine it and keep trying until it feels right, so that eventually you do it your way. It turns out never being exactly like anybody else's move. Your move in coming about becomes, most specifically, the beginning of your style.

The move itself does become necessarily intricate, though not really so difficult, once you actually set about making it. You just have to start as conservatively as possible. Say "Ready About." and take both sheet and tiller in the same hand—in either hand; it doesn't matter, and now the other hand is free—and say "Hard Alee!" and push the tiller to leeward, still holding the sheet in the same hand. Then move while the boat is in the eye of the wind. Move yourself deliberately, without stress. You have three or five or eight seconds with the boat in the eye and safely sheltered, and just the three seconds make a long and tranquil time for this. In three seconds you can move at leisure across the cockpit, even pausing to catch your balance or dodge the boom, or just to consider. You step or crouch, or you slide across, but now, in any case, you move yourself in total reference to the hand holding the sheet and tiller; you move, focused upon this place where sheet, tiller, and hand come together. And after you cross over and turn around—which is automatic now, the most basic move—the same hand instinctively retains either the sheet or tiller, whichever one of the two it holds more comfortably, and the free hand naturally takes the other. Your two hands make the exchange between themselves, very logically, and you steer the boat out of the eye and sail onto the other tack. You just work like this, almost mechanically, and you can hardly make a mistake.

Then beginning like this—from this—you invent your own personal move. You experiment with different ways: always more venturesome, not always successful, but not conservative ways after this, nor mechanical. From now on you mean to be daring and artful, always coming about more quickly and neatly. You try moving with different steps: half steps, back steps, side steps, even no steps. You do a high move, a reverse pirouette up on your toes; a low move, a duck waddle down on the floorboards. You move while exchanging sheet and tiller around

Each skipper derives his own move for bringing the boat about. The move becomes the beginning of his individual style. ***Drawing by Don Raden***

your knees, or behind your back, or while holding the sheet in your teeth, or the tiller under your heel. You devise moves just for this, inconceivable moves anywhere else. When you make bad moves, or good moves badly, then you get tangled in the sheet and can't let out the sail, which is bad; or you let go of the tiller and set the boat spinning, which is worse; or you do both at once, which is worst of all. But you work at moves, discarding the bad ones and developing the good ones; and out of this you do what works best—and out of *this* you do what feels best—so in time you derive your own move, and thereafter you refine it. You never really stop refining. You do this by yourself; nobody else can do it for you. This is how you bring the boat about.

Now you tack upwind, a useful strategy. You zig and zag. You are *here*, downwind, and you want to go *there*, upwind, and you can't get to there from here, because the way is straight up the axis. So you sail from here to there by way of somewhere else, a longer way; you go obliquely where you can't go directly. You sail close-hauled from here to somewhere else—you zig—and then you come about and sail close-hauled from somewhere else to there—you zag. And with the zig and the zag, you are straight up the axis from where you started: the zigging and zagging together comprise tacking. And when you can tack, you can go anywhere upwind or down, except you have to sail farther upwind. Sailing close-hauled, 45 degrees to windward and holding to the edge of the eye of the wind—and coming about in precise 90-degree turns through the eye of the wind—you zig and zag and tack three miles upwind, and you come to a place about two miles up the wind axis, which is less than you would like, but this is how you get there.

You learn to accept the realities of tacking upwind; they are the realities of sailing upwind—the boat at its limit sailing only obliquely against the wind it sails by. Except now there is a longer dimension. The boat at its limit has a place to go, however obliquely it must go there. And now you need a special science to find the right way there. This is the science of pinching and footing.

Pinching is sailing above the windward limit. The boat pinching tacks a shorter distance at a closer angle but sails too slowly. Footing is sailing below the windward limit. The boat footing sails faster but tacks too long a distance at too wide an angle. The science is the means of maintaining the ideal course between pinching and footing; it is the constant adjustment of the lines and angles by which the boat sails exactly at the limit—sailing not too slowly and tacking not too far; just holding to

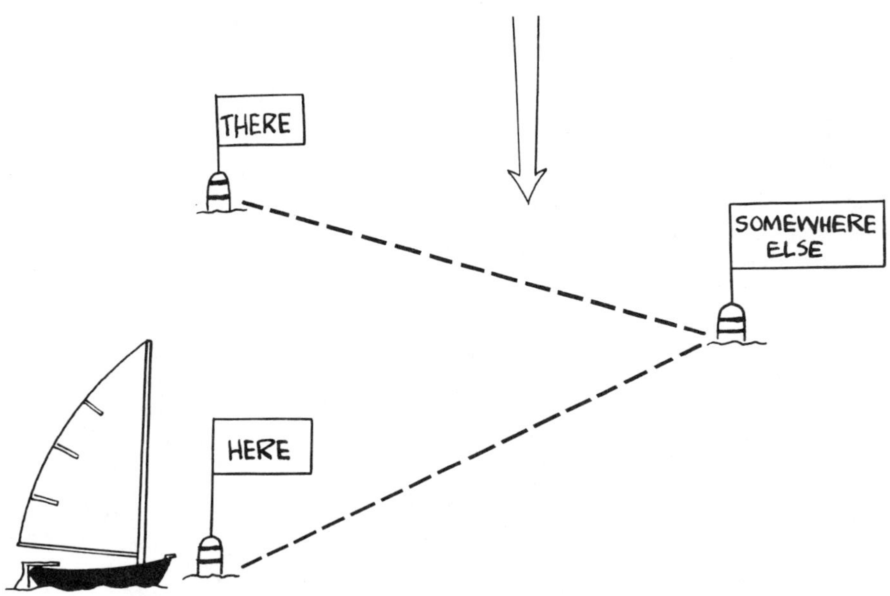

Tacking upwind is a useful strategy for going from here to there by way of somewhere else—when the boat can not go directly from here to there because the way is straight upwind. *Drawing by Don Raden*

Lateral drift

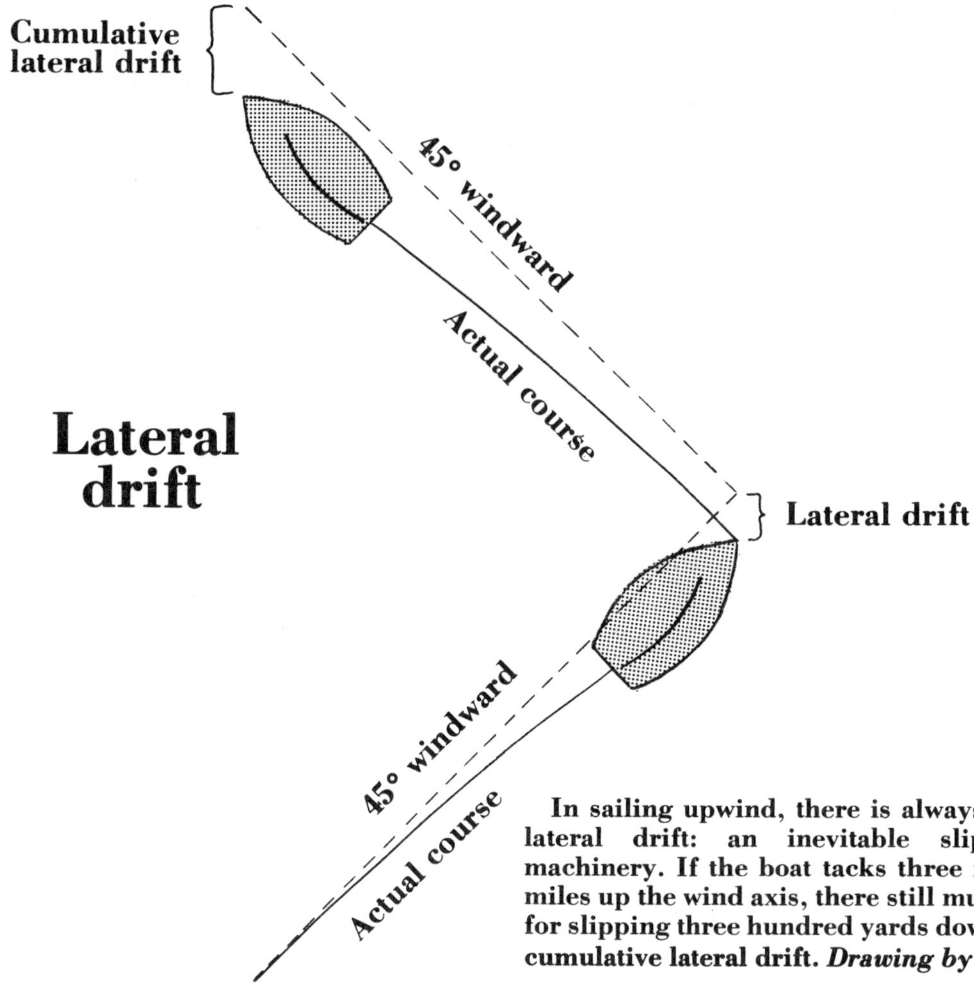

In sailing upwind, there is always an element of lateral drift: an inevitable slippage in the machinery. If the boat tacks three miles to go two miles up the wind axis, there still must be allowance for slipping three hundred yards down the axis—the cumulative lateral drift. ***Drawing by Lana Cory Hall***

the fine edge and making the minimal pattern of zigs and zags and coming to the place up the wind axis ahead of any boat pinching or footing. The science also allows for that element of lateral drift: a negligible thing until now, but suddenly a ponderable factor. The boat does drift slightly sideways, as it has all the while; just because there is inevitable slippage in the machinery, because of course the centerboard can't be absolute and won't hold absolutely. So if the boat zigs and zags three miles, then it slips perhaps 300 yards down the axis, even as it is tacking two miles up. In the longer dimension, you learn to sail upwind with the sense of the boat tacking like this.

Then you go obliquely on to places up the axis: continually testing and feeling and calculating and correcting, and steering the boat always for the limit. If it pinches above, you deliberately foot it off; if it foots below, you deliberately pinch it up. You find that you either pinch or foot compulsively; probably you pinch—most people are inclined to; they just keep pointing higher—and you have to keep chanting to yourself: "Foot, foot, foot. . ." and footing back, holding to the limit. (If people give you strange looks from other boats, you can feel superior to them.) Before you come about, you sight over your shoulder and off the windward rail, and you plot the next course in that direction: across the eye of the wind, 90 degrees from where you sail now, and you allow for lateral drift and fix upon the landmarks. So when you come about, you know where the boat will go, and you zig and zag and tack upwind.

You tack upwind more than you sail any other way, and you work harder at it: laboring close-hauled against both wind and waves. And you go farther working at it: pushing three miles up for every two miles you would run back down. You tack upwind maybe as much as you sail all other ways combined, and you feel like you do it even more than that. So when you do run downwind, you go uneasily, gauging the greater effort with which you must come back up. If you overrun yourself and go too far downwind, then you must turn around to face a prohibitive effort coming back, an ordeal of raw survival. Once you know how this feels, you tend to sail to places where you tack upwind first, so you can come running or reaching back down, your dues already paid. But ultimately you must sail both upwind and down—or downwind and up, whichever is first. You can go downwind directly, but you must come upwind obliquely, taking the zigs and zags, going three miles to make two. (Perhaps three times in your life, you may go sailing without taking a tack.) And if you do better going upwind than down, you are going to win more races than people who do better going downwind than up. You are the better sailor, tacking upwind.

11 Jibing

Now you jibe the boat. You go the other way—downwind—and across the wind axis. You wait until now for this because jibing is supposed to be a crisis: because it is dynamic and not altogether certain. It begins as something you do and becomes something that happens most powerfully to you. It impresses you and makes you respectful, and if it is wrong often enough it is bound to capsize you. But jibe the boat, and don't be afraid of capsizing. Jibing is worth that.

Jibing must begin with very basic uncertainties. In 10 knots of true wind, jibing is almost nothing. Most of the things that happen to you in jibing don't even start to happen—not so you know they happen—until the true wind rises to at least 14 knots, or more likely to 16 or 18. Just to learn jibing so that you actually experience it enough to understand what happens, you are going to need more wind: sometimes twice as much wind as you needed to learn nearly everything else. You have to assume more wind now—arbitrarily once again, but this time not momentarily. You and the boat are going to be a good while in strong wind, learning to jibe.

This much *is* certain. The boat, jibing, sails down to the wind axis, aligns with it, and turns across it; and the sail swings across and fills the other way. Then the sail is on the other side of the boat, the wind on the other side of the sail, and the boat once more is on the other side of the wind. The perspectives are once-turned. The boat comes through the looking glass. If this were still a 10-knot wind, jibing would be nothing more. You simply would do it and be done with it.

But now, in strong wind, before you even try jibing, you need a very specific new awareness of boat and wind. In a jibe, the boat will cross only the axis of the wind, not the eye of the wind. The eye is not part of this; it was upwind: only the bare line runs this way, downwind. The boat sails down to the line and turns a little more, a microscopic turn, and it is across—just like that. But it has to keep sailing all the while, still under power with full sail and forces pushing, even at the instant of crossing over. The boat going downwind can't ever stop sailing; there is no place, no respite, no sheltered quadrant. The boat must jibe fully exposed to the wind, and the wind must keep pressing. This is the way in jibing. It is very quick, with only the line to cross, and the weight of the wind is omnipresent.

(The iceboats are the exception to this. Iceboats go downwind at five times the speed of the wind; by their sheer velocities they generate headwinds at least four times stronger than the true wind astern. They jibe while sailing dead into their own head-

The critical moment in jibing: the sail is about to fly. ***Drawing by Don Raden***

winds—crossing the axis with booms bobbing and sails flapping, as if they were coming about. Iceboats never need even acknowledge the weight of any wind astern.)

You first try jibing most circumspectly, after you are quite sure you can make a good move coming about. You need that move first, just to have your reflexes working. Then you can begin your other move, for jibing—a move in the other direction, not the same move, though not entirely different. The jibing move follows well enough, except it happens faster, and you make it under greater duress. And you don't make mistakes like before. You no longer allow yourself the luxury of making mistakes.

Then just be careful going into this. Start as simply as possible; try to ease your way. Say "Stand By to Jibe!" or "Jibe-O!"—either being traditional, both universal—and pull the tiller to windward and say "Hard Aweather!" or "Helm's Aweather!" Then steer to leeward, toward the axis. Steer gently this time, don't be abrupt; sail the boat softly, don't hurl it. It isn't going on momentum now; there is no place to do that. It has to keep moving downwind under the weight of the wind pushing. Sail it like this down through the broad reaches, then run it before the wind. But keep it turning; be steady. It is going into the jibe, and the jibe is going to happen, and you are not going to flinch from any of this.

Let the sheet out as the boat sails downwind; let the sail swing out over the water. As the boat turns and runs, keep the sail broad and full and squarely across the apparent wind. This is the way you run before the wind; like this you steer the boat down through the aerodynamic nether region to leeward. You know this region. You have to sail alone in the waves once again, keeping the balance without the stable element, while the boat rocks and slides and turns slightly giddy now and then. The wind blows against the sail and spills around the edges and goes spinning around to the other side, into the widening chasm of eddies and whirlwinds just behind: the windshadow. And as you steer nearer to the axis, you point the boat deeper into the chasm; until at the axis line itself, running dead before the wind, you sail directly at the ragings and churnings of the whirlwinds themselves. The boat just glides and sways, with hardly any feeling at all, almost wraithlike at times. Then suddenly it flies into fits and seizures, reeling and wrenching and striking in open rebellion. You know the boat in this state. It is not rational; it is not stable. This is where you bring it to jibe.

(Except that in coming down to jibe and letting out the sail, you go dead against the wisest, best-established counsel—which says the boat in this state is most vulnerable, with no control of its own, so you must enforce the very strictest control upon it; you must retain the firmest grip coming downwind, pulling the sail in, not letting it out—not the true way to sail downwind, but this could be a matter of survival—and then you had better steer into the jibe with the sail under the tightest possible restraint, actually lashed down, as if close-hauled. Or else when the jibe happens, the sail will fly, and the raw forces turned loose will hurl you and the boat beyond all control, into awful chaos. Though other counsel, more enlightened and experimental, says jibing indeed should be free flight, unrestricted and unconfined, even in this tenuous state, so the sail should swing naturally out over the water as the boat comes downwind to the axis. And when the jibe happens, the sail should fly because flying is elemental—and this works without effort or impediment if you and the boat and the forces simply move together in the jibe, never needing to enforce anything, just coming around, fully coordinated, sustained solely by the fundamental disciplines of basic rhythms. There is this counsel, and there is the other, and you will consider both, but later. Right now you are only becoming aware; you are not taking counsel. This time is for effect.)

Then steer across the axis.

The boat turns, and so it crosses; and you expect more, but there is a fateful moment while the rest waits. The sail doesn't fly, or swing over, or anything. Instead, for this moment, it is in suspension, just holding in the same place, on the same side, still out over the water. And the boat still sails before the wind, except now, across the line, it comes into a strange state of gathering imbalance—where for this moment, it is even less secure than before. The boat is on the other side of the wind now, but the sail is not on the other side of the boat, and the wind is not on the other side of the sail. Across the axis, the boat keeps turning, now on the new tack and beginning to go upwind, while the sail remains on the old tack, still set to go downwind. And like this, for this moment, you are sailing by the lee, which is against nature itself and more unstable than anything.

This is a long, fateful moment. The boat turns, but it has trouble. With the turn the balance comes undone. The sail, in effect, is bent backward in the wind. The sail's trailing edge no longer trails but bends first up into the wind; more wind spills around that edge to rage in greater turmoil behind the sail. New pressures rise and fall but ultimately grow in the turmoil. The boat now must turn against mounting pressures to go upwind—still reeling and sliding and feeling uncertain, and now pressing progressively harder to go farther past the axis. And now as it turns, it begins to lean and sway more radically, almost grotesquely: not heeling this time but listing under the pressure; it leans *away* from the sail, as if its equilibrium were shifting off-center. Sailing by the lee, it turns with increasing difficulty through massing resistance, still rebelling, sometimes balking, and it becomes ominously tense and uncomfortable, being forced in these irregular ways. But it pushes for this long moment, and the pressures build behind the sail, and the state becomes more unstable and comes to a critical point. And at the critical point, the pressures behind the sail are more than the pressures in front, and the sail flies.

You get a clear warning. The boat leans over. The boom lifts high. The sail rises above you,

Flying jibe

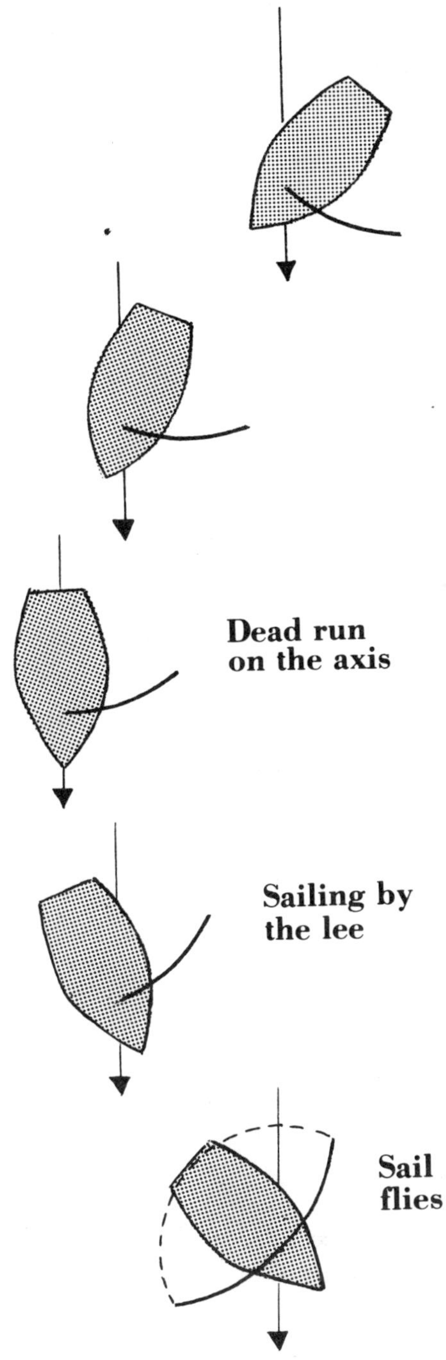

In the flying jibe, the boat crosses the axis and keeps turning—simply sailing by the lee until the sail flies because of sheer pressure imbalance. ***Drawing by Lana Cory Hall***

hesitates, and begins to curl in, as if gathering itself together. It looks to be fomenting inside, like a storm about to burst. It looms fearsomely above you, however you see it, and you flinch instinctively at first; you probably steer back a little. Then you recover a measure of resolution, as you must; you turn the boat and push once more to the critical point. And the sail surges up again, and this time it breaks loose—whipping free on the blacklash of the whirlwinds and flinging itself out into the wind. It swoops, it plunges. It flies. It comes at you like cavalry out of the storm; you duck and the boom slashes over like a saber blade. And just like that the sail flies across and out over the lee side, where the sheet and travelers catch it fully extended, and it stops with a sharp, sudden impact against the last restraints. There are no three or five or eight seconds this time; there is only the surreal frenzy of things flying, then the impact in the other direction; and then all the forces are aligned the other way. The boat jibes.

It is the flying jibe: the blind, basic, out-of-control jibe. It might be traumatic for you, except it happens too fast. You come out of it feeling at least respectful, then you find yourself grasping at things that are almost necessarily in disarray. The boat wobbles and yaws in sudden after-shock; for some moments it can't be steered precisely, being jostled in so many odd ways by so many odd forces so abruptly shifted. The sheet usually is tangled somewhere; it really is a lot of loose rope flung about, and some of it is bound to snag on something—perhaps on the tiller or rudder or travelers, but most often on the aft corner of the boat itself. The sail fills the other way, with the reverse curve, but it still shudders and twitches for a time before it will set firmly for the wind to push upon. And then, having indeed jibed, you need to recover perspectives. In jibing they must change, but of course too fast, like a blink of the eyes, and you can't be quick enough to change with them to see where you are. You have to establish perspectives afterward and fix upon them and then see where you are—and all the while you are steering imprecisely and trying to untangle the sheet and steady the sail. You work busily coming out of a flying jibe. You learn respect.

You also make your own move, though now you don't dwell upon it. In jibing your move becomes only a minor adjustment, almost incidental, and it isn't so hard if you just do it first, while steering down toward the axis—because you move much better going into the jibe, still having time and poise, than you move coming out, having neither. (You prudently dismiss all notions of superior moves upon the instant of the jibe itself.) And you move in any case while sailing before the wind, so you do everything from one place in the middle of the cockpit. You keep the balance there, and you exchange sheet and tiller between your two hands

The control jibe is executed by enforcing strict control on the sail—pulling it taut and effectively twisting it backward in the wind—as the boat turns to leeward. *Drawing by Don Raden*

and turn yourself half around. That is the move. You make it and hardly notice it; you just keep steering into the jibe, stretching one way with one arm to hold the tiller to windward, and stretching the other way with the other arm to ease the sheet to leeward. Then you come downwind like an evangelist, with both arms outspread—turning across the axis and sailing by the lee, until at the critical point the sail flies and the boat jibes. That is the way. The move is right, even though you never again want to fly out of control in a jibe.

You next jibe most conservatively, now taking seriously that wisest, best-established counsel. You do the control jibe, deliberately pulling in the sail as you steer down toward the axis. You set the sail solely by the boat; you studiously disregard the wind. And you control the sail, or subdue it in essense, like a wrestler—applying leverage against it and cramping it back into something figuratively like a hammerlock. In effect you bend the curve almost brutally, turning it backward in the wind, twisting it around to where it would be close hauled if you were sailing to windward. This indeed is not the true way to sail downward, but it is how you enforce control. You make an abberation of the boat, but you keep all the machinery firmly in hand.

Then the wind comes down on the twisted-back sail and blows and spills the wrong ways around it. And the forces push and pull in the wrong patterns upon it. So as you pull the sheet tighter, you get only a perverse, marginal sort of power from the sail—something like power but more diffuse—and this is resolved far aft in the sail and from there is exerted mostly to windward upon the machinery, while the boat is turning to leeward. So now the boat gets little more than a contrary and overburdening weather helm from the wind. It slows of course, its power compromised; and it turns churlishly at best, the tiller laboring heavily against the sheet. It feels almost mechanially sluggish. But you keep strict control; you are determined on this. You make the boat turn steadily, and you pull in the sheet regardless; and you go to leeward, however unnaturally. In a minute you come to the axis and pull in the last of the sheet and draw the sail taut, directly over the cockpit. Then you jibe.

This time you simply tug the sheet, only once, sharply; and the sail snaps across. It doesn't curl in first, or gather itself together, or foment inside. And it doesn't fly. It is very still with the tension, like a spring, and it recoils on the instant of that single, sharp tug. It snaps in one way and out the other, moving scarcely a few inches in coming over; and then it stays in place, very still, again like a spring. The boat is jibed.

With this your control is complete. You hold the boat rigidly with the sail cramped and the sheet pulled tight. The boat is on the axis. You turn it minutely; it responds precisely; and it is across and on the other tack. This time it is just machinery working. It never leans or sways or slides, never sails by the lee, never loses equilibrium. There is no after-shock, no disorder. You don't let any of that happen. You just hold tight. You begin to gather perspectives.

The control jibe seems plainly the least venturesome of all jibes, and perhaps it seems the most secure in its way, given some allowance for uncertainties. And being certified by the wisest, best-established counsel, it is of course the approved maneuver for crossing the axis to leeward. It is even considered definitive in many quarters: the only warranted jibe where others are never acknowledged, except as errors or irresponsibilities. But with all of this, the control jibe still is not altogether satisfactory. It is slow and mechanical and, indeed, unnatural; it would not even be a good maneuver, except it is so terribly effective within its limits. You do the control jibe just because it doesn't involve the

Control jibe

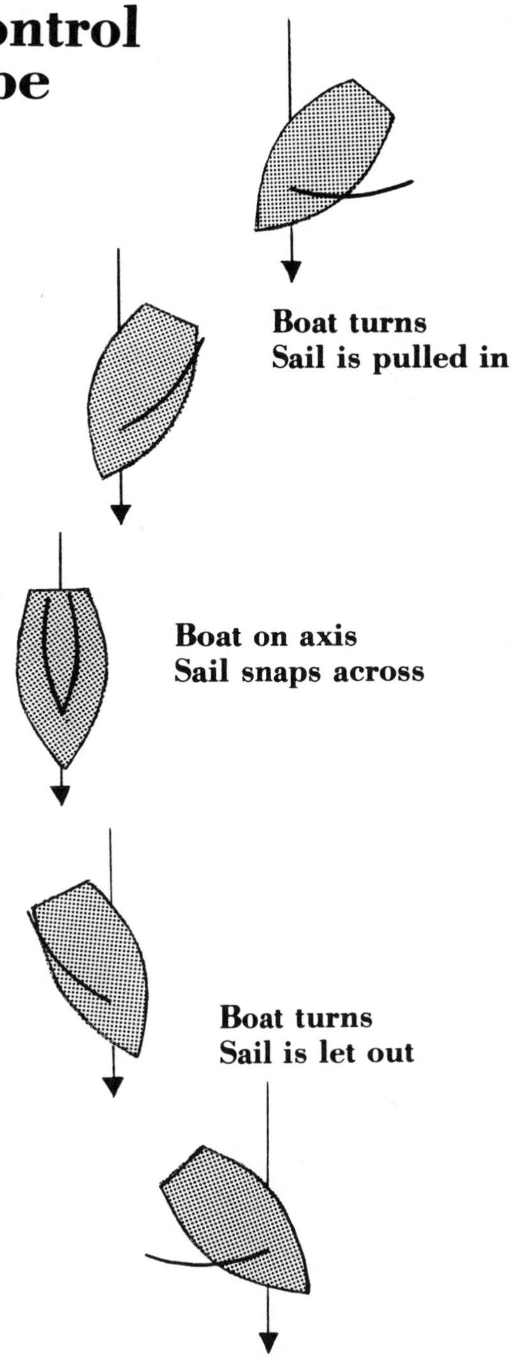

In the control jibe, the boat crosses the axis when the sheet is pulled tight and the sail is directly over the cockpit. The sail snaps across with one sharp tug on the sheet. ***Drawing by Lana Cory Hall***

Free jibe

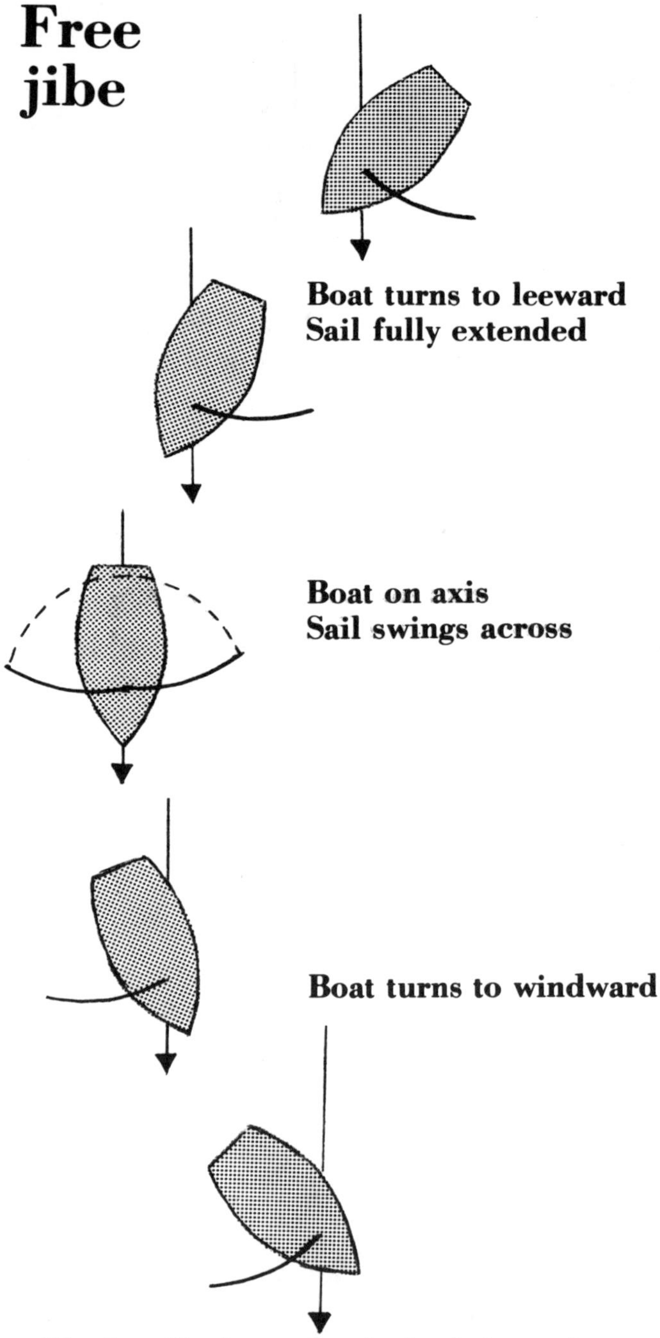

The free jibe is an exercise in timing and coordination. The sail swings across at the moment the boat crosses the axis, because everything is attuned to the rhythms of the elements. ***Drawing by Lana Cory Hall***

more extreme consequences of the flying jibe. You are particularly tempted to try it in heavy wind, when you especially don't fancy the ways sails would fly; though in many boats you find it nearly impossible to twist the sail back against such massive forces into such an aberrant setting. (You do see large keelboats control jibing in heavy wind—because otherwise their sails, set loose, would fly into impacts violent enough to cause serious structural damage—but the big boats have powerful winches to enforce control jibing; and, anyway, they jibe in more complicated ways, using relatively larger headsails and relatively smaller mainsails. You don't have to bother about big boats). You do the control jibe, most simply, because it seems conservative: it feels safe, even though it isn't really as safe as it feels. You never learn to like it for any of this. Even as you keep doing it, you never can actually like it.

Then inevitably you begin to hear the more enlightened and experimental counsel, still advocating a jibe that is free flight: unrestricted and unconfined, with the sail flying because flying is elemental—but always in a critical harmony with the overall movement of the boat crossing the axis. Such a jibe is simply the aesthetically pure, logical maneuver, with everything refined down to just the essential timing and balance, nothing ever contrived or enforced. It is entirely coordinated, never controlled: a venturesome jibe, widely unwarranted, largely radical, but indeed natural. You don't have to do it if you think you are the sort who shouldn't, but if you do it, you probably are going to like it regardless. Call it the free jibe.

So you are bound to try it. Steer down to the axis again, this time with the sail swinging out and setting across the wind—and with the wind spilling around the edges to rage as whirlwinds in the chasm opening behind, and the boat bearing slowly around to sail at the ragings in the chasm—which is the true way to go downward. The boat comes to the line and sails in the very tenuous state, just rocking for a while, then reeling and wrenching. This is the dead run. You have been here before.

On the line you hesitate, crouching on your toes, keeping the balance. You hold the course amid the turmoil; you feel the old instability and uncertainty. This time you are most intent on the delicate condition of the sail itself, again suspended between the weight of the wind and the ragings of the whirlwinds. The wind is dead weight now, just leaning on its side of the sail. The whirlwinds are fitful on their side. They come around the mast, then around the leech, swelling abruptly from one edge and surging across the surface, then receding abruptly and swelling in turn from the other edge. They keep doing this, swelling here, receding there; swelling there, receding here; and so surging back and forth behind the sail. And in this the whirlwinds strike a rhythm: a tempo obscured by the random writhings and swirlings, but still there, more fundamental. The boat rocks to this rhythm, more fixedly and deliberately than it rocks in waves, and the sail sways in slow motion out over the water, rising and sinking. It rises as the whirlwinds surge from the leech; it sinks as they surge from the mast. Its movements become quite regular, and more remarkably so, with nothing else being certain. It rises and falls like something breathing.

Then you watch this sail, concentrating on it, testing it, feeling it through the sheet. And you begin to breathe with it. You breathe in as it rises; you breathe out as it sinks. You move in rhythm.

For a moment you let the boat rock, just to be sure of the way this feels. It rocks to leeward, and the sail sinks. It rocks to windward, and the sail rises. You get ready as it rocks. You take long breaths. You let it rock once more to leeward; it leans over and pauses an instant. Then it comes back, the sail lifting. The timing is right. The moment is crucial.

You wait. The sail rises up, the whirlwinds coming around the leech and swelling behind. The mast comes erect, then leans to windward. You get the sense of the whirlwinds swelling, just from the way the boat feels as the mast leans. And you wait, breathing in, while the sail rises higher and the mast leans farther, until they both pause on the instant where you stop breathing in before breathing out—when the whirlwinds stop swelling before receding; before the new surge goes back the other way. On this instant you jibe the boat.

You steer across the axis, and you pull the sheet. You reach up and pull down, just once—a single, strong, steady pull: the critical touch, on the instant.

It is just enough. It moves the sail, if only a little, as the boat crosses the line. And the new whirlwinds come spinning around the mast, swelling large and surging around the heavy part of the sail, and the old whirlwinds recede back toward the leech. All of this starts exactly on the instant. And with this, the sail suddenly breaks out of suspension, coming free like a breath released, and rather incredibly the sail begins to drift across, against the dead weight of the wind itself. The sail nearly falters, but it seems almost metaphysically impelled, just floating over. It comes faster as more air slides in behind; it crosses above you and swings out over the other side, gathering momentum and beginning to fly—but softly now. The sail doesn't fly hard until the very end, and then the sheet and travelers stop it. You dampen the impact by letting the sheet slide through your hand. Then you just steer the boat and trim the sail, all quite easily; nothing is shaken, everything is coordinated. There is no frenzy or disarray, no contrivance. The boat sails at ease through the jibe and emerges with complete equanimity.

The perfect free jibe may be the most enlightened of all maneuvers, perhaps the highest state of the art in sailing the boat. *Drawing by Don Raden*

That is the free, enlightened jibe. It may be the highest state of the art in sailing the boat. When you do it right, it is the nearest thing to the perfect jibe; once you do it right, you never want to do any other jibe. But it has to be right within the narrowest tolerances: with everything happening exactly on the instant. The free jibe goes wrong if anything misses by half a second—because of imponderables: the boat swerving slightly, or a whirlwind taking a turn, or a wave breaking just then, or simply because you breathe half a second too long or too short. And when the jibe is wrong, by whatever margin, it does not work at all: it is no jibe. The moment goes, and the sail does not break free, and the boat is left there, muddling absurdly, off-balance and over the line. Then you either pull the sheet and try to enforce a control jibe to get out of this, or you keep turning the boat and sailing it by the lee until you push it into a flying jibe. Or you could start over and steer back and try another free jibe, which may not work either. The free jibe is like this. It could be the most satisfying single thing you can do in the boat. But you can't do it every time.

You learn the free jibe as an advanced art: the last effort of sheer feeling and balance and timing and rhythm. You just have to keep trying it until you do it right, even if partly by luck, and then you begin to get the sense of it. At first you do perhaps three good free jibes in ten tries, but the three jibes are more than worth the seven failures. So you work willingly at this, and when you are expert, you do nine free jibes out of ten, and the tenth is an impossible circumstance, so you can't be blamed. But when you are expert, you recover adroitly enough that you make even a bad jibe look good. The free jibe works to this extent, even if it is not fully sanctioned.

You choose your own jibes after this. You do free jibes if you like them best, though you have moments when you would rather do control jibes, even though you don't like them. And sometimes you even are seized with moods for doing flying jibes. You experiment with jibes and develop your own hybrids: free jibes with some control, control jibes with some freedom, even flying jibes with some vestiges of moderation. But you still go with some uncertainty into all jibes—because all the while, jibing remains the necessarily uncertain maneuver in the turmoil dead before the wind. And while you do come sailing through most jibes, sometimes handily, sometimes not, you still don't come through all of them. Now you have to consider this: now and then you aren't going to make it. Some jibes can very nearly capsize you because of the uncertainties. A few are actually going to.

There is the phenomenon called broaching. It is not capsizing: it causes capsizing. It is an occasional madness that seizes the boat as the sail swings in a random jibe—a very specific *centrifugal* madness. Broaching is a sudden, rapid, forceful, uncontrolled heading-up from a run or reach. The boat spins. And it rolls. It hurls all its drive and momentum into a wrenching loop on the water; it suddenly is up on its edge and teetering precariously, leaning over and down, toward the water. There is no restraint; everything presses over and down: no steerage; boat and rudder are simply dragged together. The boat has this total seizure of spinning around and rolling over; it ships heavy green water over the rail. This is broaching. For this moment, there is nothing but madness.

You have only the raw sensation of broaching. It is a *potent* madness: something quick and violent that happens before you can know why. And sometimes the boat does capsize while broaching—too fast to be your fault, but more than it happens all other ways—and other times it recovers and comes shakily erect with water sloshing ankle-deep in the cockpit. It may do either, but only on its own resources. You have no part in this; you are no longer sailing. When the boat broaches, you can only cling tightly until the madness passes, and then you still don't know what happened. Broaching is out of your control.

There is profound speculation on broaching. It is the flying jibe come to the ultimate bad end for being frenzied, the control jibe come to the bad end for being stifled, the free jibe come to the bad end for being unsanctioned. It is the boat caught between waves and gusts and sent reeling about; it is the boat reeling from the impacts of flying sails or under the constrictions of tight sails. It is the boat going one way and the sail another, the boat swerving aside while the sail drives ahead—the boat simultaneously turning under itself and tripping over itself, the rigging going headlong over the hull. It is simple though abstruse; complex though fundamental. It is fearfully quick and irrational in any case. All speculations eventually come down to this: the final element of madness.

Broaching is a sudden, rapid, forceful heading-up from a run or reach—an abrupt madness that seizes the boat in the midst of jibe. The boat spins and rolls, and there is nothing to do but cling and hope. ***Drawing by Don Raden***

You find scant enlightenment in this, and no reassurance. There is a logic in broaching, but it is not readily discernible. Broaching is going to happen fitfully to you in some jibes and not in others. Do a jibe once, and the sail flies with all its sound and fury, and the boat broaches; do it again, and the sail flies, but only with the sound and fury. The boat can broach or not broach in the wildest flying jibe, or the strictest control jibe, or even in the most enlightened free jibe gone wrong. And if it broaches once with you in any given jibe, then you probably can't make it broach again if you did the same jibe a dozen more times. But then you still can't be sure it wouldn't broach again if you did the jibe just once more. So when you deliberately try to make the boat broach, it probably won't. When you don't try, it eventually will, but never for any apparent reason; and of course broaching is always so damnably sudden. Once it happens you know it, even though you never realize until too late.

This confounds you, as it must. You have no control of the boat broaching, no feeling beyond the raw sensations, and you have little chance of comprehension. You know just enough to be nervous when you are going to jibe. And you have good reason.

So learn this: the best theory says broaching is an imbalance. It is things taking hold and letting go, forces shifting where other forces already are. It is a special state: the boat, about to broach, comes down to the line, rocking like always, pushing doggedly to leeward in fitful conflict with its own weather helm pulling to windward. It turns steadily despite uncertainties—against random forces and things surging up and lashing back. Turning like this, it has its seizures of reeling and wrenching; it goes easily, then hard. And this time, as it crosses the axis, it encounters some chance resistance and goes especially hard. It masses its weight and makes a great push past the line. And just then the sail comes free and comes across.

This happens too fast. The sail comes. The boat jibes. And the weather helm abruptly lets go where it had pulled against the boat pushing, and now it takes hold the other way and pulls where the boat pushes hardest. The boat effectively lunges out of the weather helm on one tack and is impelled headlong into the weather helm on the other—like a dog lunging and breaking a leash behind and being jerked just then by a leash ahead. And this is altogether too much; it is a massive overbalance. All force and impetus suddenly come together, on the instant, pushing the boat around and now pulling it too. Everything is turning the boat; nothing will stop it after this. With an awful lurch, the boat spins.

So the boat goes mad, and this is its special state. It reels under the flying sails, swerves around while still driving ahead, turns under itself and trips over itself, the rigging going over the hull. The boat heels up and swerves still harder, with the weather helm verging on overpowering. Spinning and rolling it goes over—or it doesn't quite. This is broaching. The boat is beyond your control. Now what do you do about it?

You experiment: very gingerly. You jibe some more, and each time, as you steer downwind, you concentrate on the feel of the boat turning through the uncertanties. When the boat turns easily, you steer it gently, and it is all right. When it begins to turn hard, you begin to push it, but cautiously. You don't like to push any more; you do it only to test and probe and try to sense the way downwind. You don't push the boat at all when it turns very hard and wrenches and balks against amorphous forces; you ease it back instead, and wait with it, keeping it calm until it turns easily again. You have to learn a strategy of feints and finesses to bring the boat to leeward; it is like playing very defensive chess in one sense, and like crossing a busy street in another. This requires a special restraint: a singular sort of courage in the easing back and waiting and keeping calm. But finally, before the wind, you steer the boat to the axis; and there on a moment when everything goes without effort, you float the boat effortlessly past. On the line itself, you just balance the boat and hold the tiller, and you never let yourself push anything. Never so much as a nudge.

Then the sail comes across, the boat jibes, and this time no unbalanced impetus drives it farther around. It doesn't lunge or push. It just turns effortlessly and keeps the balance, and the lines of force shift from one side to the other. Like this it does not broach. Not broaching, it does not capsize.

In time you learn this. It is a special skill, and it requires a touchy technique, but you work at it and begin to get the feel for it, as you do for everything. And after this the boat almost never broaches if you just don't push it. It broaches only when you lose restraint and push when you know that you shouldn't—when you go into the jibe pushing. Then everything is about to spin out of your control.

Except you have one last chance. You try to pull the tiller back before it is too late. Give the tiller one hard, short, urgent tug just as the sail flies—you have only this one instant for this one tug back—and if you pull in time, you quell the push just enough to hold the boat back before it would spin away altogether. Then let the sheet go completely, so the sail crosses over and swings free, spilling wind as fast as the lines can reel out; you desperately jettison wind to get the boat out from under the weight of it. This works only if your timing is right, but this once you presume it right. You hold back the boat and lighten it just enough so it doesn't spin away. It hesitates instead. It thrashes awkwardly in the water, shuddering fearfully under cross tensions; then it quiets down and rolls with the waves. This is sloppy sailing, but you do keep the boat from going mad and broaching—though of course you never are certain that it really *was* about to. In any case this works sometimes. Or it seems to.

Later, when you are good at jibing, you have reckless moods in which you deliberately push the boat hard past the axis and deliberately try to pull it back at the last second. You jibe like a dive bomber; you are incredibly daring. Sometimes you make it. Sometimes you don't.

Still later, when you are expert, you outgrow this.

12
Landing

When you are done sailing, you land the boat. Landing is like stopping the boat, except landing becomes a specific state. Stopping is letting the boat flutter and die in the wind and on the water. Landing is stopping at one place on the earth: exactly there and not four inches away. Landing is stopping absolutely.

When you land right, you stop the boat at a place three inches down the wind axis from a pier or buoy: stopping it so it never touches the pier or buoy or anything else fixed to the earth. You stop it by not sailing it, by putting it in irons and so letting it flutter and die. You land it so it flutters and dies at that place three inches from an untouched fixed object. You land by precisely pinpointing the death of the boat.

You stop the boat easily—or it dies easily. Its life forces, however potent, still exist only tenuously in your two hands, and now you simply let go after holding on all this while. Drop the sheet, and the sail swings away, flapping. The wind shakes out; the forces blow free. Ease the tiller to leeward, and the boat turns up into the eye of the wind, drifts and flounders; and it stops there. You let go, and the boat flutters and dies.

This happens between two places. The first place is where you let go: the boat stops sailing there, though it still keeps coming—fluttering and dying but drifting farther, across a certain distance—until it comes to the other place, the final one, where it stops altogether. So when you land, you stop the boat with a certain foresight. You can only get to the final place from the first, and you can only find the first place from the final. You must resolve the first place as a calculation to fix upon—allowing for momentum and counter-momentum—when you see the final place three inches down the wind axis from a fixed object. You begin and end on this.

This means, as you come sailing toward a pier or buoy, that you become preoccupied with landing strategies while still a distance off. You aim the boat at long range, measuring force, speed, drift, inertia, concentrating on the feel of all the elements together, then figuring the ways they all will go when you let them go. Coming closer, you plot the ways the boat will go, fluttering and dying, when you let go. You gauge distances and directions now, first projecting them outward from the pier or buoy, then from the place three inches down the wind axis. You calculate outward in any case; you come sailing in, and now you are very close, adjusting and correcting minutely. You feel the boat coming toward a resolution. Then just ahead you see the place where you are going to let go. It is resolved on

Drawing by Don Raden

the water, a place measured from the other place. You fix upon it, and only the maneuver remains.

(Land at a buoy this time, not at a pier. Don't try pier landings until you learn precision doing buoy landings. Find a small, lonely, weightless buoy, your own buoy if nothing else; make one like a fisherman does, from a well rinsed plastic bleach bottle anchored by a brick. The bottle afloat will be weightless like a bubble and will bob in place while you learn to stop three inches away, and when you drift four inches too far, it will yield impalpably before you and gently forgive you. Until you learn the precision, you need the forgiveness. The pier would not yield you an inch. It would have no forgiveness at all.)

In landing you don't really dwell on the actual maneuver; you are intent just on the precision of it. The maneuver is the simple letting-go, and the landings you make with it differ only by the variations you do on it. And the variations are so limited that your most conservative landing would be little different from your most radical. This would be the easiest maneuver of all, except—in this state of incessant mobility, where everything rolls and heaves and blows away—you must commit yourself to the ideal landing, precise within three inches. This is indeed where landing becomes its own specific state.

First do a half-hedged landing; or an idiot's landing, or a diddler's landing—there being only these unkind tag names for lack of an adequate real name—a semi-maneuver that is something less than a real landing but does come after a fashion to the same end. It is rudimentary enough: just set the

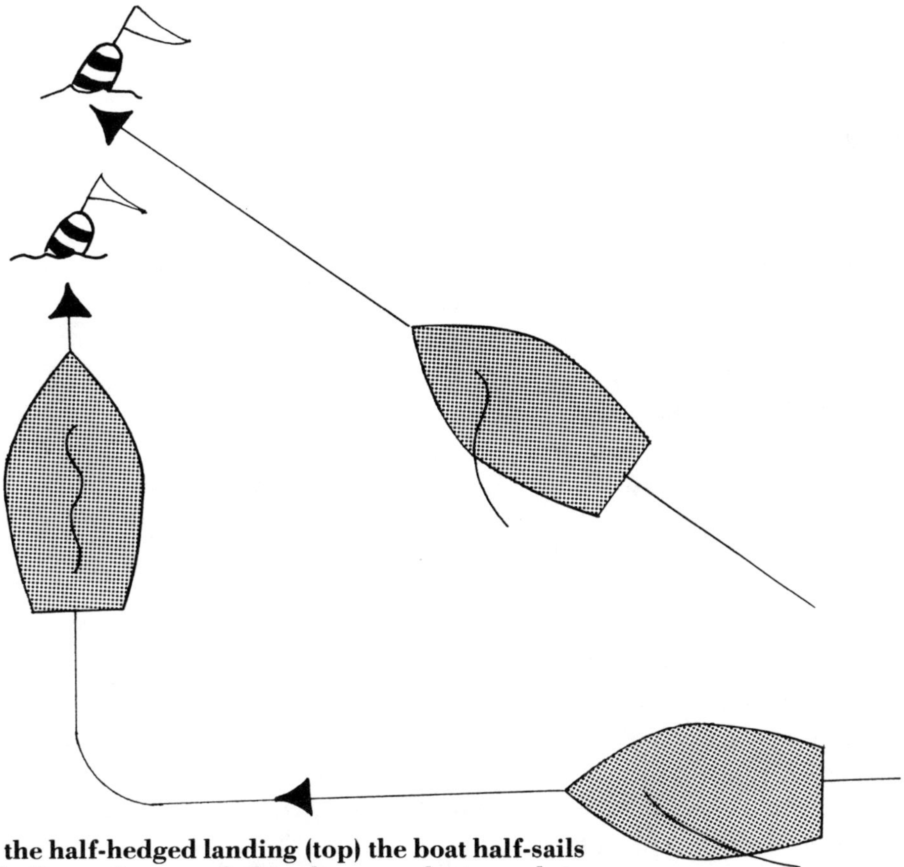

In the half-hedged landing (top) the boat half-sails half-luffs, and comes haltingly up a close reach to the buoy. In the true landing (bottom), the boat turns deliberately up the wind axis and drifts directly to the buoy. ***Drawing by Lana Cory Hall***

boat on a close reach, pointing up toward the buoy; steer ahead, straight at the buoy. And now let the sheet slide, so the sail swings out quivering, about to start flapping. But don't let go completely; this is where you half hedge. Steer into the wind with the boat half-adrift, the sail half-fluttering. If the boat is about to stop short of the buoy, then pull in the sheet just enough to harden the curve very slightly in the sail—and keep going on this. Then let the sheet slide again, and let the sail soften before the boat can gather any serious momentum. Then pull the sheet in again, and let it out again. Keep the boat moving like this, just on the verge of dying but always aimed dead at the buoy. You begin to feel almost cruel.

This is what you mean to happen: there will be a moment when you know that the boat, by its inertia and direction, must go to the buoy. On that moment you will stand up and let go of the sheet and tiller—this time simply dropping them and leaving them; you won't need them. You will take three steps forward to the bow, and when you are there, the boat will stop still in the water, three inches from the buoy. You will tap the buoy three times, slowly and symbolically, and the boat will stay floating in place.

With that you would make one perfect landing; though with your allowances so minute, you won't make many more like it. You land, finally, by learning the balance between momentum and counter-momentum—by figuring action against reaction: by anticipating measures of impetus even as you come half hedging toward the buoy. You need to reckon that the boat is drifting with a certain momentum, and as you take the three steps forward, you will carry a certain counter-momentum; and in fact your three steps will set the drifting boat three feet back. So in half hedging, you must allow the boat the added momentum to go three more feet to the point three inches from the

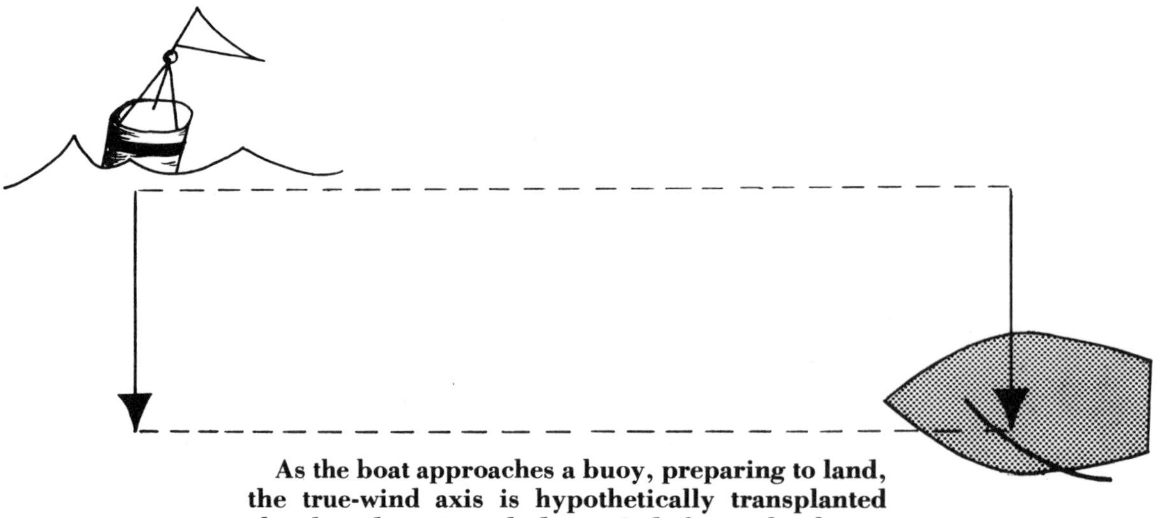

As the boat approaches a buoy, preparing to land, the true-wind axis is hypothetically transplanted ahead and projected downwind from the buoy. ***Drawing by Lana Cory Hall***

buoy. Then you will land.

Try several half-hedged landings. Do them from both tacks. Do them right. Make the allowances; feel the momentum. If you don't actually stop three inches from the buoy, you still should stop within a foot of it, which is close enough so you can tap it three times. (Or if you weren't just practicing, you could tie the boat to the buoy and be secure). Do the half-hedged landing just enough to know how it works—which is enough to learn not to like it, which is all you really need of it. You do it only to start landing, before you learn real landings. When you are done with it, you probably never will do it again.

When you do real landings, there is no hedging. You make the total commitment and go dead into the wind—straight up the line from the place where you let go to the place where the boat stops. From now on you do all landings up the true wind axis, the first line of reference.

From the first, you apply your foresight specifically to the true wind axis: this line, integral to the boat all this while, now advances even before the oncoming boat itself. As you come sailing in, you hypothetically detach the axis from the boat and attach it to the buoy ahead—perhaps fifty or one hundred yards ahead—and project the line downwind from the buoy. So just for landing, the axis-reference line is displaced forward where it lies across the course you would sail. Then steer toward the line, resolving it, gauging distances on it, and fix on a place down the line and aim the boat there. And when you get to the place, let go. Ease the tiller, drop the sheet; turn the boat up the axis. Steer directly at the buoy, dead into the eye of the wind. The boat drifts, fluttering and dying, until its momentum is gone, and it stops. When you learn the precision for this, the boat stops three inches from the buoy.

Hereafter you acquire precision. You do many landings. You learn how the boat feels, doing landings, and you gradually derive still another new feeling for it, a very particular sense of its speed and momentum. By feeling, you come to know distance. You feel the balance between the impetus of the boat and the force of the wind, and from this you reckon how far the boat will drift against the wind by how hard it drives with it—or how far the boat will go up the line by how forcefully it comes to it. You learn this with practice. Because of the balance, the boat has a certain headreach: a certain distance it will drift upwind. The headreach varies with different winds; it shortens in heavy winds. It is affected by how sharply the boat turns upwind. But in headreach there still are certain constant factors—things you begin to sense, almost like the boat's own inertia. In figuring headreach, you learn the first elements of precision.

Then come sailing in, calculating headreach along the axis line transplanted ahead, measuring it downwind from the buoy. Assume for the first landing that headreach is double the length of the boat: that the boat will drift twice its own length against the wind. You are half-arbitrary, half-intuitive on this, but mostly you are right; most little boats do drift about this far. You gauge this distance by sighting proportions or casting projections along the line, or by doing triangulations if you are clever that way—or you just learn by feel, which eventually works about as well. This is a science now however you do it: twenty yards from the displaced axis line, you measure the three inches from the buoy; you allow the momentum for the three extra feet, and you fix upon the place two boat lengths downwind. Aim there, sail there, let go, and steer the boat upwind.

Then you have done it, and you can only drift toward the buoy to see if you have done it right or wrong. If the boat stops three inches from the buoy, you have figured the exact headreach. If the boat stops short, and you can't reach the buoy to tap it three times, you have figured too long a headreach; next time measure a shorter distance down the wind axis. And if the boat drifts too far and overruns the buoy, you have figured too short a headreach; next time measure a longer distance down the axis. You learn precision by measuring distances longer when they are short and shorter when they are long.

At first you are not precise at all. You drift the boat six feet past the buoy; then you stop five feet short. Sometimes you miss the turn and come upwind wide of the mark. But soon you come closer. You make the large, easy corrections, then the small, hard corrections, and then the very small ad-

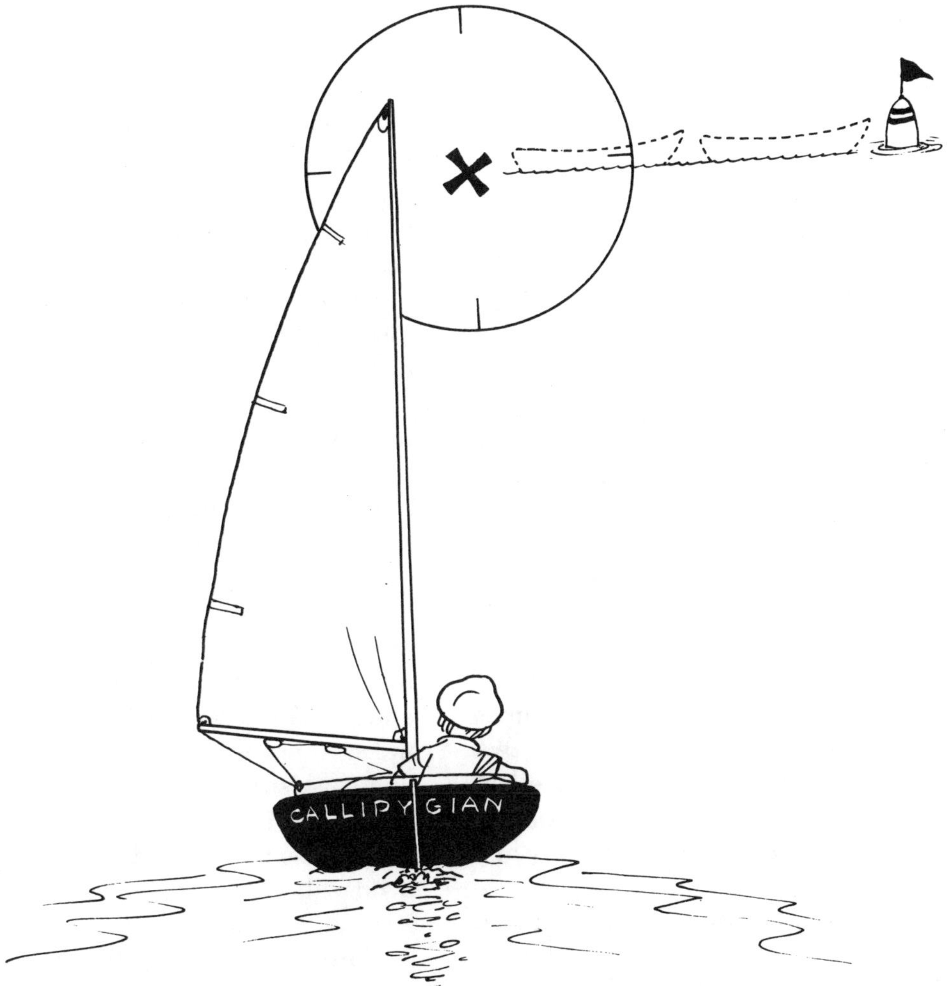

The skipper figures headreach. He calculates that the boat will drift twice its own length up the wind axis to the buoy. He fixes upon a place two boat lengths directly downwind of the buoy; he will sail to that place and swing the boat from there directly upwind to the buoy. ***Drawing by Don Raden***

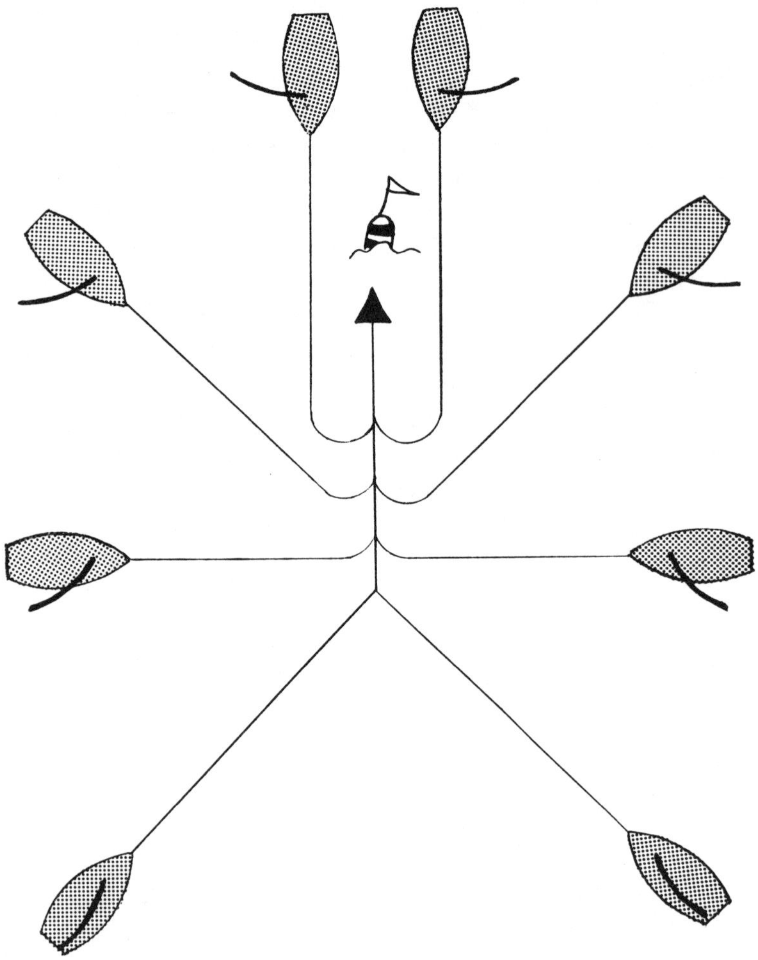

The boat approaches the buoy from nearly every direction. It lands from port tack or starboard tack, from dead runs, broad reaches, beam reaches, and close reaches. *Drawing by Lana Cory Hall*

justments: figuring just the last few inches up and down the axis. Do fifty landings—dedicating yourself, concentrating each time on that place three inches downwind of the buoy—and in the last ten landings you should stop the boat four times within a foot of the buoy and five times within two feet. You probably do miss one landing in the last ten, but you are becoming precise even so; you are refining the particular feeling for the boat's headreach.

(As you do landings, you discover that you also must undo them; because after you bring the boat to a landing, you must back it out. Backing out of landings is the same as backing out of irons, because in landing you put the boat deliberately in irons, three inches from the buoy; and after you tap the buoy three times, you still are there with the boat in irons, floating dead in the water. So you back out of this; you have backed before. Wait until the boat begins to drift backward, then steer very cautiously in reverse, pointing the tiller where you mean to point the boat. The trick, as always, is to stop the impulse to steer the other way: a simple trick when you do it, but still a trick. The boat, drifting aft, swings around and comes across the wind; the sail fills, and the boat moves forward. As often as you land the boat, you back it out like this, just so you can do it when you really have to. Backing out is easier than landing, but in critical moments it can be equally vital.)

From now on you practice—hovering about the buoy, coming to it like an insect, then backing off and coming again: serving the apprenticeship in landing the boat. Sail to the axis line on port tack and on starboard, until you are precise landing both ways. You become precise sailing close hauled to the line and landing that way—and sailing the close reaches to the line and landing that way; and sailing the broad reaches to the line and landing that way. Finally you run dead before the wind and swing the boat completely around and point it up the axis and become precise landing even this way. For a while you just work at this.

Sometime in this, usually after a long time, you discover the dynamic landing: the kind that experts do. They come to the axis, and they let the sheet go, but they don't ease the tiller, which would be the natural way. They force the landing. They swing the tiller hard to leeward, pushing it almost violently to its limit, setting the rudder nearly flat against the transom. (You tried this coming about, and it was wrong then, because the boat stopped, but this is landing, and the boat means to stop.) With this they set a boat into a sudden, forceful swerve, spinning it to windward in a great flurry, driving mass and impetus sideways against volumes of water. On the axis they wrench the tiller back—hard—and the boat just seems to pause there dramatically, as if suspended on that instant. Then it comes straight toward the buoy, moving very slowly, advancing as if on will power alone. Its momentum is abruptly gone in volumes of water.

This makes a splendid landing in a flourish of surging water and rattling sails; this *looks* like something experts would do. But try it yourself, just once—push the tiller hard and pull it back—and you can do it too. It isn't even difficult. You figure about the same headreach as for any landing (though you also can do this in tighter quarters; in moments of stress, this may be *all* you can do in tighter quarters). You swerve the boat, driving its momentum against the water; you set the boat on the axis. The boat shakes itself, comes erect, and comes forward straight up the line. It moves steadily, not really even drifting like before; this time it seems somehow drawn toward the buoy, as if self-guided. The boat, having dumped its momentum so abruptly, now gives you an extraordinary feeling of control. You could be steering by sheer concentration, knowing just by cause and effect that the boat must come very near to the place three inches from the buoy. This is why experts land this way—not just because they are experts; simply because the landing works so well.

When you are done practicing landings, you come back to the shore to land at the pier. This time you are not practicing. You come to the pier when you really are ready to land. When you know you are going to make it.

There can be no compromise. You expect none. The boat comes. The pier stands. If the boat doesn't stop, the pier doesn't forgive. If the boat stops short and doesn't back out right, it will flounder toward the shore, which is rock and doesn't forgive either. You don't propose to be forgiven, or to need forgiveness. You mean to bring the boat with all certainty to the pier and to stop it there in the water, only inches away. And you mean to do this before the inevitable board of review: an omnipresent committee of critics, commentators, and informal faultfinders who make themselves ever-vigilant in solemn clusters on the shore. They have no actual sanctions or authority, but they are always there, passing judgment, and you establish your whole reputation by this first landing you do before them. You must never show the slightest awareness of their existence.

(By the way, you aren't about to try landing on the windward side of the pier. You don't ever want to put the boat on the windward side of anything that doesn't forgive. You would be placing it directly between the force of the wind and the mass of the unyielding fixed object—between hammer and anvil—and the boat, even made of plastic, would not survive for long. Not there.)

Choose the largest open space on the lee side of the pier. Allow all possible landing room. Then project the axis line downwind from the pier. Measure along the line, gauge the headreach, figure the momentum. Fix upon the place for letting go, sail the boat there, and make the landing. Do this dynamically. Swing the tiller hard. Spin the boat, driving its momentum against the water. Set the boat on the axis—shuddering, coming erect, and moving forward. It moves inexorably. It impels itself upwind toward the pier. This time you know it is not going to stop.

Let the critics have this one instant to savor blood and wreckage, anticipating the crash.

Then swing the tiller once more, hard, and spin the boat half around—just before it would hit—swerving it sideways and turning the last of its impetus against the great weight of the water. The boat comes alongside the pier; you set it here deliberately, and it stops here abruptly. This is in fact the best way to land at a pier. The boat lies exactly three inches from the pier, never touching the pier. It is perfectly still, except for the sail flapping.

Be completely casual now. Set the tiller down and leave it there; you are done with it. Stand up, straighten your collar, and move forward most leisurely, as if you were just taking a stroll about the decks. Pick up the painter as if you simply happened upon it. And very calmly reach over to the pier and make the painter fast. Leave it hanging slack between the boat and the pier. Never even acknowledge the critics on the shore.

13
More Wind

At the end you learn about the real wind.

All this while the wind has been constant: the true wind, a fair wind from the north—blowing steadily for you at 10 knots; blowing arbitrarily harder when you needed—wind presumed this fair and constant for you to learn to sail in. But wind isn't going to be like this from now on. It really isn't ever like this. Wind is wind, unfixed and incessant; it is shifting, spreading, changing, turning; it is completely volatile, blowing heavy and light, one way and all ways. This is what you learn in the end: the real wind is not constant.

You begin to know the real wind just by sailing in it. It has definite traits from the first, even as it is not constant. It can blow heavy or light, or it can shift about, blowing heavy or light. In moderation or in extreme, it is heavy wind or shifting wind or light wind. It blows in these three particular ways, and you come to know it when you learn to sail in it.

First, then, the heavy wind, the special one: the ultimate confrontation. When you consider real wind, you really mean heavy wind; you can't help it, you invariably leave other winds for afterthoughts. There is no mistaking heavy wind. You know it by its force. It howls with force; it bends trees, it bends people trying to walk. It is the kind of wind in which the Coast Guard's red flags are up and rattling. Great, green rolling waves are rising up with white crests and driving against the shore with fearful impacts, setting the spray flying. This is magnificent wind. You could reckon it greater than twenty knots, or higher than force five on the Beaufort scale. But you don't need numbers: this is an emotional experience. You have a very basic feeling for this wind when you are about to sail the boat in it. You know without asking—this is heavy wind.

There have been times—there still are times, persistently recurring—when conservative counsel says you never should sail a small boat deliberately into heavy wind. Because you are plainly unequal to heavy wind. It is at least ten or twenty times greater than you and the boat together. Its force could summarily overwhelm and overpower you; it can seriously endanger you. Conservatives dwell ponderously on the awful magnitude of heavy wind. They know heavy wind as a predator from the abyss. It is always out at sea somewhere, just waiting. Eventually it must descend on you as you drift unguarded. And only then would you actually sail in it. But you would mean solely to survive in heavy wind—to reef down the sails, hold down the boat, and just beat for shelter, reducing all efforts to the primal struggle for self-preservation. By conservative counsel you would limit yourself this rigid-

Drawing by Don Raden

ly: learning only to sail the boat out of heavy wind and into safe refuge. You would never even allow yourself the alien thought of sailing the other way, out of safe refuge and into heavy wind. Not into that sort of force.

But you also must hear the other counsel, more enlightened and experimental, advancing more objective attitudes toward heavy wind. It is indeed a force of considerable magnitude, certainly a most serious force, not to be exaggerated. But for all of that, it is not a sinister force: not intrinsically, not specifically. Heavy wind has a certain rudimentary fairness. It means only to blow hard where it will: to be always a simple, indiscriminate force, having no actual grudge against you. It tolerates you to a degree for being in its way, but it makes you no allowances. It quickly blows you down when obliged to—when you turn too *much* in its way—though even then it blows you down benignly, meaning you no harm. By enlightened counsel, you would sail on the fairness of heavy wind, having a sufficiently cautious respect for it without wanting to be afraid of it, knowing you are not equal to it but still keeping a trust in it. You are going to learn now that you need a very basic maturity to sail in heavy wind: because now, with just the boat and the skill to sail it, you find yourself suddenly less intrepid than you would like to be.

You have your first reassurance just in the way a good boat feels in heavy wind. A boat can be wood or plastic, but you know by feel alone if it is built by the rules of heavy wind. A good boat still is vulnerable—in heavy wind everything is ultimately vulnerable—but it always feels somehow competent, regardless of how capably you actually sail it. For your own boat, the glass and resin hull is strong and inert to the point where it seems quite numb to the stresses of heavy wind. It can heave and strain and pound interminably through the great waves; and it just keeps going, insensible and uncomplaining. It takes stress better than you do; you feel the pounding, it does not. In this boat you will sail deliberately into heavy wind—and really sail this time, not just survive—because you know the boat will go, and you need to know how far you can go with it.

Then understand this at the start: In heavy wind you sail as you would in any wind, except you do all the compromising. You derive a whole strategy of compromise—and concession and conciliation, and often outright sacrifice. You have to make all the allowances the wind can't, and still you have to feel secure about sailing the boat. In heavy wind you have to be more prudent than proud. This is where you need maturity.

First you must recognize that heavy wind is not the final wind. There is a point, very subjective, where it swells to an upper capacity and verges on overpowering, becoming a survival wind of gale strength, about to blow with more force than you can compromise. You know a survival wind by the feeling of forces about to overwhelm—something you don't mistake—but you concentrate specifically on this point where heavy wind turns to survival wind. This is where the wind presses your own limit; it is where you want to know your exact limit, because survival wind allows you only a narrow margin, giving you your last chance to survive—beating for shelter, trusting the strength of glass and resin—before still greater winds would rise up, growing by stages to hurricanes. Hurricane winds are beyond survival. They would simply blow you away.

You would like to be sure of your own limit, so you could fix upon it and measure it precisely—by a wind speed or force, something over 30 knots or force 7 on the Beaufort scale—but it can't be like that. Your limit varies at any given moment with the boats you sail and the skills you learn, and then it shifts erratically with the moods that come upon you in the emotional experience of heavy wind. Moods become powerful now, with this much force in the wind. If you could hold always to the right sequence of moods, you would set out a romantic, starting at a high limit, being fresh and strong and eager for the challenge, yet tempered by the measure of prudence. And you would return a pragmatist, sustaining a high limit, being wet and battered but well-seasoned now, keeping just the essential measure of strength and sailing with a grim, hard, tired competence. But in heavy wind you never can progress so rationally, keeping your moods so well ordered; moods change as you do, and you are very complicated. You have your moods in sudden shifts, the right ones raising your limit, the wrong ones lowering it. You are willful, dogged, sometimes exultant, occasionally fearful, and at moments, near despair. You never can be so sure of so many moods that you could actually fix your own limit by them. You come to an understanding with your own limit; you still would like to know it but not enough to try it. You know it to the extent that you are not about to test it just to get its measure in heavy wind, not when you consider what is just beyond. You come to realize that you never are going to be *exactly* sure of your own limit.

Instead you settle for an abiding awareness. The limit is there; at least you are sure of that; and by keeping aware of it, you do get definite feelings for it. You know when you are near your limit, just by the way the forces gather for a crisis. And you intuitively sense crisis; the feeling is strong and clear and imminent. You just need to know this is the feeling of your own limit, even though you can't be precise about it. Then you can come to know your limit at least enough so you can begin to allow for it and learn to keep away from it. You can connect your limit in heavy wind to your instinct for self-preservation, and this is all you really want to do with it anyway. With abiding awareness, you set this margin.

In fact you probably could measure your own limit by that wind of 30 knots or force 7, and often enough you would be quite close. Assume that limit in any case, just to have it to fix upon, if only arbitrarily. Then allow less—a margin for error—when you actually go sailing in heavy wind. Start in a wind below 25 knots: or still more safely, in a wind of 25 miles per hour (about 22 knots) if you feel surer of it that way. Call the weather bureau before setting out, and the recorded voice quotes you a figure in miles per hour. Or listen to the weather on the radio, which quotes you another figure; or watch the TV weatherperson, who may quote you still another. Just get some sort of word in advance, if only to have it—though don't trust it implicitly; it usually is for weather somewhere else—then allow the extra margin on your limit for when the word is wrong. Then go sailing in heavy wind.

Always rig the boat as quickly as you can in heavy wind, because a boat is most painfully vulnerable in the rigging process—being both tethered and tossed, tied to a pier and thrashing at the end of its painter, caught between elements in the stress and conflict of fixed objects and moving forces. The wind blows the boat; the waves lift it and roll it. But the painter abruptly jerks it back, and the pier never yields or forgives. In heavy wind this becomes distressing. The boat is lifted high, rolled far, and jerked back hard. It can't move its natural ways; it is jarred the wrong ways, just held there and shaken incessantly; in time its machinery would begin to chafe and loosen and crack at the weak points. So now you work fast to raise the sail and get the boat underway while everything still can be intact and healthy. The boat plainly is not healthy tied to the pier in heavy weather. Don't keep it there any longer than you must.

The sail goes up the groove in the mast, now as always, hoisted by the halyard. But this time it goes with gathering convulsions: writhing and lashing and flapping hard—taking a pounding from the wind—and making a racket, snapping like gunfire along the leech. You feel the distress of the sail even more than that of the boat. The sail seems mindlessly bent on self-destruction; left like this, it would flog itself to rags and tatters. Often you have to fight it up the mast. It stalls or tangles or jams in the groove. It struggles against you; you struggle back. Concentrate just on raising it fast; once you start it up the mast, try only to contain it and keep it going up, even if you have to fight it all the way to the top. Once you have it there, secure it tightly, cleating down the halyard with a very good knot. But never stop for a moment.

Draw other lines taut. Pull the halyard tighter than before (or pull the downhaul tighter if you have one), stretching the luff another fraction of an inch along the mast. Pull the outhaul more: just short of the point where the tension would make stretch marks across the sail. Drawn this tight, the sail may fill out in a slightly flatter curve, which is aerodynamically better in heavy wind—just as birds with flat, knifelike wings are aerodynamically better at high speed. But more important, the higher tension must hold this curve firmly and rigidly against the greater stresses of heavy wind. A sail under less tension would belly out into a deep curve with the sheer weight of heavy wind. The sail, in effect, would drag its belly in the wind and become severely burdened by it; whereas a sail with a leaner profile, a flatter curve, still will turn the wind dynamically without getting in its way and so will generate real sail power. Some fancy boats even have special sails cut flat for heavy wind. On your boat you just tighten lines.

Now rig the boom vang. It is a restraining line, a piece of rope lashed diagonally between the foot of the mast and a point on the boom, three or four feet aft: And you especially need the boom vang in heavy wind. (Boats should have special fittings for attaching boom vangs, but yours probably doesn't because boom vangs are dismissed too often as specialized toys for racers. You have to rig yours with a rolling hitch which is the same as a tautline hitch in Boy Scouts—a very creative knot that doesn't slip under tension. This is called jury rigging.) Pull the piece of rope tight and secure it at about a 45-degree angle, (See illustration) and you make a right triangle of mast, boom, and vang; the vang is the hypotenuse. The vang lets the boom swing across but not up; it keeps the boom down and the curve flat. Without the vang, the sail would belly out with the sheer weight of the wind; in bellying out it would form a deep curve and lift the boom. But now, with the vang attached, the sail can't lift the boom, and without lifting the boom it can't belly out, and with the sail not bellying out, the curve stays flat. The boom vang becomes part of the boat's working machinery; it really is a much better thing than it is given credit for. You ought to use it all the time.

Understand one more thing, very basic and physical. Heavy wind bends farther around the sail than does lesser wind; the outer current turns upon a longer arc forward and separates from a shorter arc aft. This means, as lesser wind becomes heavy wind, that the center of effort moves several inches aft on the sail—and then moves much farther aft as

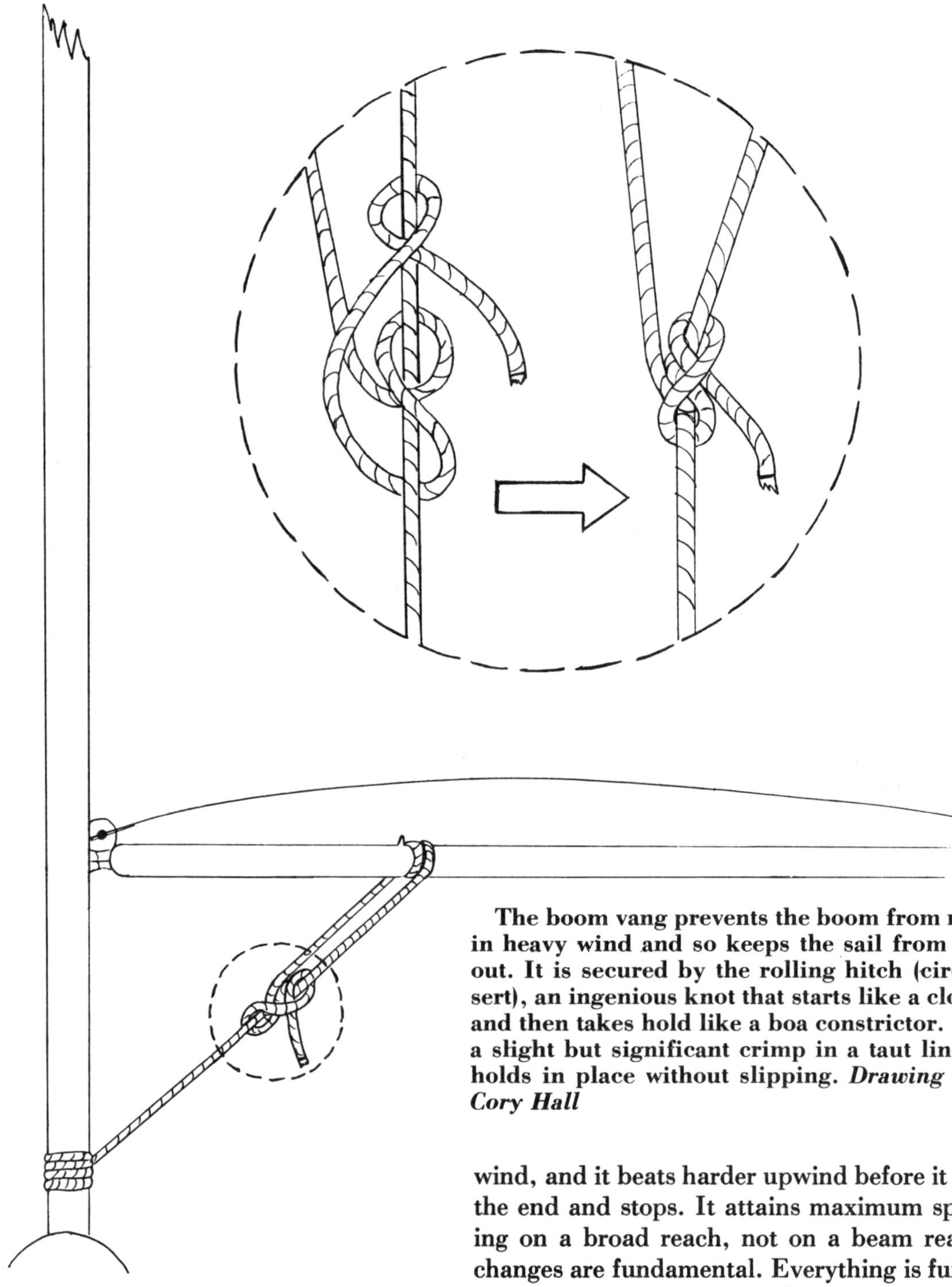

The boom vang prevents the boom from rising up in heavy wind and so keeps the sail from bellying out. It is secured by the rolling hitch (circular insert), an ingenious knot that starts like a clove hitch and then takes hold like a boa constrictor. It makes a slight but significant crimp in a taut line and so holds in place without slipping. *Drawing by Lana Cory Hall*

the boat heels; and the boat nearly always heels in heavy wind. And *this* means, this time without further involvement in cause and effect, that the dogleg angle opens several degrees wider between the wind axis and the force axis, and the boat sails by very different force patterns. The boat reaches farther downwind before it begins running downwind, and it beats harder upwind before it comes to the end and stops. It attains maximum speed sailing on a broad reach, not on a beam reach. The changes are fundamental. Everything is fundamental when you sail in heavy wind.

(You could calculate forces down to a completely rearranged polar diagram, spread much wider to leeward, but now the fundamentals themselves would disrupt the calculations. You are pressed so hard by fundamentals so urgent and immediate that the polar diagram becomes only a paper pattern. In heavy wind you don't pretend to sail by patterns or calculations. You sail by fundamentals.)

Something else is a fundamental element to remember in heavy wind. The balance changes. On the sail, the center of effort shifts a significant distance aft. And now, on the centerboard, the center of resistance makes a very pronounced shift forward—for reasons having to do with increasing boat speed and greater sideways pressure—and with both shifts the total force and total resistance come farther out of alignment. Then as the boat heels steeply, it takes on a truly massive weather helm. You have never felt anything like this—a far greater force exerted with much harder leverage. It becomes sheer hardship, an unrelenting strain on the tiller, just pulling against you. The boat feels like a horse that loses equilibrium and leans heavily to its weather side, trying constantly to wheel upwind. The only way you can ease the weather helm is to move the center of resistance aft and in doing so shift the total resistance back to near-alignment with the total force. But to do that, you must move the whole centerboard aft; your boat has to have the kind of centerboard that swings aft, or pivots aft, as you raise it up. If you raised it all the way, it would pivot up into its housing like a jackknife blade, but in heavy wind you raise it only part way, to the point where it swings a significant distance aft and sets at a rakish angle. (Because of the way things pivot, the centerboard first comes most of the way aft, then goes most of the way up.) Then indeed the center of effort moves several inches aft, and force and resistance come back near alignment; and this restores the balance.

Of course right now the boat is tied to the pier, and the centerboard *is* all the way up and in its housing. When the boat isn't sailing, the centerboard always should be up and in its housing. And from there you *lower* it to the rakish angle—so it swings out of the housing and most of the way down but holds at the setting where it still is most of the way aft. It comes there regardless, whether you raise it or lower it.

Except your boat may have the other kind of centerboard—the dagger board—which can't move aft to ease a weather helm; it can only move up and down. You plunge it straight down into the water at the beginning and pull it back up at the end. In heavy wind all you can do is sail with a dagger board a third of the way up and hike yourself desperately over the windward rail. The weather helm should ease somewhat, and the boat should go better into the wind—because it heels less, though it slips sideways more, slipping where it would have heeled—but you still feel a considerable weather helm, and you can only endure the hardship as a natural reality. The dagger board plainly isn't good in heavy wind, where you plainly need all things to be good, but it is simple and cheap, and the current trend is to build it into the machinery of small boats. If it is in the machinery of your boat, try to be strong.

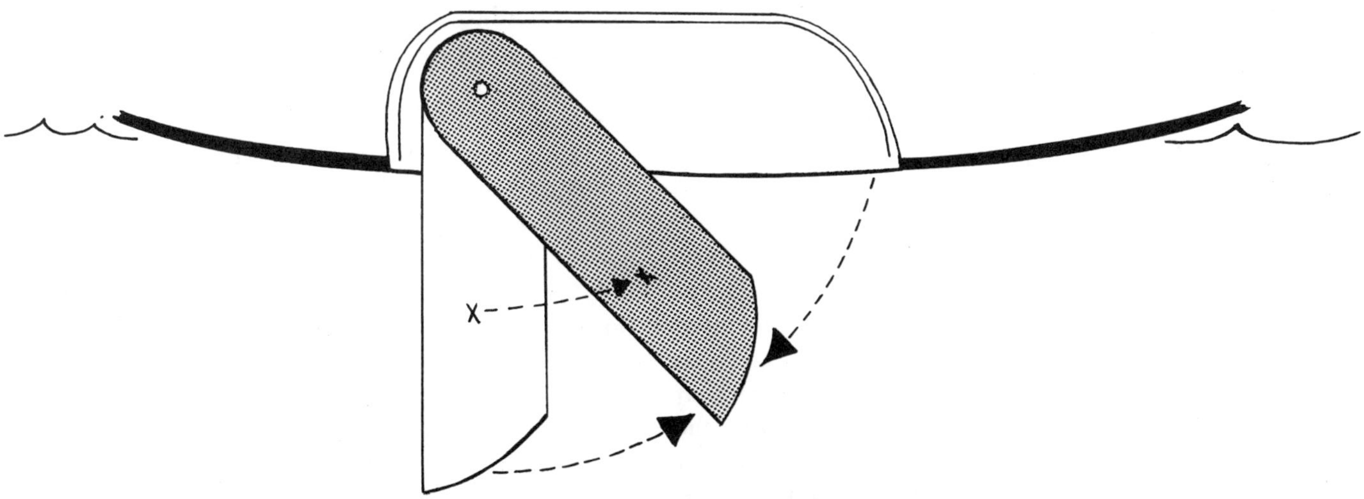

When the centerboard is partly raised—or partly lowered from its housing—the center of resistance *X* is shifted aft to keep a better balance with sail forces that shift aft in heavy wind. *Drawing by Lana Cory Hall*

Setting the centerboard is the last thing you do before casting off. It is easy to do and easier to forget to do; so don't forget. Or forget just once, and the wind will blow you sideways, and you never will forget again. The centerboard is essential machinery, good or bad, in heavy wind or any wind. Even the worst centerboard keeps the boat from being blown sideways, and for that alone it has to be better than no centerboard.

Then cast off the painter, back the boat away from the pier, steering in reverse; swing the boat back and around—very competently, before critical review—and sail it forward into heavy wind.

The wind hits. Very simply. It is no surprise. It is a great force, far stronger than you, more than you and the boat together. It is serious force: direct and uncomplicated. It is exactly what it seems to be, the last and largest reality; now you come to it and don't need to wonder about it. This is heavy wind.

The wind hits the sail. The force hits the boat. And the weight hits you: massively and resolutely, wasting no time, leaving no doubt. You feel the strain double immediately and instantly redouble and perhaps redouble again—and press hard upon the boat, abruptly pushing it up on its edge and pushing even farther. You hike to the rail and lean beyond, stretching to your limit, applying all your leverage, and the boat still heels, the wind remorseless upon it. The wind is most serious now. Everything is completely serious.

This time you know you are not enough, however strong and determined, to bring the boat back down; you could be two people and still not be enough, because heavy wind remains straightforwardly overpowering, and in another moment it must dispassionately capsize you for getting in its way. You could capsize without compromise, holding rigidly to your sheet and tiller, knowing you haven't a chance but still keeping the sail at full power and driving to the end—which would come very quickly, at best within a dozen heroic yards; at best you would have a magnificently abbreviated cruise. But of course you do compromise, and you don't capsize; the alternatives are plain enough that you don't have to think on this. You let out the sheet and loose the sail in the wind, or you push the tiller and turn the boat toward the wind—luffing up in either case: coming into the wind to get out of its way—deliberately causing the curve to soften and sink and sweep aft, dumping out the heavy wind and most of its force and power. The boat does come back down, compromised but still sailing, and with this you begin the strategy of compromise—and concession and conciliation and, indeed, outright sacrifice—being so definitively outweighed and outmatched by heavy wind.

Then this is how you sail—in various states between luffing and heeling: constantly working the sheet and tiller, luffing up when the boat heels over, heeling over when it luffs up. You sail with the curve always going soft and usually sinking and sliding aft, the sail freely dumping raw force. You feel the great preponderance of power blowing away. In effect you shrug the main stream of heavy wind out of the sail; you catch just an edge of the wind in the last vestige of the curve, and you sail with that.

In fact you deliberately squander energy: something which all this while you have resolved never to do. You sail with only fractional efficiency, casting away the entire principle of wind and sail at maximum force, wholly abandoning all notions of fine adjustments and precise alignments and 5 degrees tighter than trim—everything with which you once kept the last feasible ounce of maximum force driving the boat. In heavy wind you rarely can withstand maximum force; you don't meticulously conserve ounces, you creatively waste tons. You sail on just the leavings and remnants of heavy wind—and indeed you find them quite enough. When you first feel the weight of heavy wind, you know that whatever part of it you must dump, however you must reduce your straits, you still are left with all the driving force and sail power you can manage. There is no way you ever will be shorted on that.

Consider: if you can sail handily in a fair wind of 10 knots, and if the total sail force increases with the square of the wind speed, then in a marginally heavy wind of 20 knots—double the wind speed—you get four times the total force (and probably much more with the currents turning farther on the curve), and you can sail handily, dumping at least 3/4ths of it. In a very heavy wind of 30 knots—triple the wind speed—you get better than nine times the total force, and you can sail handily dumping at least 8/9ths of it.

(By the way, some people think they can outmuscle heavy wind by ganging up on it, and this is catastrophic. These people would load themselves four or five at a time into a little boat—a skipper

With the boat overloaded in heavy wind, catastrophe looms. ***Drawing by Don Raden***

and three or four robust passengers exerting their cumulative bulk, everybody hiking strenuously beyond the rail to hold down the boat. And the skipper, with a great lust for sail power but a decidedly deficient vision, would wrench in the sheet and see himself sailing flat and balanced and 5 degrees tighter than trim: driving ahead under maximum force doubled and redoubled and more. But he would put four or five times the weight of the crew against four to nine times the weight of the wind—and so put sixteen to forty-five times the stress directly upon the boat's machinery. And the machinery would directly come apart. Cables would break. Screws would tear loose. Or the mast suddenly would buckle; a wood mast, under extreme stress, would snap like kindling—breaking with an appalling crunch and crashing down with boom, sail, shrouds, and splintered fragments: everything falling into total wreckage. The ruin would be so awful and abrupt that it would catch the skipper and his rowdy crew still hiking out and looking smug, fancying themselves most dynamic.

(Besides, the boat still wouldn't sail fast or well, even if it could hold together between such awesome force and human flesh. Even with sail power doubled and redoubled, the boat still would only muddle down, awash almost to the gunwales, and sail at best like a bathtub with club feet—trying to push its way through water it rightfully should float over, expending all its tons of sail power just to push tons of water. If anything, it would go slower now, laboring ponderously, more overburdened than overpowered, and with gunwales nearly awash, it would go in constant peril of being swamped by each wave—provided, of course that it first wouldn't break apart.

(Enough then. Overloading the boat in heavy wind is both destructive and self-defeating and has to be one of the worst things you possibly could do; so surely you aren't going to. In heavy wind you set the strictest load limit: at the last extreme you never would carry more than 400 pounds of people in a little boat—so better still, in heavy wind, you never would carry more than 300 pounds or a modest equivalent of two medium-sized adults. In fair or moderate wind you could carry more, not well but at least safely because the force is less, but that is the necessary irony in this. You can load more in less wind, but you must load less in more wind.)

If you are to have a single word for sailing in heavy wind, you finesse. If you are allowed two words, you finesse and survive. All the arts and strategies of heavy wind sailing come finally to this: you dump the weight of the wind and catch an edge of it; you compromise. And like this you finesse and survive—getting wet and tired, which is essential. You learn this like everything else, and when you actually do it, it is easier than it looks. Then there are just a couple more things in heavy wind.

There are the gusts. There nearly always are gusts, in almost all winds, but gusts are serious in heavy wind. They are random surges in the wind, coming suddenly with the wind and blowing even harder for a moment, then gone. You feel them first in your ears, and then you see them by their shadows. They blow patches of dark crepe-like ripples across the water—shadows, in effect, moving over the surface, sliding and spreading and shifting about, looming larger and smaller, their substance never appearing quite certain. The shadows grow darker as the gusts grow stronger; the shadows of really powerful gusts are almost morbidly black. By the shadows, all gusts look ominous. In heavy wind, coming abruptly at the boat, they always are.

The gusts are more than heavy wind. They come at you on top of heavy wind—after you have made all your allowances to finesse the wind and all your commitments to survive it—and they hit you again, still harder, with very real substance. They catch you luffing and heeling on your edges: sailing by the edge of the wind, at the edge of your margin; and they thump you once more, a quick, sharp, extra thump pushing you past the edges, and the rest could be messy. Whether the thump is large or small, it very nearly capsizes you; it probably would capsize you if you didn't keep the margin. In heavy wind it would need only this moment.

Because of the gusts, you have to make allowances beyond even finessing and surviving in heavy wind. You don't sail on your edges, nor even near them; you sail with special reserves just to anticipate gusts—setting margins on margins, keeping options on options, never drawing anything completely tight, nor leaving anything completely loose. You hike to the rail but still hold back a part of yourself when you lean past. You luff the boat when it still could heel, heel it when it still could luff. And you always know somewhere to turn with the tiller; you always have something left in the sheet to pull in or let out. To do this, you must dump more wind and compromise still more driving force and sail power, but out of this you save your last commitment for when the gusts come with their black shadows. Then you are ready for them: you can hike out and hold firm and go to the edges with them. You still will be there when they are gone.

In time you gain insights on gusts. You learn to be always watchful for shadows, which move erratically in the distance but acquire direction and dispel all doubts as they draw nearer—coming almost invariably at you, scudding across the water and right up to the boat. By their shadows, you would swear that the gusts are guided like missiles, deliberately homing in on the boat and seeming almost certain to hit. You see little charity in them; they very likely would veer across half an ocean just to give the boat a thump. But by watching the shadows at least you see the ways the gusts come. And after the first half-dozen gusts come and go—passing in quick succession—you begin to plot and measure the gusts by their shadows: gauging speed, strength, and directioin by the movements and textures of the dark, tiny ripples. You see gusts swelling as they close in, or taking sudden twists at the last instant: the tiny ripples going darker or spreading wider or turning abruptly as they reach the boat. You learn to read ripples this way; it becomes a special skill. With practice you can read ripples well enough to know almost exactly where a gust is about to hit, and how hard. That gives you just a moment's foresight on gusts, a momentary advantage in the timing, which is most of what you need.

When the timing is right, you discover that you actually can *ride* the gusts. The discovery just happens to you. You see the gusts come surging; you turn slightly to meet them—and suddenly you surge with them. Beating upwind, close-hauled, you meet the gusts and steer up into them, and you feel them bearing more powerfully upon the boat: driving it harder ahead, forcing it higher upwind. Or sailing across the wind or downwind, beam reaching or broad reaching, you meet the gusts and steer down with them; and you feel them lifting and carrying the boat: as if somehow, figuratively, they were getting under the boat and rising up with it and scudding over the water with it. The timing alone does this; the timing is momentarily transcendent.

In riding gusts, you begin to reorder and restrict your strategies in heavy wind. You learn that the boat, sailing close-hauled, can meet gusts most heroically; It swings up and hits first, seemingly almost straight on—riding hard into the gusts, driving even past its usual limit and into the eye of the wind itself—and holding there for just a critical instant, safely sheltered as the gusts blow past. And you learn that the boat, sailing beam reaches and broad reaches, can meet gusts most handily: It turns down and goes with them—simply picking up and riding them out, sailing across the wind and downwind—being securely buoyed up for the moment on pure, headlong force. Riding the gusts, you learn a strategy of survival by hairbreadth escapes: turning up from close-hauled, turning down from the beam reach. In heavy wind you make a practice of hairbreadth escapes.

Then you discover, hopefully not the hard way, that you can't ride gusts with the boat close reaching—sailing up in the windward sector, above the beam reach and below close-hauled. In that sector there is no survival strategy for heavy wind: There is nowhere to turn when the gusts hit. Try steering just once, hypothetically, from a close reach up into a gust, as if here too you would hit first with the boat and drive up toward the shelter of the eye. This time the gust would hit you twenty times as hard before you were barely started. Or try steering from a close reach out of a gust just once, hypothetically, as if you could swing the boat around and sail ahead to a course safely below the beam reach. The gust would catch you fully exposed—again before you were barely started—and would come down on you with all its weight and force. All you could do then, as a last effort, would be to let go of the sheet and loose the sail, just trying to hold down the boat and spill away the wind, if this alone could save you. But these high-powered gusts come much too hard and too fast for the sail to dump them out in time. In the close reaches you are in trouble wherever you turn the boat. You nearly always are too little and too late.

So be certain on this. You are not allowed hairbreadth escapes in a small boat in the windward sector in heavy wind: You make hairbreadth escapes only from the very edges of the sector—from the upper edge, where the boat is close-hauled, or from the lower edge, where the boat is beam reaching. In heavy wind you never would even venture into the windward sector, except sometimes to cross very quickly from edge-to-edge: And then you must seize upon chance moments between gusts and just steer across as fast as you possibly can. You go between gusts like you ride them: always by the timing.

And still be careful. Even when you know all of this, you still have the upwind urge. Your own raw self-preservation instincts want you to go always upwind, because you know the most certain shelter is there. You have the compulsion to turn the boat always upwind, regardless of where it is when the gusts hit. The upwind urge is right and good enough when you are close-hauled; the upwind turn indeed brings you into safe refuge in the eye of the wind. But when you are sailing off the wind, beam reaching or broad reaching, this same upwind urge would verge almost on a death wish, your best instincts notwithstanding. The turn would set you all the wrong ways into everything you should be going away from. You would be driving blindly up into the windward sector itself, swerving the boat at the very gust that is coming down on it. You would stand only a negligible chance of getting past the beam reach and up into the close reaches, where you shouldn't go anyway. And certainly you would have no hope of ever bringing the boat on across the close reaches, up through the gusts—all on this single compulsion—and finally, very theoretically, into the eye of the wind, if you still could believe in such a thing. You would never even come close to the eye. You would not make it in any number of ways, meeting several different disasters of different sorts that you needn't dwell upon. So understand this—a surprising number of sailors don't—in heavy wind, when you sail on a beam reach or broad reach, the eye of the wind is only a mirage to windward. Believe in it, but only in principle not in practice: not at this distance.

So again, for the last time: in heavy wind, when you sail on a beam reach or a broad reach and the gusts hit, you steer the boat *downwind* to keep it sailing; not upwind. You steer downwind even against your own instincts for self-preservation—away from the eye, where you know there is shelter and security. You need a certain resolution to be able to do this. You have to understand why.

Then besides the gusts, there are the waves. There always are waves with wind, but with heavy wind there are great green waves with deep green troughs between; and in the waves, like in the gusts, the boat is vulnerable. The waves are the other element in heavy wind.

The great waves are like heavy wind: plainly the manifestation of heavy wind. Like the wind, they mean only to go where they will, and they go with a force stronger than you, more than you and the boat together. And you must get in their way just to sail the boat; though when you turn too much in their way, then indeed they are obliged to roll the boat over, just as the wind would be obliged to blow it over—without malice: with only their necessary mass and momentum. The waves, like the wind, have this basic fairness: they bear you no grudge for being in their way, but they make you no compromise. You sail at the sufferance of the waves, as you do of the wind, allowing that you are outweighed and outmatched but still sustaining a degree of trust. You are going to make your way in great waves as you do in heavy wind: sailing with the same caution and keeping constantly aware of mass and momentum.

You come hard against mass and momentum in the very first wave—a most ponderable volume of gray-green water rising up and rolling at you and now looming immense above you, breaking into white foam at its crest: its mass and momentum accumulated from here to the horizon. You drive the boat into the very substance of this. And you can't mistake the impact. You and the boat hit together, hard, driving with everything at once. But the wave hits back, many times harder; its sheer weight is awesome. If the wave were put in barrels and set rolling, the barrels would roll straight through the boat, summarily shattering and flattening it—and you, and probably anything else—and would just keep rolling without pause or remorse. The real wave, unbarreled, rolls just as certainly and forcefully and is perhaps only technically less destructive, and a thousand waves of equal magnitude come rolling just behind. This is what you must get in the way of when you sail the boat in heavy wind.

Clearly, the boat and the wave must have their unequal encounter and must get past each other to go their different ways. But they can't go around each other and won't go through each other; so one has to go over the other, and one must go under. And most simply, you want the boat to go over the wave so the wave doesn't go over the boat.

This seems a near thing, though it isn't exactly, but it never can be easy in any case. The boat and the wave come together: the boat sailing, the wave still rolling. The wave will not be dissuaded; it goes where it will, as it must, rolling implacably over anything in its way; in a moment it would roll implacably over the boat for being in the way. But the boat, in this moment, sails up the wave and over the crest and gets out of the way just in time. The wave rolls past, under the boat, not over it. The wave doesn't care.

Then all the while the boat has been a straightforwardly good boat just to perform as well as it must, but now it becomes quite an incredibly good boat to sail in a moment, on its own resources, up a great, green wave. This is simply the architecture of a good boat; you can't even take much credit. You just turn the boat slightly to leeward as you drive it at the wave—footing it off at the last instant, gathering a final, extra measure of speed and power—and then you steer the right way into the wave: obliquely, though you want to go directly. (You need to quell a self-destructive urge that would have you driving squarely into the main force and weight of the oncoming green water; as if you wanted to think the boat would go straight up for coming straight in—and you know it won't, not at all well, at least). So obliquely, the boat meets the wave and takes a half-turn, half-roll aside; half deflecting the impetus of the wave while still retaining an impetus of its own. And with this, and an integral buoyancy, and a very strong effort, the boat slants sharply across the wave and sails abruptly up it—obliquely, like a goat going up a mountain. You feel only the effort and the sudden lift and the boat wrenches precipitously upward. Then everything hangs at the crest for just an instant, barely time enough, and the wave rolls beneath and rolls away with no hard feelings. And indeed this is not easy; this does seem a very near thing: the boat and the wave must have a most serious reckoning. But the boat goes up and over on its own resources. You only steer.

That is the first great wave. The second comes just after, an equal volume, with equal mass and momentum. The third comes, immense and gray-

The boat sails obliquely up great waves—not directly. It turns half aside as it meets the waves; it rolls slightly and goes up and over with a measure of impetus, an integral buoyancy, and a very strong effort. ***Drawing by Don Raden***

green. The rest follow: a dozen great waves, a thousand. You lose count; you don't want to count. The waves just keep rolling inevitably: each wave rising up and looming before you, a private reckoning for the boat, a separate crisis for you. You steer obliquely in; the boat sails obliquely over—turning, wrenching, lifting up and hanging on—just in time, before the wave would roll implacably over. This never gets easy. With each new wave you feel the weight of all the others. You steer into ten thousand successive waves one-by-one, and the boat sails over them, one-by-one, but you still come to the reckoning and the crisis at the ten thousand-and-first. You have hard, rough sailing in great waves, and you wonder if this is all too precarious—if the boat really should keep going like this on its own resources; if after ten thousand waves it should meet just one that it doesn't get over, just in time.

Because of the waves, your strategies become still more restricted in heavy wind. You sail nearly always close-hauled or on broad reaches: going across the wind diagonally, so the boat meets the waves obliquely. You rarely go anywhere directly: You go most places by tacking—zigging and zagging, sailing close-hauled and sailing broad reaches, tacking not just upwind now but across the wind and even downwind—though you do this as the most minimal kind of tacking by making the longest possible tacks with the fewest possible maneuvers between. You sail on the beam reach sometimes, but only in limited ways: either very carefully or very recklessly. And on occasion you run dead before the wind, but you never like it at all. All this is for very good reasons.

You have to feel threatened sailing a beam reach across heavy wind. The boat is dramatically vulnerable, lying squarely across the waves, its flanks exposed. It doesn't move to meet waves; it just goes passively in the troughs between them. And the waves come like broadsides, rising up in all their mass and momentum and pounding with awful impacts into the side of the boat. Each wave sets the boat reeling and tries to roll over it: When one wave doesn't quite roll over the boat, or roll the boat over, it drops it back into the trough for the next wave, and that wave has its roll and drops the boat back for the next. This might be exciting if you are in the right mood; you can keep sailing breathlessly and precariously on the beam reach, holding the boat up so long as you keep dumping wind from the sail. But more often this just becomes demoralizing, or at least discomforting. Most often you tend to turn the boat very quickly past the beam reach when you make your zigs and zags. You try to time the turn so the boat always comes to the crest of a wave for that instant when

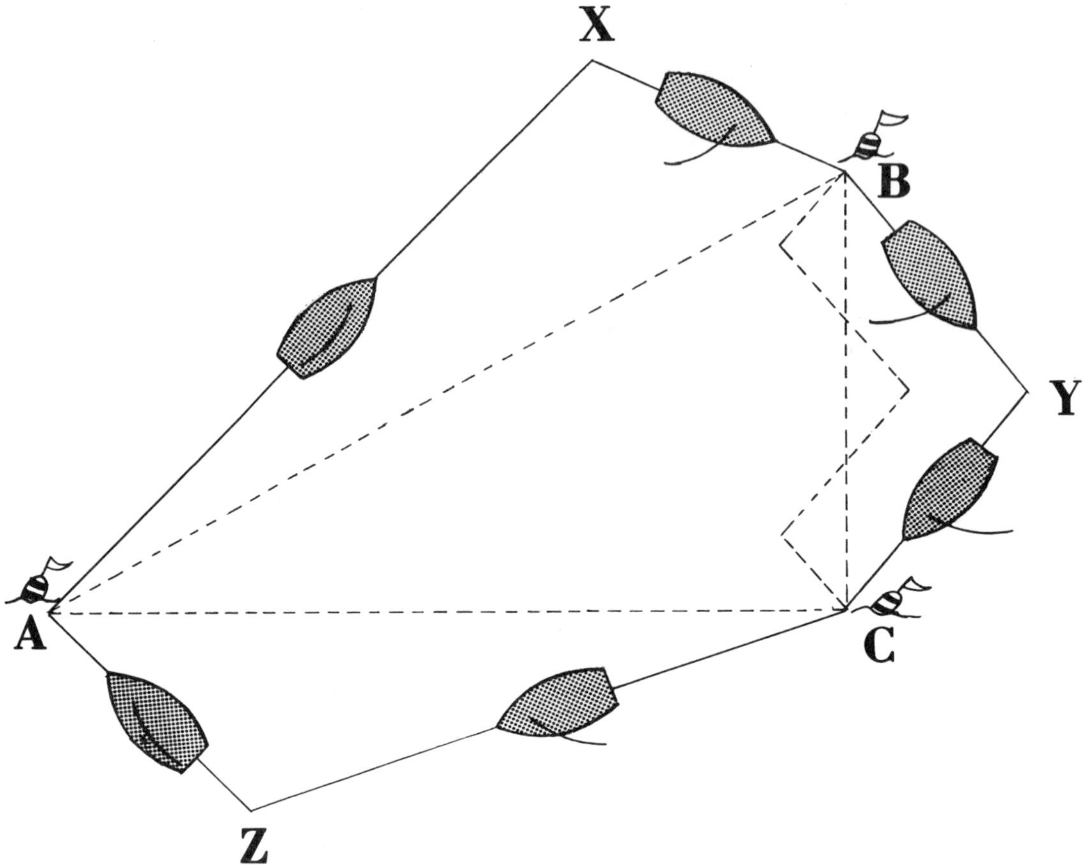

Heavy wind requires a special strategy. The basic idea is to avoid the dead run and the beam reach as discreetly as possible—and to regard the close reach as altogether impossible. This means the boat must tack more often in heavy wind to go places where it could sail more directly in lesser wind; though it still must keep all tacking as simple and as minimal as possible. Thus:

Rather than sail a close reach along the hyphenated line from buoy A to buoy B, the boat instead sails close hauled up to point X, then sails the broad reach down to buoy B.

Rather than run straight downwind from buoy B to buoy C, and rather than take many tacks downwind, the boat avoids all hyphenated lines. It takes a single tack down to point Y, jibes once, and then takes the single tack down to buoy C.

Rather than sail a beam reach from buoy C back to buoy A, the boat sails a broad reach down to point Z, then sails close-hauled to buoy A. *Drawing by Lana Cory Hall*

you do steer past the beam reach. You usually avoid the trough like the black pit. That is another skill you learn.

Sailing on the beam reach may be the third-worst thing you can do with a small boat in great waves. The second-worst would be sailing on the beam reach with the boat overloaded. The worst thing would be to sail on the beam reach between great waves and concrete seawalls. You don't even want to think about what would happen between great waves and concrete seawalls.

You do run downwind in great waves now and then, but you don't like to, because you must run in following seas, and large ships founder in following seas. The waves have an abrupt and unpleasant way of overtaking you and catching the boat from behind and seizing control. They would pick up the boat, swing it around, and set it across the wind, on the beam reach—a phenomenon called "broaching-to" because it seems somewhat like the broaching that occurs in a jibe, though the actual causes and effects are altogether different—and they would hold the boat in the trough and pound it and roll it there until you could regain enough control to steer it out. So when you don't *have* to run downwind, down the axis, you learn instead to tack downwind through great waves, sailing the broad reaches and zigging and zagging across the axis—even jibing between the zigs and zags in the full force of heavy wind—all this just so you don't risk broaching-to in the following sea. You feel that you make a very good exchange.

Then you sail. When you make the necessary compromises for heavy wind, and ride the gusts and meet the waves and allow for strategies and adjustments—then for the rest you sail in heavy wind very nearly like you do in any wind. Except you work harder at it and are more careful about it, being indeed so vastly outweighed and outmatched. Sail close-hauled first and keep hiking beyond the rail, still exerting enough of yourself to maintain the balance—and restraining enough to keep the margin. Even now you remain minutely ponderable as a counterweight. The boat goes hard, as it always must into the wind. This time it must pinch and heel and luff its way to windward, dumping the great preponderance of forces just to keep sailing, but still going, more burdened than driven by forces, just to keep sailing upwind. You pull and strain, and the boat turns higher and loses power and never has any real speed; there is no way it will ever go fast against this much wind. But it labors doggedly up the waves and against wind, pushing its way to the end. It comes to the end, in heavy wind as in any wind, sailing on the edge of the eye of the wind and surging momentarily higher in the gusts. Beyond the end, it goes into the eye and loses the wind—heavy wind or any wind—from the last trace of the curve in the sail; so it dies as it must, a good boat regardless.

(If you come to windward to bring the boat about, you find that coming about works far better than you expect in heavy wind. Just swing the boat decisively as it is turning toward the eye and is rising up to the crest of a wave; give it a measure of momentum going into the eye, and it goes across just as surely as it would in any wind. And if you come to windward to land the boat, you find this works perhaps best of all in heavy wind. Drive the boat squarely into the heavy center of one great, oncoming wave, and it stops cold, exactly on the spot where boat and wave meet. For your part, you need only avoid the obvious mistakes when you do the upwind maneuvers, and the boat, for its part, is competent and precise. It surprises you.)

Then sail back down through the close reaches. Go quickly past the beam reach and down into the broad reaches. And be ready. This is where the extraordinary thing happens in heavy wind.

The boat comes around. The forces come together. Boat and forces come into alignment. All forces—total forces, doubled and redoubled and more—converge on the boat, and in this direction they go with it, driving it, not burdening it, singly and collectively thrusting it ahead. You feel this; everything goes into one cumulative forward impetus. You start to ease the sheet; then you reflexively tighten it; you steer to leeward, pulling in the sheet and letting it out, then deliberately holding it against the weight of the wind, gathering new, raw power. You begin instinctively to trim the sail; this is the only time in heavy wind—right now, with everything together and aligned and exerted ahead, nothing in the way of anything else. The boat wouldn't withstand this, except it isn't in the way either; there is nothing for it to withstand. It goes ahead with all forces, where all forces go. Just this once you trim to maximum force in heavy wind. Nothing is going to stop you.

The boat goes fast through the water: driving hard and driven still harder. Then it is driven too hard even to stay in the water. Many small boats reach their breaking points right here; they abruptly plunge straight down into a wave, like submarines going under. But your boat is a good one. It surges up and breaks free and skims over the water. It begins to plane. And on the plane it finds new kinds of speed, beyond maximum speed. It skips and skitters, as if on the verge of flight; it rides on sheets of spray, skidding like a bobsled up and down great waves. As you trim to maximum force, the boat seems about to leap off the very crests of the waves. This is a new state; there never has been anything like it; this is maximum force driving past the limits of maximum speed. And this is an emotional experience. You are caught up in the passions of sheer, driven, headlong velocity—and you feel precarious. All you can do is steer the boat and hold the sail 5 degrees tighter than trim and maintain the trust—at this speed, with these forces greater than you and the boat together—that nothing is going to slip out of alignment. Then you catch your breath, and you never want the boat to come down from the plane.

It will come down. All boats must come down. Each boat has its own range for planing at maximum force. A boat stays up and planing for as long as the conditions are right—the alignment, trim, drive, balance, even the angle with the waves—and different boats stay up longer than others, but ultimately they all come down. While your boat is

The boat finally planes. It surges up, breaks free, and goes skimming over the water, beyond even maximum speed. ***Drawing by Don Raden***

up you have the grandest ride of all; if you could keep it always up, you would have no further reason for sailing in heavy wind. You never would want to sail in any other wind. But your boat, like all others, eventually must sail other ways than this. So steer it on to leeward now, out of the broad reaches, and set it running before the wind: down into the aerodynamic nether region, where you never trust anything to be right. Sometimes you have to go this way.

The boat is still up and planing. Having reached the plane, it sustains it for a moment—planing even over the following sea, running ahead of the great waves themselves—though it loses power all the while, being only pushed by heavy wind now, not driven by maximum force. But even as the boat planes, it turns toward the windshadow: sailing down toward the chasm of whirlwinds behind the sail. This time there is real violence in the chasm. Those whirlwinds are now vastly larger and altogether fearsome, still surging and lashing about, their sheer weight doubled and redoubled and more. You never know what is going to happen with them; the uncertainty is the worst part of this. You just come into the run as if into combat against unknown odds. The boat comes in at planing speed, running reckless and wanton, and the tail of a whirlwind can swat it like a silly shuttlecock. One swat can send the boat reeling across wind and waves, bringing it down from the plane into the troughs of the following sea. And you may or may not have a chance to save it; you need all your combat reflexes, and you have to be very fast and strong and must fight through all the elements to bring the boat back on course—just to hold it there, waiting to be swatted again. You fight all the way down the axis like this, constantly outweighed and outmatched and never certain of anything; you just keep wondering how long you are going to struggle before one hard swat simply upends the boat, and the waves roll over it. You become nervous about running in heavy wind. You run when you must but never farther than you need. The odds are not dependable.

This is why you would rather tack downwind on the broad reaches—like the iceboat—riding up on the plane and zigging and zagging, always following the easiest possible strategies, taking just one long zig and one long zag and jibing only once between. You have to go farther this way, but you sail much better, especially when you ride up on the plane.

In heavy wind there is real violence in the aerodynamic chasm behind the sail. The whirlwinds keep surging and lashing about, but now they are vastly larger. *Drawing by Lana Cory Hall*

Except now you come to the place where you jibe the boat in heavy wind, and this makes you anxious. If jibing was an impending crisis before, in lesser wind, then jibing now becomes a crisis of a whole new magnitude. To a small boat in great waves, jibing can seem the coming of the cataclysm and the revelation: the apocalypse—an anticipation momentarily grown to biblical magnitude, if no other description is adequate. However you see this, it makes you *very* anxious.

You do jibe in heavy wind, but you derive unlikely ways of doing it; and while this indeed makes an extraordinary experience, you find that the jibe itself finally must turn out to be less than biblical. It is a flying jibe. A very rough and rudimentary one, actually a violent jibe, the kind you liked least of all in lesser wind. It is the very last jibe you ever would expect to work in heavy wind. But it works in its own improbable way: just because it is fear-

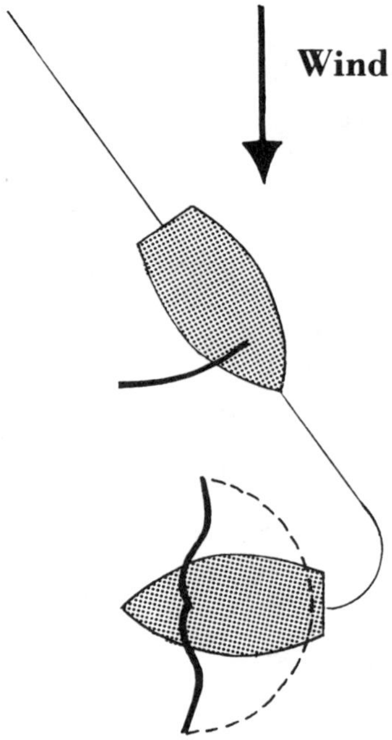

In the super flying jibe—done only in heavy wind—the boat swerves sharply across the wind axis and comes all the way up to the beam reach before the sail flies. ***Drawing by Lana Cory Hall***

somely simple. You jibe by powering the boat as hard and fast as possible across the axis—simply plunging over the line ahead of any uncertainties, anything that might get in the way—and then you hold tight and weather the consequences and just try to keep the boat where it won't broach. You know you haven't a prayer if the boat broaches in heavy wind.

Jibe like this: push the boat to leeward. Steer it down to a deep broad reach, nearly to a run, and hold it there and sail it hard, forcing all possible speed and momentum on it. And all on an instant—without even waiting for a sign—loose the sheet, free the sail, and heave the tiller all the way to windward. Swing it savagely this time; don't hold back. Put the tiller hard against the stops, the rudder flush against the transom. This would be wrong anywhere else; here it is imperative. The boat spins. Abruptly. Convulsively. It swerves around, enraged and distressed; it leans, rolls, pitches. It hurls itself both forward and sideways across the axis. And it keeps on, mostly sideways, reeling into the wind, laying itself across the wind: pushing volumes of water. The boat is over the line and nearly around to the beam reach all in a moment, before the sail even flies, and you still are holding the tiller against the stops. Then the sail does fly, and you straighten out the tiller; and you stay down in the cockpit, keeping the center of gravity low. Don't even think of raising your head until you know the boom has gone over.

Then hold tight. The boat stops against the water and undergoes massive shaking spasms. The great green waves come rolling and breaking and pounding against the side of the boat. The sail hangs out to leeward, spilling all wind, flapping prodigiously, making noise like cannon fire. You are jibed in one forceful moment, but the effort is traumatic on the machinery of the boat. Now you and the boat both need a much longer, less disquieting moment to recover from the effects.

The boat doesn't broach. For this moment it is in a precarious state—badly shaken, dead in the water—but broaching, at least, is the one thing that doesn't happen. The boat is forced past the point of broaching before the sail flies, and this is the whole reason for such a seemingly improbable jibe. Not broaching, the boat weathers everything else, uneasily but effectually. It stops most of its shaking, it survives the waves; it stays up, being a good boat. Pull in the sheet now, and hike to windward, and the boat begins to sail again. The jibe worked.

Call this the super flying jibe, or the power jibe, or the plunge jibe, or the heavy weather jibe. It has no specific formally acknowledged name of its own. It does have inevitable detractors who call it unkind things like the suicide jibe, or the madman's jibe—probably because they are appalled at the sight of it, or offended by the grossness of it—but this jibe remains true and functional, regardless of all detractors; it works in ways that no other jibe can work in heavy wind. Its failing is only that it *needs* to be artless: You make it work by being completely crude and simple. You would disrupt it with the slightest attempt at grace or style; such things would only get in the way and cause complications and uncertainties that you dare not allow. That is the principle of it.

The free jibe is the only other jibe that can work in heavy wind. It works, being the other extreme. It is nearly everything the flying jibe is not: consummately artful, completely attuned, the pure and natural movement of the boat within the patterns of wind and force. It is all balance and rhythm and timing and coordination—like always, but now with the wind blowing harder. In heavy wind, like in any wind, you do the free jibe as the nearest thing to the ideal jibe. You make it work by doing it more skillfully than all other jibes. Then sometimes it still doesn't work and the boat broaches, and in heavy wind you are always especially mindful of this.

Do the free jibe. Just try to do it right. Steer downwind through the broad reaches, then on downwind running: coming cautiously toward the axis, making yourself attuned. Watch waves. Feel forces and rhythms. Breathe. Sail by the sense of timing, riding with the boat rocking. And don't ever push, even with the wind blowing harder. So come to the axis, wait there for your moment, and pull the sheet once—the firm, strong, steady pull—and steer across. The sail swings. The boat jibes. When the jibe is right, the boat never even slows. It just shakes itself once like a spaniel dog and keeps sailing. When the jibe is perfect, it might indeed seem almost biblical. The boat never even comes down from the plane. This is rare; it may never happen to you, but if it does, it is the best thing you and the boat and the elements can ever do together.

When the free jibe works, it is clearly—aesthetically—the only good jibe in heavy wind. When it doesn't work, it can capsize the boat. You can learn to make it work nine times in ten tries, and you may do even better. But on that fated tenth try you get swatted by the tail of a whirlwind for being off by a hair's breadth. This needn't be your fault, but the odds are that one swat out of every six or eight will broach the boat or capsize it outright. You could learn to accept these odds as a condition for sailing in heavy wind, but of course you should never even go out if you don't think you will stay up. So in heavy wind—in any case—when you consider values, you tend to do most free jibes when you know the rescue boats are standing by. For when the odds go bad.

There are no more jibes in heavy wind. The control jibe, for all the authority it carries, doesn't work. It remains an aberration: a lot of grotesque heaving and floundering and trying in vain to pull in the sheet and bend back the sail—altogether hopeless against forces doubled and redoubled. It just becomes an awful muddle: plainly futile.

Finally there are times when you can't do any sort of jibe in heavy wind. You know just by feel as you steer down toward the axis that conditions are wrong and any jibe will be bad, and the effects will be worse. Then you have one last alternative. You turn the boat back and bring it about—the hard way: the long way, up and around. Sail it all the way back upwind, up through the broad reaches, very quickly past the close reaches (steering watchfully between gusts) and on through the eye of the wind and onto the other tack. Then sail downwind on the other tack, across the close reaches, and into the broad reaches. You sail in a large loop to come about this way, steering around at least three quarters of the circle just so you don't have to jibe the other way across the axis line. You are not being cowardly. You make a very wise and practical judgement; the best and bravest sailors all do this most gratefully. For your trouble you come by the most certain way to the new tack and the new heading; you take the best possible odds against capsizing in heavy wind. Sometimes you are taking the only odds left.

Eventually you probably *will* capsize in heavy wind. You know enough not to capsize, so you have

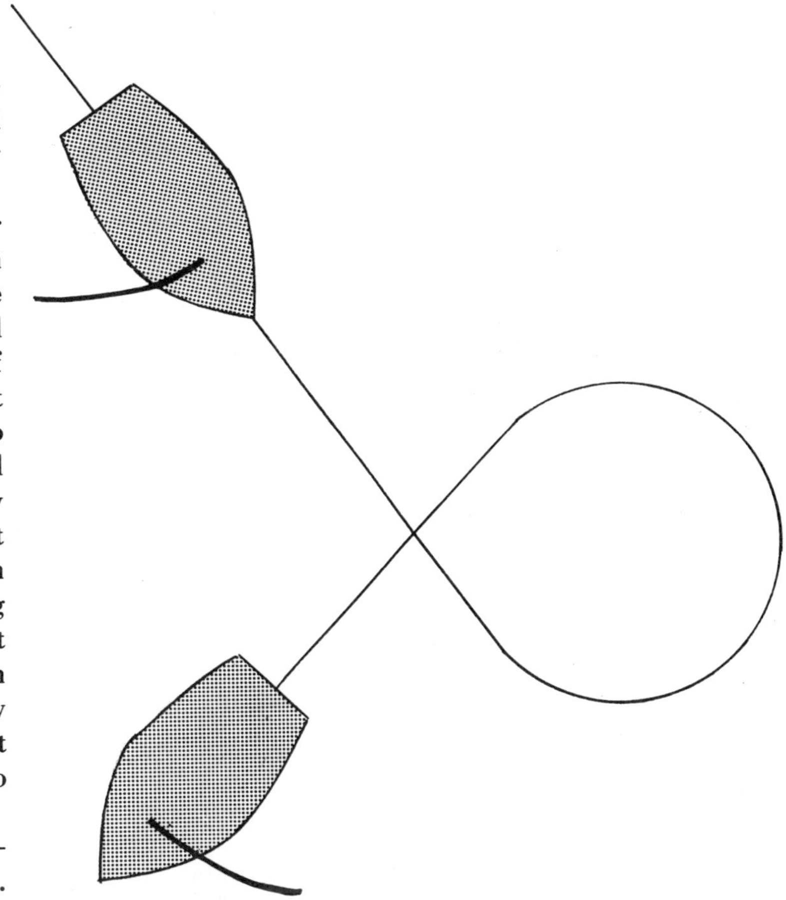

When jibing becomes unfeasible—or impossible—in heavy wind, the last alternative is to bring the boat about, steering it the long way around, all the way from broad reach to broad reach: sailing through a complete loop to come through the eye of the wind. *Drawing by Lana Cory Hall*

to make a mistake to do it, but ultimately you expect it. The boat is vulnerable. The risk is constant. Capsizing finally happens. Though when you first do capsize, it doesn't happen at all like you think it will. You expect it to be suddenly and violently overpowering; actually it is slowly and mystically overpowering. You are swept up in wind and forces; the boat is rolled over—but the boat pauses on its very edge. It just stops; it holds absolutely still, suspended palpably, almost metaphysically, over the water; everything hesitates like this. You can only wait; you feel the pause, nothing more. Then everything simply relaxes and sinks slowly. All the lines go slack. The mast sways in a long, languid arc down to the water; the sail settles like a dying swan on the surface. The boat just rolls up and over and lies down very gently on its side. This is capsizing.

You find it does not have to be a marine disaster in a small boat. It needn't even be destructive—like breaking the mast, or sailing into a seawall. You capsize the boat, and it goes down intact and unhurt. And you bring it directly back up. You slide quickly over the side, even as things still sink slowly, and you perch yourself on the centerboard. The move is not at all improbable in these straits: the centerboard now juts like a balcony from the underside of the rolled-over boat; it is actually the only place left to stand on the boat. And from the centerboard you exert leverage, getting a grip and pulling back and down, and the boat swings up like a bobber: the same boat, just wetter now.

If the boat is the kind that fills with water when it capsizes, then things get messy. The boat comes erect in a sodden state, swamped to the gunwales and lying awash, the waves rolling over. You can't sail it like this; you can't bail it out with the waves coming in. It becomes a vessel in a nominal sort of distress. You have to pull down the sail and wave to passing motorboaters, trusting that one will pull you to shore. (Motorboaters tend to be very decent about this.) Then you have to dump out the water, dry out the boat, spread the sail out in the sun, and finally you go sloshing home to change clothes. You become defensive sailing this kind of boat in heavy wind—and justifiably so. You can't help brooding about the capsizing.

You do better to capsize the kind of boat that has longitudinal flotation: special air chambers that buoy up the boat as it lies on its side, so it floats there, even upturned, with the cockpit well above water. You are, or should be, up on the high rail now—precariously perched as the boat goes over, just teetering on the edge but hiking to the very end. The first wave nearly jars you off the edge when the boat settles; you clutch at marginal handholds and recover barely in time. Then you swing quickly over the side and down to the centerboard, and you begin to exert your leverage to pull the boat back up. You have to work at this. There is difficulty breaking the sail free of the water's surface tension; there is trouble with the great waves pounding

A capsized boat can be righted by standing on the centerboard and exerting leverage. This works best in the kind of boat that has special flotation that allows it to float well above water, even when lying on its side. ***Drawing by Don Raden***

against the boat and pushing it down as you are pulling it up. Then you have still more trouble just staying on wet slippery surfaces as the boat thrashes and plunges. But you can manage several strong heaves on the boat between waves. You bring the mast slowly up out of the water; it hesitates at one point, nearly horizontal. Then you heave once more, and the entire boat abruptly rights itself, coming up like the bobber, light and dry. If you are very nimble you can be back aboard and working the sheet and tiller without even getting your feet really wet.

You just have to be especially prompt at getting yourself out on the centerboard. You could be there quite unhurriedly in six seconds—soon enough—but you do much better to be there in two seconds or less, applying all your leverage. After six or ten seconds (or sometimes twenty; some boats might give you more time), the mast begins to sink under the weight of things generally pressing down. The mast drags the sail under, and you are too late with your leverage. The boat slowly, inexorably turns over: turning turtle, finally floating belly-up. The waves wash over the boat; the centerboard protrudes absurdly up into the wind. Because you were a few seconds late, you need the help of several motorboats to set your boat right. You have to be acutely aware of seconds when you capsize.

Finally you must try not to fall off the boat when it capsizes. You fall most innocently, in any number of ways. You are up on the edge, holding only by that tenuous balance, and you become so caught up in the urgency of going over that you can fall at any moment without even realizing it. You can fall down into the cockpit and bring the boat down on top of you. Or you can fall back over the side and leave the boat to turn turtle by its own weight. However you fall, you make a mess of everything; so try to remember this when you capsize. And hold tight.

When wind is heavy, you accept it for that. You ask no favors of it; you take no liberties with it. You don't pretend to hide from it, or presume to trifle with it. Just understand the fairness of it, and this is how you sail in it. Later you realize that you have very good sailing in heavy wind.

There is less for you to know about shifting wind—and much less for you to like. Shifting wind changes direction, and you adjust for it. Sometimes it changes slowly, and you adjust slowly, which is easy. Other times it changes fast, and you adjust fast, which is harder. You must learn to sail in the wind that shifts fast; then you automatically can sail in the wind that shifts slowly. Then you are this far ahead.

Wind shifts for its own reasons. The slow shifts are meteorological; you mostly contemplate them at long range. The fast shifts are happenstance. They are the gusts; or more specifically, they are the twists and turns of the gusts, the immediate symptoms of the gusts. They become the most persistently prankish elements of the gusts, being always quick and devious in heavy wind and in lesser wind. You can't plan deliberate strategies for the fast shifts of the wind. You can only meet them tactically and try to be as fast as they are—to steer as fast as they turn and trim as fast as they twist. You learn this, as you must, though you find little accomplishment in it. You only do necessary combat when you sail in shifting wind.

It would help if there were some underlying, fundamental, definitive formula for this, and you could learn by the formula. But there isn't, and you can't. You learn about shifting wind by concentration and dedication—by going out and sailing in it, and staying out until you find the right reflexes for it. But this is hard, so go out and sail alone; don't make your friends endure this with you. Take a long afternoon, when your wordly affairs are in good order and you are generally free of frustrations; you can set out feeling stable and secure and dedicated. Then go sailing in an offshore wind, which is a wind blowing off the shore and onto the water. Find a strong, likely wind blowing off a shoreline of large, blocky buildings, unevenly sized and inconsistently spaced. Or likeliest of all, find a wind blowing off a big-city shoreline. The wind comes writhing down the corridors between skyscrapers, wrenching around the corners, bending through the tight places, and constantly bouncing and shattering against great, gray walls. It comes through the skyscrapers in a state so tangled and fragmented and traumatic that it really isn't even wind any more. It is a plague of ten thousand gusts, all fomenting mindlessly, going everywhere and nowhere at once—except they seem to gravitate more or less in the direction the wind is supposed to blow. Then steer into this; steer toward the shore. This is exactly what you want: something utterly confounding to sail in.

At first glance the water looks calm here, not con-

The best way to learn sailing in gusts is simply to sail into a plague of ten thousand of them coming off a big-city shoreline, where the wind has become traumatically tangled and fragmented bouncing between the skyscrapers. ***Drawing by Don Raden***

founding. This is just because there are no large waves; there isn't room for waves to start rolling so close to shore, nor is there a constant wind to set waves rolling. You could be fooled by the look of the water if you didn't know better; you could sail too gullibly into the offshore wind: coming into chaos, mistaking it for shelter. But now you see the shadows of the gusts—ten thousand dark spots shifting on the water, no spot shifting like any other. You have no illusions. You know what you are getting into.

Sail across the wind first, or more or less across the direction the wind is supposed to blow, so that in theory the boat should go more or less across most of the gusts. In theory this should be the most probable direction to sail in shifting wind. Then when you have the boat trim and balanced, a gust comes, and the wind shifts. Then the sail is too tight, and you have to loosen it, or too loose, and you, have to tighten it. Or the boat is on the wrong course, and you have to steer it to the right one. Then the wind shifts again, and the sail is tight where it was loose, or loose where it was tight, and the right course is abruptly wrong. You sail into three quick gusts and three radical shifts while trying to trim and balance just once; you are on a beam reach, then a close reach, than a broad reach. Then you are in no wind at all. This happens too; the wind simply veers around you for a moment and leaves you stranded. Then it comes again and catches you off balance and out of trim again. Now you know you are here.

You get no real insights into this. When the wind shifts, it just shifts and doesn't say where. But you do get one observation. Concentrate just on the wind shifting upon the boat. The wind shifts two ways: forward or aft. A shift forward is a header: the wind swings farther ahead, and the boat goes harder against it. A shift aft is a lifter: the wind swings farther astern, and the boat goes more easily with it. A header heads the boat; a lifter lifts it. In shifting wind, you either are being headed or lifted. When headed you trim in or turn down; when lifted you trim out or turn up. Except it isn't that easy because you have to be so fast when you actually do this. You can't even be thinking about it.

Of course you do watch the shadows of the gusts gravitating toward you: not the nearer gusts—they already are past watching—but the farther ones, coming just after. You try to derive an early warning system from the shadows, divining, however uncertainly, which gusts might be headers when they hit and which might be lifters. In fact now you become preoccupied almost entirely with projections on distant dark places; you already are too late to consider anything closer. For that you are on reflexes alone.

So now you dedicate yourself to this long afternoon of groping through the offshore wind, searching for the right reflex. It could be very nearly your worst afternoon. You hardly even sail. Mostly you flounder amid the gusts, and however frantically you turn and trim and try to balance, you still are always two or three shifts behind, so long as you keep stopping to think. But you see how you are supposed to do this. You should know by a single reflex if you are being headed or lifted, and with the same reflex you should be turning and trimming even then. And you can have only this one reflex; you must do everything on one reflex; two reflexes together would be too slow. You have to find the reflex now and train it into yourself just for shifting wind. All you can do is work at this, taking the boat grotesquely through ten thousand shifts and gusts throughout the long afternoon.

You do find the reflex, but not as if you could simply claim it and put it in your pocket. You come *into* it more than upon it; you happen into it very gradually. And when you have it, or think you have it, you never are quite sure that you control it, or should control it. It just happens, after a long time in the offshore wind, that you finally begin to turn and trim and keep a balance of sorts in some of the slower, less radical shifts. You tend to turn when headed and trim when lifted, never really knowing why but generally maintaining the balance. Still later you begin to hold the balance even in some of the harder, faster shifts, and here you don't even know how; you just seem fortunate at having the boat and sail in the right places when you meet the gusts, as if you somehow become lucky with practice, and your luck improves with more practice. This should be the reflex working.

But often it proves faulty. The actual reflex never can be as simple as it is supposed to be: not so completely simple and yet so readily functional with every shift of the wind. Now and again the reflex must become unaccountably complicated, if only by circumstances and only for an instant, and then it must go wrong and set you at odds with a gust and leave you unbalanced and floundering, one shift behind. When you have the reflex, you have to allow that it is necessarily imperfect, and you never are going to make it work as well as you think it is supposed to. But you do get it working well enough to bring the boat through shifting wind: often muddling but still sailing better than by pure, blind luck, which isn't feasible but is the only other way.

Then having found the reflex, turn the boat against the shifting wind—or against the general drift of the gusts which make shifting wind—and learn about sailing upwind, which is harder than sailing across. Pull the sheet tight, and sail close hauled, and when you meet a lifting shift, you steer higher with it, which is usually intuitive. But when you meet a heading shift, you stop abruptly in the eye of the wind, which is nearly inevitable. You have to decide very quickly—by reflex—if you should steer back from the header and wait for a lifter, or if you should steer into the header and on through the eye of the wind, and bring the boat about, figuring that this gust which headed you on the old tack will lift you on the new. In theory it will: a header on one tack is a lifter on the other, by definition. But the gust could blow away even as you come about, and you might meet a new gust

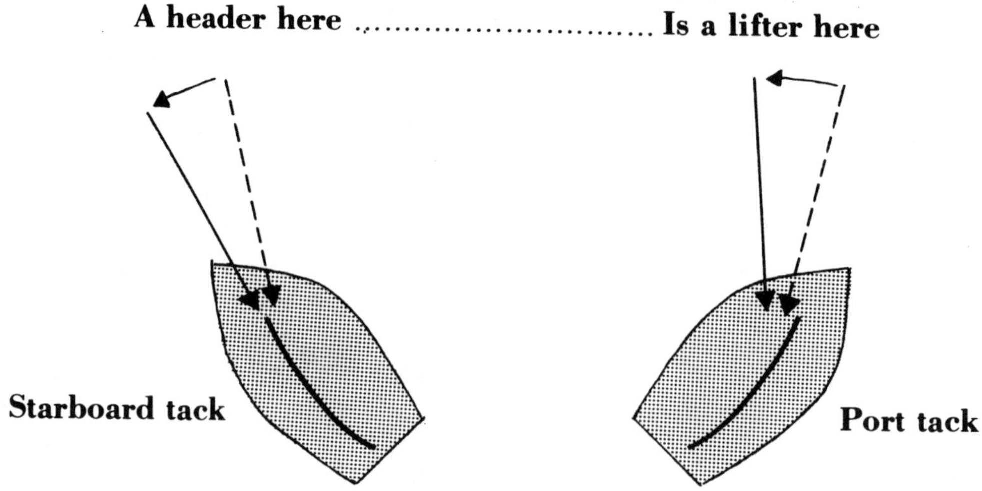

When the wind shifts with a sudden gust, it heads the boat on one tack but lifts it on the other. ***Drawing by Lana Cory Hall***

which would head you on the new tack where you could have waited for it to lift you on the old. You go upwind on speculations like this, trading headers and lifters, and when you speculate wrong, the boat dies in the eye of the wind. You need an uncommon equanimity to sail for long against shifting wind.

You do run more easily downwind through the gusts, but you go more precariously, because the more radical shifts occasionally catch the boat from behind and suddenly jibe it. Then you are beyond even sailing by reflex; you are on trust alone, so never mind the rest. (Actually you don't capsize too often because these radical shifts usually don't carry much weight, most of them being more mobile then potent. Most of them.) So for the rest of the afternoon sail into and out of the offshore wind: tacking into the shore, then running back out. And when you think you can do it well enough, come back and try it all again when the wind is heavy and shifting. Try even doing buoy landings in heavy gusts. After that you never sail in shifting wind unless you absolutely have to, and then you never like it for a moment. It probably is the second worst kind of sailing you ever will have to do.

The worst is sailing on a windless day, in a dead calm—a misapplied variation on existential nothingness, a metaphysical ether that you conjure out of exaggerated hopes and, with exaggerated charity, call light wind. Always call it this. The name may be the only thing that might move the boat.

You never mean to sail in light wind. You set out in other winds, and the other winds die. The sail hangs. The stillness descends. the day grows hot, and the flies come. The flies always come; they would find you like carrion if you were only a speck in a stagnant ocean. You are adrift now, without forces; nothing in the machinery of the boat means anything. You are becalmed.

You could whistle for wind. You could scratch the mast. Sailors have whistled and scratched masts for a thousand years, and now and then they have raised wind. Whistle, scratch; either is better than just wishing for wind.

Probably you should paddle home, swatting at flies and wishing the boat were a canoe. But not yet. You have to make one last attempt at sailing; you must try drifting the boat home, which is what sailors do. Heel the boat. Hike to the rail: in light wind hike to the lee rail—even if you arbitrarily must presume a wind direction to determine which *is* the lee rail—and just make the mast and the boat lean over together. Then from the tilt of the mast, the sail sags passively into a curve of sorts: the shade of its old curve, hanging vaporous in the air. The curve by its presence might generate a vestige of sail power from the random stirrings of the molecules in the air. The stirrings collectively might become light wind, or the metaphysical ether that you call light wind. And the boat may drift home on the vestige of sail force. In theory this might work.

You have to be perfectly still for it to work,

The worst sailing is in very light wind or no wind. There is nothing to do but hike to leeward and lean the boat over, so that the sail sags passively into a curve of sorts that might generate a vestige of sail power from the random stirrings of the molecules in the air. *Drawing by Don Raden*

because your slightest tremor would send waves across the sail and would disrupt the curve, and the vestige of sail force would simply evaporate. You must keep hiking out, though now you get no speed for your effort. You just lean over the lee rail—the low rail—holding yourself only a few inches above the water, and you study the water very closely to see if the boat really does move past the particles of algae and plankton. You could become profound and scientific doing this, but if you just hold still and keep hiking and withstand the heat and flies, then the boat should drift home: passing the particles, one-by-one.

It is a long drift home. You have time to meditate on the way.

Afterword

The essence remains. You sail the boat and experience the elements. You belong to air and water. This is rare.

All this while, the boat does what it does because it is what it is, and where it is—the machine: the presence in air and water, the resolution of forces of air and water. It works because you keep the balance. You hold the sheet and tiller; you steer and trim. And you sail. You experience.

After this you broaden the experience. You sail bigger boats, faster boats, different boats with more machinery. You fly spinnakers, ride trapezes; you become fluent in the language. You sew sails, splice lines, scrape paint, and you learn to repair with glass and resin. You should race; you will become a far better sailor. Perhaps you will cruise oceans. You do many things and go many ways. But you retain the essence. On an ocean or a pond, in a little boat with one sail or a big boat with a dozen the essence holds constant: the air, the water, the boat. When you have it, you are established.

Now you must share essence and experience. The last reward and final dimension is simply that you can share; you can sail with people. Together you will belong to air and water. You will keep the balance. This will be the fulfillment.

Index